WAITING

FOR

MORNING TIME

A Novel

CHRISTOPHER BOWRON

South Shore Publishing

© **Copyright 2023** Christopher Bowron
Print Version

ISBN: 978-1-9994413-2-6

All rights reserved. No part of this publication may be reproduced, stored in a retrieval system, or transmitted in any form or by any means – electronic, mechanical, photocopy, recording, or any other – except for brief quotations in printed reviews, without the prior written consent of the author.

This work is based upon true events. The characters are actual. Most of the historical events within are verified and all persons, all incidents, descriptions, dialogue and opinions expressed are both true but may be products of the Author's imagination such as dialogue and the Author's poetic license.

Published by:
SOUTH SHORE PUBLISHING INC.
7330 Estero Boulevard
Ft. Myers Beach Florida, 33931

This material is protected by copyright.

Christopher Bowron

Praise for Waiting for Morning Time

"5 Stars- This story is based on a true story and events that were told to the author, a friend of the family. This is a tantalizing story, and even if you are aware of the story (it was pretty widely told) of the harrowing events that occurred that stormy day, in Florida, in the Gulf of Mexico. The reader meets Lew, Bill, and Neal, but not only the men in the story, but the families while they were trying to be strong. Three missing men, and not a lot of support because of the impending storm. It would be a storm for the family, bringing them closer, and showing strength and determination. Read it from the beginning all the way to the end, because you just want to know why and how what was going on. Both thrilling and intriguing, all the way to the end. A wonderfully told story. Brilliant writing!" -*Amy's Bookshelf Reviews*

"*Waiting for Morning Time* by bestselling author, Christopher Bowron is a shocking, yet inspiring story of faith and the ultimate test of survival. After a violent storm, three men are stranded at sea in the Gulf of Mexico, desperately floating in shark-infested waters for a total of 49 hours before they are finally found. It sounds like a dreadful, horrendous fiction movie, but it really did happen, and their story will have readers held in suspense while reading, turning the pages faster than one can blink.

Waiting for Morning Time by Christopher Bowron is the harrowing true story of the longest-known survivors stranded in the open sea. A father, a son, and their friend go out for a relaxing time of fishing and diving, but when a storm quickly hits and upturns their boat, they are left floating at the mercy of the terrifying ocean. They are forced to take drastic measures, and one man even uses his dentures as a vessel to drink rainwater. Meanwhile, their wives scramble to get help from the Coast Guard, friends, and new stations.

It has been more than 20 years since these heart-wrenching events took place, but reading about the trials that these men went through is incredible. They were suffering intensely, but so were their families on shore. It is incredible to learn just how difficult it was for their wives to get cooperation from the Coast Guard, which is much harder than you'd imagine. The unwavering faith and determination of the families back on shore was so inspiring and incredible to read about. Author Christopher Bowron has done an excellent job of writing from different perspectives, and his writing style with descriptions of all the scenes, characters, and all they had to endure makes the reader feel like they are right there with the men and their families at the time of the unforgettable life changing event.

Waiting for Morning Time is a truly impressive, thrilling, and meaningful story of real-life survival, faith, hope, and perseverance. Readers will absolutely enjoy and be thoroughly satisfied with that aspect of the story. But, along with the passion and suspense written perfectly into the story, Christopher Bowron brilliantly keeps readers on the edge of their seat from start to finish." - *Chick Lit Café Review*

Christopher Bowron

PROLOGUE

The sun-drenched, barrier islands of Gasparilla, Estero, Sanibel, and Captiva or the coastal towns of Sarasota and Venice, offer a slower pace than the built-up East coast of Florida. The Sun Coast provides a playground for those who enjoy fishing, golfing, and sun worship. Pull up to a seaside bar and you will likely hear one of Jimmy Buffet's songs being crooned by one of the many island Bards-- almost like a religion. Southwest Florida is a happy place, for the most part. People travel there to chase their dreams and search for a better place to live out their days. Some are lucky enough to find their dreams. I'm Lew Lipsit. I moved here thirty-odd years ago with my sweetheart and second wife, Merry, to what we both saw as our heaven on earth, miles away from the cold north.

I soon learned there is a Ying and Yang in any tropical paradise. For every great four or five-week period of amazing blue-sky weather, there will be change. March is a dry month in southwest Florida. It had been hot for the past few weeks and the warm air fed off the Gulf of Mexico, blowing strong from the south. A cold front was moving in from the North. When the two weather masses met, the collision would result in an occluded front. The two natural forces mashing up into a nasty cyclonic storm. The weather would be

Waiting for Morning Time

terrible for several days, high winds in excess of 50-60 miles per hour. There would be rain accompanied by violent storm cells full of thunder and dangerous lightning. For those who were used to the occurrence, it meant an excellent time to stay indoors with a good book or perform that indoor chore put off for a rainy day.

On the day we left Venice to go spearfishing, a small craft advisory was issued by the Coast Guard before the storm moved in: *Boaters to stay off the water.* The warning should be heeded unless it would be impossible to do so. Hundreds of boaters lose their lives to the sea each year in the United States. Most of the deaths are due to bad judgment and malfunction. Three of us, me, my son Bill, and my friend Neal decided to grab a blue hole in the sky before the storm moved in.

CHAPTER ONE

7 a.m. Saturday - North Fort Myers, Florida

NO ONE plans on calamity. These unfortunate occurrences often start innocently enough; often a series of events leading up to the crisis—sometimes with premonition.

"LEWIE! We gotta get going, babe." I tramped around noisily in the backyard trying to remember what I might have forgotten. Merry couldn't blame me for not being ready, though, as the plans had been changed. We were supposed to have spent the day boating off Venice Beach. Good friends, Neal and Jackie Obendorf, offered to take us along with our visiting family for the day. However, it looked as if a storm front would be moving in from the North later on. Bill, Neal, and I planned on diving for a few days off North Captiva Island over the next week. After some deliberation, we decided to do a pre-trip run out to a dive site to spear fish in the morning and come back in before the storm hit. The girls decided to take the kids to *Busch Gardens* in Tampa. Jackie said that it wouldn't be a good time for the kids out on the water, since it would be hot and wavy. The last thing the girls wanted would be to cut the boy's dive short because of cranky seasick children.

Waiting for Morning Time

"Here it is," I said, appearing with a big red Colman cooler so Anna, Bill's wife and Merry could pack lunches for everyone before leaving. Merry could see the way that I rubbed the back of my neck, followed by a deep breath that I was irritated and in turn, I picked up her somber mood. We were in tune that way, seldom apart in the fifteen years we'd been married. The morning was organized chaos as everyone rushed around with no real purpose, trying to remember what might have been forgotten.

"Why don't we all go to the beach for the morning?" Merry said. "This is beginning to get a little too complicated and hurried." By this time the kids were running amuck, and she could feel the beginnings of a headache creeping up the back of her neck. She didn't feel well, and her stomach began to cramp. Something wasn't right… she couldn't put her finger on it.

I knew it wasn't Merry's kind of thing. She'd have preferred taking the kids to the theme park with me, leaving Bill and Anna a little free time, possibly going with Neal and Jackie out on the boat. Merry didn't cope well with the kids… without me. I like to think I had a way with the children, probably because I'd raised my own, where Merry never had children.

I cleared my throat. "I promised Bill. I can't let him down. He's excited."

Bill had been talking about the dive trip for months. Merry knew I couldn't say no. She shook her head submissively, seeing the pleading in my eyes. Bill and Anna lived in Niagara Falls, Ontario and were visiting on vacation. Bill and I hadn't seen a lot of each other in recent years and I wanted to make the most of things; I was caught between a rock and a hard place. Bill recently took his dive course and couldn't wait to get into the deep water somewhat warmer than the forty degrees when he'd made his last dive back in Canada.

It was a herculean feat filling up Bill's minivan; four large adults and two kids with what seemed enough stuff to last three days. We made the half-hour drive up I-75 to Venice, packed like sardines in a tin can.

***

Neal and Jackie lived seven miles inland from the Venice shore, on a few acres of property with its own lake. The drive in from the main road took us down an old tunnel-like laneway, moss-filled trees arching over the roadway to meet overtop. Merry and I had worked for Jackie as sales reps before her meeting Neal. Jackie, after dropping out of college started her own business, creating hand-painted Florida postcards. Merry and I were always on the lookout for a good product to sell and had contacted her cold. At the time, she hadn't been looking for new salespeople. We had asked for a small sample to sell in order to showcase our abilities. We had sold a similar product back in Canada for our own lucrative business. It didn't take long to become Jackie's number one team. Both of us were excellent salespeople. After working for Jackie for a few years, we parted ways but had kept in contact as is the "Merry and Lew" way-- seldom breaking a friendship.

Our caravan arrived a little before eight that morning, the driveway a beehive of activity. The kids, Billy and Ashley, expelled themselves from the cramped van. They were eager to meet Kayla and her baby brother Robbie, who was only thirteen months old. They weren't familiar with each other, only hearing names spoken by parents; but kids will be kids and they made friends within minutes, very glad to be away from us older people.

The adults were in full scramble mode. Bill, Neal, and I were grabbing all of the spearfishing and dive tackle from the minivan and transferring it to the boat still hooked up to the trailer behind Neal's truck. Bill appeared awestruck by the boat, a 30-foot *Wellcraft Scarab* with two brand new 250-horse *Evenrude motors* on the back with a six-inch thick red stripe running its length. His eyes didn't leave the craft even as he performed his packing duties.

It seemed a bit of a rush job, but the window of open time had been cut short due to the oncoming storm. Merry could understand how the men were eager to be free of the kids and the women and eager to shuffle them off to the amusement park... in a hurry to do their *male* bonding thing out on the water. To be honest with herself, she would later say, she wished we were taking her with us. She was none too pleased that the tasks had been decided; the men going fishing while the women brought the kids to Tampa, sexist roles decided without any discussion… and they were my grandkids. It may have been the first time Merry and I hadn't at least kissed on the cheek... maybe since we first met many years back in Canada. She might have made more of a fuss, but there was another issue, which had never been vocalized. She knew it bothered Bill the way she monopolized my time when he was around. Thus, she sighed heavily and deferred to the men's wishes, deciding to keep her thoughts to herself, something she'd never done with me.

The process of transferring items took thirty minutes. Afterward, everyone stood in the driveway looking at each other quietly until I spoke up, "Don't worry about us. We'll be back on land before the sky turns. Now you," I turned to Anna, "be careful driving. You have precious cargo on board." I looked at each kid's face before turning to Neal and Bill. "Well boys, let's get going."

Within a few minutes, the driveway emptied; a cloud of dusty exhaust trailed down through the tunneled exit to the property.

CHAPTER TWO

I KNEW my wife was not happy when we parted on the driveway. To the best of my recollection, she seldom showed negative emotion towards me. I'd seen her become agitated at the odd time with a supplier, or in the early days when we'd talked about her first husband. The situation in the driveway made me feel really bad. I'd sworn to myself that I would do my best to never let her down. To this point in our relationship, it had seemed an easy task. It didn't appear a grievous foul in the beginning, but I swore never to let it happen again. I'd made my sweetheart upset, and I didn't like myself much for doing it. We'd never taken liberty with each other and always making sure we were on the same page.

At the time, I'd had half a mind to tell Neal to turn around and bring me back. I'd call Merry up and tell her how I didn't feel up to the whole thing, blaming it on my wonky heart and the medication. I wanted to tell her to come back as soon as she could. I missed her already and wanted to make up, I was feeling sorry for myself.

Now, of course, hindsight being 20/20, I reckoned this to a man swimming halfway across a lake and deciding to turn back. The foul had been committed and I may as well live with the consequences at this point. The other side of the equation and probably the crux of

Waiting for Morning Time

everything is how I'd most likely let my son down. Bill had been looking forward to getting out on the boat for weeks. I took a deep breath and washed the thoughts from my mind. Merry would get over it, never to happen again... I made a promise to myself.

Neal's voice brought me out of my thoughts. *"Seven-Eleven?* I need a coffee; I don't know about you guys." Neal, a tall thin, dark-haired man, was soft-spoken with a Florida drawl only people who'd grown up in the state possessed. I heard a low rumble emanating from deep in his throat. Though much younger than me, we had grown to be good friends over the years due to our mutual connection with Jackie and Neal's father-in-law: photographer, Clyde Butcher.

Bill voiced his mutual need. "I put my coffee down when we were packing up and forgot to finish it." Bill Lipsit, like myself, was a large individual, pushing three hundred pounds. To this day, he'd never given me a moment of grief. Born and raised in Niagara Falls, Canada, Bill grew up to be a good guy, who liked to have fun and maybe drank a little too much. Above all, he loved his family. Since waking that morning, he'd been bouncing around like a kid, unable to hold his excitement for the ensuing boat ride and dive.

We stopped to make caffeine a top priority. When Bill spotted me carrying a couple of sugary donuts, he couldn't resist and followed suit. There was a good reason why Bill and I outweighed Neal by a hundred or more pounds.

As we pulled out of the convenience store parking lot, Neal gave us the agenda. "Once we leave the dock, we'll head to M-16 which is only nine miles out. We'll see how the Grouper are there. If it's no good, we'll head over to M-9, which should give us three or four hours. We can get off the water before the weather hits. Cocktails will be ready for the girls before they get back. Rub their feet a little, no foul committed."

I chuckled and would have been in total agreement with Neal's assessment had I still been married to *Janet.* Merry and I didn't operate that way.

There were a number of manmade reefs in the Gulf, part of a revitalization of the coral reefs created by the state of Florida. The sites were well-plotted and marked by GPS coordinates. M-16 and M-9 were created by the erection of manmade cement blocks and pilings. In conjunction with the U.S. military, several old tanks and troop carriers were dropped to the ocean's floor. Coral needs something to adhere to, and over time the spot had become a hot destination for scuba divers and fishermen. The manmade reefs were now teeming with marine life including large Grouper-- Neal's target.

***

The three of us arrived at the Venice public boat ramp a little after nine. It took half an hour to transfer what we would be taking to the *Scarab*. It was a handsome boat, out of reach financially for most. The craft was extremely seaworthy and able to cut through the heavy chop we'd be facing on that day. Bill couldn't keep his eyes off its sleek lines, running his hand down its beam.

***

Within half an hour, the Scarab knifed its way through the light surf near shore; wisps of morning mist still hanging around the fringe of the marina. A couple of bottlenose dolphins played with us for a few minutes, jumping through the wake of the boat until Neal opened up the twin engines. Since Neal had recently bought them, it was the first time they'd been run. While he had been happy to go diving, Neal was just as eager to try out his new toys. They didn't disappoint him, purring like twin Florida Panthers.

As the boat moved away from shore, waves began to escalate making for a bit of a rough, but fun ride. I chuckled seeing Bill thrown around in the bow, holding on for dear life as the boat shot up and became airborne on several occasions. Neal and I thought the ride was a blast, while Bill endured more than he had bargained for not being accustomed to slipping across the top of the water. I had no fear, knowing Neal had always been an expert boatman. I was also experienced, owning my own thirty-footer, kept in the canal behind our house.

Neal smiled, seeing Bill bounce around, hammering the motors a couple of times as they crested a wave to fly airborne once again. Neal was a gentle soul, born in Venice, Florida, he ended up spending his life in his hometown. He was virtually born on the water; his parents always owned a boat of some sort for as long as Neal could remember. The Obendorfs were third-generation Floridians. His parents had always been connected within the business and social community of Venice. Neal had spent a lot of his time sailing, qualifying for the nationals in his eighteen-foot Hobie Cat. At age fifteen, his parents entrusted Neal to sail their forty-one foot Morgan back from the Keys to Venice with his thirteen-year-old brother and a friend, navigating the hundred fifty-mile trek using a Loran. Today's ten-mile-ride out to M-16 had to seem like child's play to Neal. His biggest concern was how many Groupers he might catch.

They arrived at M-16 twenty minutes later, roughly ten miles off Venice. Neal slowed the engines, allowing the bow to rise and then slowly settle. There were several other boats at the site, surface fishing.

Neal had to speak up over the rumble of the engines. "This is no good. There's an unwritten rule you shouldn't dive or spearfish at a fishing site where there are other boats. Scares the fish away and the fishermen get right angry. Let's see what's up at M-9 a little further out, thirteen miles total and a bit deeper, sixty feet, the Grouper will be thick. A lot of these smaller boats won't want to risk going out that far with this bad weather moving in." He pointed up at the mass of dark clouds looming over the Gulf far to the North. "It won't take us long though." He patted the gunnel of his boat. Bill and I nodded, deferring to Neal's judgment.

Bill decided to take a seat in the back, proving to be more comfortable for him. He moved up close to Neal so they could chat. I was happy to stay quiet while listening to the two of them. It sometimes took a little work to get Neal to converse, but after a few minutes of constant prodding by Bill about fishing, boating and the variances of the ocean water, Neal was ready to open up.

Bill looked proud to tell, "Completed my last open water dive just before Christmas."

"In Canada?" Neal looked sideways at him; his brows lowered in disbelief.

"Yep! And it nearly killed me. We could only see four feet in front of our noses and the water… nearly zero Celsius. Real cold."

"I don't get it. How can that be any fun? You Canadians are nuts. I guess all I know is diving in the tropics where the water seldom gets lower than the sixties. In fact, most of the time, the water temp stays in the eighties, uh, Fahrenheit. I'll warn you; it might be a little on the cold side today."

Bill smiled. "Then I'll be okay… thin Canadian blood. I'll be honest, though, we do wear dry suits ... keeps us warm enough. It's sometimes tough to get the weight right, but worth it in the end, eh."

"You said it nearly killed you?" Neal threw back Bill's exact words and chuckled.

"Yeah, my regulator froze up a couple of times. I couldn't get any air and had to ascend with a buddy sharing his."

Neal shook his head smiling until his eyes shifted to the depth finder and GPS on the console. "Nuts." He slowed down the engines. "I think we're pretty much there. My GPS reading isn't exact. We'll have to check the Depth Finder to pick up the shoal. The bottom of the Gulf of Mexico is basically flat, with the odd ledge here and there. That's why these reefs are so important in sustaining the fish population." He glanced at the electronics. "No problem, we'll find er'."

They continued to search for the shoal, losing ten more minutes before finally locating it. Neal became frustrated at the waste of precious time, but the chop was pretty good, and the Depth Finder had a tough time settling down.

Finally, Neal said, "Okay, there it is!" He pointed to a blip on the bottom of the sea floor. Shifting the motors into idle, he shuffled around in a cupboard, eventually handing Bill a Javex Bottle with a long string and weight on the other end. "Throw this over."

Once the marker was tossed, the white bottle became difficult to spot, due to the waves. Neal motioned to me to take the wheel. "Keep'er into the wind while I set the anchor." After another five minutes of jockeying, the boat jolted. The bow settled directly into the wind on its own, the anchor thankfully taking hold.

Neal knew it could take several attempts to find something on the bottom to grab onto. A boater doesn't want to drop anchor directly onto a reef, which might cause damage to the structure and possibly become snagged. In this kind of chop, it would be dangerous to try and free it, even diving with scuba gear. The boat drifted from side to side, the Gulf's currents counterbalancing the wind and waves from time to time. When that happened, the waves banged against the transom of the boat, making things uncomfortable.

Bill watched the water splashing up into the boat. "Is that normal?"

Neal nodded. "We don't usually dive when it's this choppy, but we won't be out here long. If we take on some water, we have the pumps."

Bill nodded, accepting Neal's explanation ... verbatim.

Neal seemed pleased to find the site vacant. He looked at Bill staring out over the Gulf at the oncoming front. Neal realized he shouldn't have said anything earlier. Smiling at the worried look on Bill's face, he tried to relieve his stress. "Don't worry. We can be back on land in half an hour. We see a storm coming in ... we're outta here, besides, that's gotta' be half a day away to the north, way past Tampa! The girls have a better chance of getting blown around. Look at the sky now, clear and sunny; it's beautiful."

I didn't mind the idea of snorkeling over the shallower reef at M-16 but having just recovered from a quadruple bi-pass, the doctor warned me telling me not to go scuba diving, which would be required at M-9. I made the decision to hold down the fort on top, drinking *Mountain Dew* and… maybe one… or two scotch and waters with lots a lot of ice.

Bill and Neal were ready to put on their scuba gear. As the sun climbed higher in the sky, it began to get hot ... coupled with the higher winds rocking the boat, it made things a little more difficult for them. Bill had to work hard to fit into the tight wet suit and began to sweat profusely.

Neal suited up quickly and decided to do a short pop dive to see if they were indeed over the old tanks while Bill got ready. He came back up after six or seven minutes, a big smile on his face as he spit the regulator out of his mouth. "Hurry up, Bill! There's more Grouper down there than I've ever seen. It's gonna be like shootin' fish in a barrel." Neal pulled himself up onto the boat and retrieved the spear guns.

Bill was still having a hard time at this point, exhausted from the struggle of getting the gear on, his face turned red with exertion and the intense heat. Neal eyed the heavy weight belt around Bill's waist and shook his head, as he handed him a spear gun. "When we get down there, make sure you keep the fish away from your body, especially on the way up. You don't want em' too close in case we get into some sharks. You might get nipped."

Neal taunted him a little and now Bill looked uneasy, "I'm not so sure about these waves, I've never tried to dive in anything like this."

While I helped put the tank on his shoulders, Neal did his best to

Waiting for Morning Time

cheer Bill up. "There are no waves at the bottom, buddy. Once you're down there, you'll love it. You've been talking about this for weeks now, just a little primer for the rest of the trip. Everything will seem easy after this." He smiled offering encouragement.

Bill nodded; the apprehension etched upon his face. He rolled his shoulders several times to loosen up. "Okay... great." He stood hesitantly, preparing to jump in flippers first.

"We don't have a lot of time, so let's get down there. Follow me. We'll bag a few Groupers and call it a day. If we don't bring dinner home for the girls, we'll never hear the end of it." Neal slipped back down into the dark waters and to my eye, a cold uninviting Gulf. Neal treaded water with the help of his buoyancy control vest (BC) and flippers.

Bill followed, jumping away from the side of the boat. However, he dropped straight down… not floating for a minute to tread water!

Neal and I looked at each other, eyes wide. In a mad scramble of bubbles and flailing arms, Bill finally surfaced, having to completely fill his BC to get back to the top. He looked none too happy having nearly drowned.

He pulled his regulator out of his mouth, barely able to keep his face above the water. Normally with that much air in the BC, anyone could keep their body buoyant in the water, floating like a cork. "I've got too much weight on this BELT!"

I offered him his spear gun and he shook his head.

"I'm not feeling good about this." Bill said, paddling his feet aggressively to keep his head above the salty waves. Using up all of his energy in an effort to make this work, Bill was losing the battle.

Bill and I could see the frustration on Neal's face. Neal read the situation correctly and gave Bill an out. "Hey, Bill, diving's all about being in your comfort zone. You don't feel right… don't worry. I'll go down and get us some dinner. There'll be calmer days next week."

Bill looked upset at his own inability to rise to the occasion. Still, he nodded in resignation. He looked as if he was ready to get back on the boat, but worried about Neal going down on his own. Bill felt he was not holding up his end of the buddy system, remembering his diving courses and how important it is to never dive alone. Neal showed his intent to make a quick jaunt to the bottom and Bill didn't want to question the expert diver's judgment.

Neal and I helped Bill up onto the edge of the boat, *no small chore.*

Neal took the minute to spit into his mask and spread the saliva over the glass before putting it back over his eyes. "I'm gonna take a few runs down there and see what I can get. I saw a couple of Gag sitting under the boat at the edge of one of the tanks, and there's a giant Goliath in the middle of the reef holding court. Can't shoot em', but I've never seen one so big, must be 5-600 pounds." Neal turned and disappeared in a flourish of flippers and bubbles.

Bill's mood continued to deteriorate. His slumped shoulders showed how much he wanted to be down there on the hunt with Neal. Bill's sorrowful face caught my attention. I turned to face my son.

"Dad, can you give me a hand." Bill looked exhausted and needed help getting the tanks over his shoulder. As Bill unbuckled the weights, they slipped out of his hands into the water sinking quickly to the bottom of the Gulf. Both of us began a round of cussing until I finally helped Bill struggle out of his wet suit.

As I extracted him from the rubber top, Neal surfaced, with two large Gag Grouper on the middle of his spear. As he popped the regulator out of his mouth, it was impossible not to see the toothy smile on the quiet man's face. "Like I said, shootin' fish in a barrel."

I pulled the fish off the spear, throwing them into a large cooler with ice. "Gee, Neal, they have to be fifteen pounds each."

"At least. I'm going back for more. We'll have lunch when I come back up. Have one of those craft beers you brought ready for me."

"Roger that."

Bill spoke up. "Hey Neal, I dropped my weight belt over the side. Any chance you could bring it up if you spot it?

Neal nodded, but he did so with a look of irritation, his face drawn tight. He handed his spear gun up from the water to Bill. "I'll get the belt first, back in a few minutes." Once again, he spat into his mask, popped it back on his face, and disappeared under a big wave.

CHAPTER THREE

NEAL FOUND the weight belt directly under the Scarab. It must have sunk fast. Trying to pick it up, he couldn't believe the weight of it. He examined all the lead pieces. Each weighed two pounds. Adding them up-- *Forty-eight pounds!* Even for a dry suit, it would be a lot of weight. It was a good thing Bill didn't go down wearing the belt. If he'd found any trouble, he would have had a hard time floating back up to the surface. Had Bill ditched the belt, he would rise too fast, which is very dangerous, possibly causing the Bends. Neal put the belt over his shoulder and headed back up. He needed to completely inflate his BC to get any upward momentum. It took all of his energy to bring the weights back up to the surface. Normally, the BC would have been all he needed to ascend. Now, he needed to kick his flippers with all his strength.

When he reached the surface, he barely had the breath to hand one end of the belt to me. He spat his regulator out of his mouth. "Man alive, Bill, you owe me. This belt is almost fifty pounds and could've caused you trouble if you had gone down wearing it!"

I reached over to grab the weight belt. "Holy smokes, I might need a little help here, Billy. This thing nearly pulled me in with it," I laughed, gesturing towards the belt.

Waiting for Morning Time

Bill looked over at me, and then down at Neal floating in the dark water wearing a smirk on his face. The junior member of our three-man team could tell we were making fun of him. Although he smiled, Bill mumbled something under his breath.

I helped Neal out of the water along with his tank and BC. The three of us sat in the shade of the canvas Bimini top and opened our bags from *Publix*. We relaxed together eating our sub sandwiches.

Neal seemed intent upon going back down and spearing a few more Grouper. He spoke with his mouth half-full. "Sorry, you couldn't see what's going on down there. It's like the reef is untouched over the winter, there's Grouper by the handful. Strange, it's like they are curious to see me." He smiled making a shooting motion with his hands.

Bill took a bite. "You're making me feel like dirt," he said with his mouth half-full.

"Not my intent, sir, I've never seen so many fish. I'm going to go back down one more time and see if I can't catch the mother lode. I can freeze the fish we can't eat."

I looked out over the Gulf at the storm clouds brewing to the west.

Neal followed my gaze. "I don't think we have to worry about them. That cloud mass has been hovering out there all day. It may not move this close to shore, if at all... not until tomorrow. Lived here all my life, Lew, I think we could have brought the girls out today."

Bill winced. "It's a bit rough for kids?"

Neal nodded. "Maybe?" Might have been crowded bouncing around like this."

"We'll have a better time later in the week." Bill added. "Weather's supposed to be nicer right?"

Neal nodded. "Once this front passes through, the air pressure will moderate and the fishin' will be even better. Clearer water as well. It's really dark right now, almost black." He finished his last bite and moved back into the sun to fiddle with his spear gun.

I spoke up. "I'm perfectly happy to sit out here and have another scotch and water. My biggest concern ... I didn't bring my heart medicine. I'm due for a pill in about an hour." I smiled, taking another sip of my drink. Still thinking about the importance of my heart meds, I shook my head. "Hell! I've survived this long; a few hours won't kill me and I'm sure the booze is doing a fine job of thinning my blood." I chuckled at my own joke.

Neal and Bill looked at each other. Neal frowned. "We can call it here, no problem… can get us back in half an hour."

I shook my head. "The stuff I'm taking isn't critical, it's preventative. I'll be okay. You go get us a couple more and we can leave after that." I held up my drink. "I need to finish this. Take your time."

Bill nodded, cracking open another beer.

Neal suited up again and jumped back into the chilly water. Bill leaned over and handed him his spear gun. "Good luck. You sure you're okay going down there alone?"

"I'm not moving around much and going straight down. I've been doing this most of my life, don't worry. You enjoy that beer."

"Just wanted to make sure." Bill held Neal's eyes looking for the truth.

Neal spotted Bill's concern. He nodded and once again disappeared into the depths below. He was happy Bill acknowledged the buddy-system protocol, though, it didn't necessarily make it right. Neal had done this a hundred times with Jackie and Kayla onboard.

***

We hadn't talked much since Bill arrived in Florida. We made ourselves comfortable, easing back into the Scarab's plush seats. "I'm sorry it didn't work out today, Bill." I could see my son was churning things over in his mind. I knew the look. "Things happen for a reason.

You might have gotten yourself into some problems with all that weight anyway as Neal said." I reached into one of the coolers and grabbed a few more ice cubes for my glass. I like lots of ice.

Bill lowered his eyes, dropping his chin to his chest. "I'm not bothered. I'll get out when we go to Captiva next week. It's my fault anyway. I should have known I had too much weight." He paused. "Hey, I'm a beginner. I won't do that again." He smiled, offering his drink in a salute with me. I clinked my glass against the beer bottle. "I keep getting the feeling Neal's mad at me, that's the worst part."

I thought about the remark, having had the good fortune to know Neal over the past few years. "No. You have to realize that Neal does this stuff all the time. He's out here as a favor. He's having a good time, I can see it on his face, but we've all maneuvered ourselves to make this day work out, the girls included. Maybe he feels guilty he's the only one going down and having all the fun. Neal's pretty quiet and hard to read. Jackie's the spokesman for the couple. First time I met Neal, it took half an hour to get him to say a word past ... nice to meet you."

Bill grinned, "I can see that. He's a pretty quiet dude."

"That he is, but he's the salt of the earth. So, how are you doing? ... really... no bull."

Bill sat in his chair for a few minutes, taking the odd swig from his bottle of beer. He looked me straight in the eye, and I prepared for the truth. "I've been better. I've been struggling the past few years. I can't really put my finger on it."

"I've been there... midlife crisis."

Bill ran his hands through his slightly wet hair. "I suppose. Maybe I haven't recognized it as such."

I poured another finger of scotch into my drink. "You spend your life doing things you feel you are supposed to do. Then all of a sudden, you're getting older ... happens to all of us, Billy. You have to do something about it. Otherwise, you fall into a depression." I looked at my son and could tell there was more that needed telling. "Anna says you've been drinking?" I could see his smile sour.

"What's she saying?" He crossed his arms over his chest.

"Just what I said."

"Nothing crazy."

"Hey, I'm not one to judge, I like my booze too, but I've never let it affect my family life. You have a winner bride, Bill, and she's reaching out. That has to tell you something."

Bill's shoulders drooped "I didn't feel I had a problem."

"Most don't and I'm the last one to tell you ... you're wrong. I'm concerned, and I love Anna of course, and the kids. You're my family."

"You haven't been there much since you met Merry... moved to Fort Myers." His eyes dropped to the deck.

I hesitated, making sure to choose my words correctly. I could see Bill trying to deflect the conversation. Most alcoholics are good at it. I didn't think of my son as a classic drinker, but I knew once it starts to affect your marriage and your mental state ... it's time to get a grip on it, no matter how much you drank. "Life goes on, Bill. When I met Merry, you'd started your family. Merry is the answer to my midlife crisis and I love her dearly. I didn't know you felt resentment toward her."

Bill took a deep breath. "I really don't. It's... I miss you, sometimes. Even though I'm getting a little older, I look up to you and need your help. Is that strange? It's like you are my dad ... who's always there. Then all of a sudden you meet Missus wonderful, and I feel not important anymore."

I felt a tear burning behind my eye. Standing up, I moved over to Bill and gave my son a hug. "I'm always here for you... you can count on that. Your mother and I had nothing in common in the end. We were on a treadmill going nowhere. Then I met Merry. This might be too much information, but..."

Bill put his hand up smiling. "Then don't say it, I think I know where this is going. Maybe I should cut down on the booze a little bit."

I smiled. "Nothing wrong having the odd drink here and there. If you can't drink with your bride, make sure it doesn't affect her. You have your family and that's it. Nothing else is important." I was quiet for a few minutes, until I spoke again. "Say, how's Hoss?" Hoss was Bill's childhood and lifelong friend. Hoss had been the *extra child* in the Lipsit house, Bill and Hoss had gotten into more trouble than most kids ... to include brawls, police chases and an endless parade to the principal's office. The two were always being called out for this or that by the powers that be after figuring out: If one was involved, so was the other.

"He's doing well. Sure, wished he could've come down here with us ... no doubt. Remember when you bought all that wood for us, and we made the speedboat? It wouldn't have lasted a minute out here in the Gulf."

"Yes. You two little brats fired up that old *Evenrude* in an old oil drum in the basement and fumigated the whole house. Your mom was so mad... it might even have been the beginning of the end of our marriage." We both laughed.

"Yes, the good old days."

I changed tacks. "Say, we have a new minister at the Church, Pat Thurmer, I'd like you to meet."

"Yeah, you mentioned him the other day. This Sunday for sure." He spoke without conviction.

The Church to this point in our lives played what I would like to call, an active role. We were not Bible thumpers, or at least I didn't think of myself that way. Merry was a bit more demonstrative in her faith. I went to church every Sunday and enjoyed the fellowships formed with the rest of the congregation. I am a social animal, no matter the venue. I was never a saint for most of my life, probably disappointing a few in the process. I felt I needed a dose of faith to balance the good with the bad.

I felt happy to see how Bill had found a new hobby in diving. People need healthy diversions in their lives. Somehow, I hoped religion might even fill a small space with my son. I'd had often heard Pat Thurmer talk. He liked to say, "to crowd out the bad influences, fill them with good cause. It will lead a person down the path to being well-rounded and a better person."

If Bill went to church with me on Sunday, I knew that he would only do it to placate me. You can take a horse to water, but you can't make him drink. In my mind, this is what dads do, or what concerned people do when they see the people they love going in the wrong direction. God has his way of finding you when you need him most. I wondered if Billy would be ready for Him to this point in his life.

***

The religious talk had been a buzzkill for Bill. We sat contemplating our own thoughts and letting time go by.

Bill didn't think he'd been drinking too much, but then people who did drink too much seldom thought they did, until they incurred a related problem. I hoped he would take my words to heart. In my mind, I had always been a drinker, but to the best of my memory, I had never seen it in a bad way or where my drinking caused a family crisis. I felt that I had a handle on things. I hadn't realized Bill had been hurt by my new life with Merry. I remembered my own words to Merry in the beginning. "The kids will be fine. They have their own lives and families now." It had been a selfish statement, the fact I remembered the remark, validated the point.

The noise of a thrashing fish caught both of our attention, pulling us out of our daydreams. A large gag Grouper, half in and out of a cooler, the spear still stuck in its side made a last gasp for life. The spear gun jammed the last time Neal went below. I had forgotten I'd promised to take a look at the damaged weapon. When Neal speared the particularly large Grouper and it had messed up the release on the spear. After fiddling with the barb for a time, I freed the spear, pulling it out of its side. I pushed the bleeding fish along the deck over to Bill.

"I'll throw that one in the big cooler." Bill stumbled towards the back of the Scarab.

I nodded as I coiled the line, placing it on one of the consuls. Looking to the back of the boat, I saw Bill amble along to get hold of the slippery fish. It took a few seconds to acknowledge what appeared wrong with the picture. When it hit me, I instantly felt a wave of panic as if a hundred fire ants just crawled up my spine and into my scalp.

Bill looked to be up to his ankles in water, trying to catch the fish as it swam around the back of the boat. The floorboards were floating, and the water level appeared to be rising quickly.

"Forget the fish, Bill! Look down at the water." My white face appeared to startle Bill more than the actual water in the boat. Pitch white, my eyes darted here and there, not knowing where to look first. To the best of Bill's recollection, it would be the first time he'd ever seen anything but calm or mirth in my eyes. Bill still managed to toss the fish into a cooler before he hurried over to me trying to turn on the engines.

I fiddled with the keys to the boat. "We need to get the pumps working, but I'm not sure that'll be enough." I began to flip switches frantically. "Go to the front of the boat and get ready to pull up the anchor. I couldn't remember if I'd tried the pre-ignition to warm up the motors. In my urgency to get the boat fired up, I was aware of the pre-ignition process, but it may have been too late at that point regardless. Once again, I tried the bilge pump switch.

The boat kept taking on water at an alarming rate. I moved one of the floorboards out of the way. As I figured, both of the batteries were submerged under the salt water. They would be fried. I tried a few more times, with no luck, to engage the twin engines. I yelled at Bill. The boat swung hard with the current, taking on an especially large wave in the stern. The water flooding the aft of the boat forced the motors to sink even lower in the water. "This boat's going down. I want you to stay up at the bow!"

Bill nodded, looking meek. Bending over, he put his hands on his knees, trying to catch a breath… his eyes wide open.

For some reason, I felt a calm returning ... as calm as could be possible under the situation. Being a practical man, I figured that I needed to keep my wits about me if the situation was going to become a disaster. The bow rose up to point to the blue sky, three or four feet. Soon, the heavy motors would drag the stern under. Fumbling with the VHF radio, all I could get was silence. Of course! There was no electricity to power up the device.

I needed to send out a MAYDAY!

Where was my cell phone? It was in my bag, but I'd thrown it there after using it earlier. Still searching around, I kept trying to remember. Spotting it floating on the deck, half submerged in the rising water, I clamored to bend down and retrieve it. Some time ago, I'd made it a point not to curse. Still, a few choice expletives passed through my lips as I flipped it open only to find a dead screen.

I yelled to Bill, who now held on for dear life as the bow rose even higher. "Bill, where's your phone?"

Bill felt around in his pockets, a look of realization crossing his face, his eyes widening. He pointed to the left side console. I could see the phone precariously balanced on the edge, the lip being the only thing stopping the cell phone from toppling into the water. I didn't know if the shifting of his weight to that side of the boat did it, but as I got to within inches of grabbing the device, it slipped off the ledge. With zero leverage to move forward, I couldn't jump toward the phone fast enough to stop its fall.

Waiting for Morning Time

"Plunk," Bill's cell phone slipped into the water and under the floorboards. I struggled for a moment to try and find it, but it would be of no use now. Cell phones don't like salt water. I took a quick glance around the center console to see if I could locate Neal's cell phone. I didn't have a clue where it might be stowed. I'd remembered Neal putting a bag into one of the side storage compartments towards the back of the boat, which was now… fully submerged.

I heard Bill pounding his hand against the hull. Bill yelled. "I'm trying to get Neal's attention!"

Okay, I thought. If we were going down, we needed to make sure there was a fighting chance at survival until we were rescued. I didn't have the heart to tell Bill the banging could also attract sharks. He soon stopped, however, having hurt his hand in the process. I began firing things out of the boat: bumpers, life jackets, and anything that could float.

I yelled to Bill, "Hey," getting his attention and tossing a life preserver to him. Unfortunately, it appeared to be a youth's size. Bill could barely get it over his shoulders. *Neal must have the adult life jackets stowed somewhere*, I searched again to no avail. I tried to find some of the water they'd brought. After a quick scan, I could see the case submerged against the transom. If I went down there, adding my weight to the back of the boat, we would be under in seconds.

I looked up at Bill, who held onto the bow, probably ten feet above where I stood near the console. I decided I had better start climbing up there now or I'd never make it. All of my strength would be required to find a way to the peak of the boat. It took a lot to get this big frame where it needed to go, especially when that place was straight up.

It was a struggle, but once I reached where he clung to the gunnels, Bill put his free arm over one of my shoulders. I could see his eyes welling up. "I love you, dad." His chin started to tremble, quicker breaths as if he couldn't get enough oxygen.

"Settle down, Bill. This sort of thing happens and once someone figures out we're missing. We'll be rescued in no time." I paused for a moment. "I'm a little more worried about what Neal's going to say when he comes up and finds out what happened. This boat is his pride and joy... the brand-new motors."

Bill shook his head. "I get that, dad, but I saw what's going on down there, you weren't able to get out a distress call. Unless someone happens upon us, it could be tomorrow before anyone rescues us. It'll be the girls who notice we're missing, and that could take some time. We could be late for dozens of reasons; this isn't very good... it's really bad actually if you really want to know." He struggled to pull himself further up onto the bow, looking down at the dark water as if it were acid.

I hated to admit it, but Bill was right. If I'd been able to send out a MAYDAY, the Coast Guard would have been here within the hour. It could be dark before anyone really took notice. I looked down at the black water, which would be cold- in the mid-sixties. I wondered how long we would be able to survive... overnight? I looked back at Bill.

Bill nodded. "I can tell by the look on your face, that you're thinking the same things I am." He paused, trying to gather his thoughts. When they came out, his voice was very quiet, which is not normal for Bill. He stuttered. "I...I don't know if I can do this." He looked as if he was about to cry or fall into a full-blown panic attack.

I looked at him sternly feeling my cheeks burning. "What do you mean? Let's get a grip, Bill. We're going to be fine. We may have to take ourselves out of our comfort zone for a while. I am a little worried, I'll admit it, but we're going to have to remain calm."

"Comfort zone... are you whacked? Dad, there are sharks in these waters. I've seen documentaries and movies about people lost at sea and how they had to fend off the stupid things. Most of the time, I'm sorry to say, they get eaten... by the stupid sharks. I'm not doing

Waiting for Morning Time

this." He began to hyperventilate, bending over again trying to catch his breath.

It was at this point I realized that I had a real problem on my hands with Bill. I also wondered where the heck Neal could be. The boat lurched, the stern sinking further into the water. I wasn't sure how Bill would take what I would say next. I looked around in the water. Some of the stuff I'd jettisoned out of the boat began to drift out of the cabin.

I steeled myself. I needed to be the adult in the room and yelled at Bill, looking him in the eye, holding onto the scruff of his shirt. "This boat's gonna flip any moment. We don't want to be on it when it does, which means, we need to jump into the water now!" I could read the trepidation on Bill's face... no, it was not trepidation, it was terror. I decided to attack the problem from a different angle. "Look... it's too wavy for sharks." I had heard they didn't like being on the surface when it's wavy, I couldn't cite a particular source, but I needed to calm Bill down or he was going to get clunked on the head and drown if he got in the way when the big boat flipped. It was imminent.

"Listen to me. I'm counting to three, and then we're both going in the water. One, two, three." I grabbed Bill's arm, and to my surprise, my son followed me feet first into the cold Gulf water. Our heads bobbed under, the children's lifejackets doing little more than keeping us semi-buoyant. We surfaced, coughing up seawater. Within minutes, the Scarab heaved and flipped over, exposing the bottom of the hull and the motors briefly. I remember thinking once again, *Neal is gonna be quite angry.*

The water was cold... *too* cold. I experienced my own pangs of panic... I didn't know if I would be able to do what lay ahead for us either... things I was asking of Bill. I felt my heart flip in my chest... *my medicine.* In time, I settled down a bit, once my body became somewhat used to the temperature of the water.

Bill started flailing his arms, kicking his feet, and swimming towards the back of the boat. He scampered around the hull and tried to get up on top of the hull by the transom. In the process, he managed to cut his leg pretty badly on one of the props. He made it onto the V at the bottom of the boat, only to slide back into the water. His eyes rolled up into his skull as I tried to make him look at me, both hands on either side of his face. "Don't try that again."

"I'm bleeding… I can't believe it, sh-sh-sharks can sense blood from miles away. I'm not doing this." He rolled his head back, looking up at the blue sky.

I laughed, if that's possible. "What do you mean *you're not doing this?* You have no choice. You're here right *now*… in the water with me." I couldn't remember from where, but I visualized Bill as a young boy doing the same thing… swimming lessons? Learning to skate? I remembered him not doing what he was supposed to do at the time, and I had a bad feeling about my son's attitude… these distant past experiences flooded my memory. In the present moment, he was locked in and scared, perhaps in shock. I hated to admit it, but it helped me out to a degree. I reverted back to the father looking out for the child. As a parent, sometimes you have no choice with small children. It swiftly took my fearful thoughts away from the crisis ... at least for a short time.

Bill didn't listen and tried to climb back on the boat. That time, he managed to stay on for a time, blood from his leg kept running down the white hull in a small, thin water diluted stream. I followed him up. We sat for a bit, thankful for the blistering sun shining on our cold wet bodies. The bliss was short-lived, as we both slipped off when a rogue wave slapped up against the side of the overturned boat, tossing us back into the water. I knew I didn't have the energy to try getting back up on the hull again, my recent bi-pass surgery weighing on my mind. I settled in a few yards away from the boat, holding on to the bowline. Bill seemed obsessed about the sharks and continued

Waiting for Morning Time

to clamber up the transom. I yelled at him as he nearly skewered himself on an engine again. "You're gonna use up your strength! The waves will keep getting bigger, this ain't getting any easier. YOU WILL FALL OFF AGAIN!"

As I predicted, Bill slipped back off the side of the boat. I pulled myself around, grabbing Bill's shoulders so he could look me in the face. Bill stared back, his eyes vacant of cognizance or reason. He blinked incessantly. I knew for certain that Bill had lost his senses, but I wasn't sure I knew how to deal with the situation other than keeping a close eye on him— he wasn't listening. When I let go of him, Bill wrapped his arms around his chest. I pulled one of his hands free and forced him to grab onto the bowline, wrapping it around the width of his hand twice. I turned and looked up at the bright sun and said a quiet prayer to our savior, Jesus Christ, hoping he would listen.

CHAPTER FOUR

MERRY FELT off her game. Priding herself on being a glass half-full, her glass felt half-empty today. Merry wished she had gone with the men ... plain and simple. She could tell Jackie and Anna detected a degree of resentment as she kept to her corner of the vehicle. The bad feelings were not directed at her friends. The van was quiet, all four kids relaxed in various modes of slumber and boredom. Everyone stared out the window as they traveled north on I-75, a monotonous straight road sided with pine trees and a swamp. It would take one and a half hours to reach *Busch Gardens*.

After an hour, Merry decided she needed to change her attitude, to be in the present for the kids—they deserved her attention. Once she came to this realization, her mood improved. She felt bad for Anna. Merry hadn't spent any time with her since her arrival. Anna's father recently passed away from Cancer at fifty-two. To make matters worse, her father's closest brother died a week later of a heart attack. It was only reasonable for Anna to be emotional. Merry had forgotten to be cognizant of her needs riling in her self-motivated funk.

When Anna offered her a bottle of water, Merry accepted.

"You know, Merry, you could have stayed home." Anna,

chomping at the bit, opened up the conversation, not knowing what she had done to the woman to deserve the silent treatment. She felt isolated enough.

Merry chose her words carefully. At the onset of the car ride, Anna seemed happy enough that the kids were occupied. She was on a much-deserved vacation. She didn't want to upset Anna for obvious reasons. Anna Lipsit was a genuine sweetheart and didn't deserve Merry's quiet negativity.

"No, I'm fine," Merry lied.

Normally, it would be difficult to get the two of them to stop once they got to talking. Conversely, Anna could be pretty quiet, a byproduct of her extensive hearing loss. It took a bit to get her out of her shell, and not a lot to put her back in it.

Talking out of character, Anna wouldn't let it go. "I can tell that you don't want to come with us. Jackie and I could have done this on our own." Anna put her hand on top of Merry's, looking at her out of the side of her eye as she drove.

Merry tried her best to put on a genuine smile. "No, honestly, I'll be fine once we get there. I'm just feeling a little off. I've got a bad feeling about *something,* and I can't put my finger on it." Then it hit her. "I'm sorry," she looked back at Jackie sitting in the middle seat, then back up at Anna behind the wheel. "I feel as if the guys pawned this off on us... feeling guilty they were still going out on the water, and we weren't. It might have been better if we'd come up with the idea together. I could tell Lew knew I was off when we went our separate ways. He never lets things fester." She paused, trying to think of the best way to put it. "For the first time since Lew and I have been together I feel... he left me behind and... I feel resentful. There's something else not quite right. It's like I have a premonition pulling at me. When I think about the fellas out there in the Gulf, my stomach clenches. It's as if they shouldn't be going out on the water. I've never felt this way before. Lew and Neal are water buddies, they do this all the time. Why do I feel so off?"

Jackie sighed, deflecting the negativity. "Okay, girls, let's make the best of it. I'm excited to be going. It's for the kids and you know... we might have some fun! Merry, you and Lew live in a fantasy. Let it go. It's okay to be apart. Let that cord stretch a little. You can do it." She giggled. "Suck it up, buttercup! Being apart is normal." Narrowing her eyes, she gave Merry a sly smile.

Jackie was a no-bull kind of gal, who possessed a way of cutting to the chase. She gave Merry her marching orders and she was right. Once Merry acknowledged her behavior, having it pointed out to her, her foul mood began to swing. She could see the look on the kids' faces. They were so excited. Kids can sense unease. She shouldn't have been so selfish, cheating them of their day. She also knew the boys were looking forward to the dive. Simply put, Merry wished she and Lew had made the decision to go different ways ... together.

"You're right." Merry blurted out suddenly. "We're almost there anyway. Let's make the best of it." She turned to Anna, placing her hand on her knee. "I'm sorry, sweetheart, I know you've been through a lot lately."

"It's okay, Merry. I'm working my way through it. Please don't worry."

Jackie spoke. "What's this all about?"

"Is it okay if I tell her?" Merry looked at Anna.

Anna took a deep breath and nodded.

"Anna's father recently passed away after a long battle with cancer."

Jackie put a hand on Anna's shoulder.

Merry continued. "To make matters worse, her father's brother, who Anna had been very close with, also died... perhaps of a broken heart ... a week later."

Anna added. "Yeah, my uncle suffered a heart attack, very sudden."

Jackie frowned. "That's terrible! I feel so bad for you. How's your mom?"

"She's getting through it. Mom's tougher than I am. I cried for two weeks straight." She sighed. "I still have a hard time holding back my tears."

Jackie shook her head. "Let's get our minds off all our sadness and have fun today." She clapped her hands. Jackie's positive attitude became contagious and soon, everyone was high-fiving and jabbering about how much fun they were going to have.

***

The packed minivan pulled into the massive parking lot. Once they got past the commercialism and the long lines, there were some interesting attractions. *Busch Gardens* is all about its African theme with the different sections representing various parts of the Continent: Pantopia, Nairobi, Morocco, and the Congo. The main attractions were the roller coasters and the fabulous Zoo, interspersed throughout the different sections.

All seven of them rolled out of the van and stretched after the long drive. Anna went to the back door to retrieve the picnic baskets, sunscreen, and hats. Merry and Jackie could hear her jiggling around with the back door latch, soon to be followed by a very clear swear word directed at her husband. "&%$@, Bill!"

Suspecting the problem, Merry walked back to help and Jackie followed.

Anna stood fiddling with the latch. "I told him to get this fixed before the trip."

Jackie shook her head. "Let's be fair, he didn't know we'd be coming here today."

"No. I asked him to fix it before we left Niagara Falls. It's been stuck for months now." Anna kept fiddling with the handle, which slowly progressed to banging on the back of the hatch with the side of her fist.

Merry moved forward and stopped Anna when she looked as if

she intended to dropkick the back of the door. "That won't help."

"True, but it'll make me feel a lot better." Her resentment towards Bill's negligence could be seen etched on her features.

Merry smiled, finding some humor in Anna's facial expression. "Here, let me have a try. Can I see the keys?" By this point, Anna had been fiddling with the door for a few minutes. The kids were getting antsy, standing in the shade of a Palm Tree. Merry tried turning the key in the lock, but it seemed to be stuck with something blocking the key from making a full half-turn like normal. She fiddled with it for a few minutes longer and would have continued to do so if Jackie hadn't come up with the eventual solution.

"Billy, come here." Jackie yelled. Billy made his way over to the women in no real hurry. "Jump in the back and crawl over the seat. See if there's an inside latch."

Pay dirt! When the back hatch popped open, Billy nearly spilled out onto the ground along with the bags packed in tightly against the door.

***

After nearly an hour of messing with the van, they encountered a long entry line to the park. Everyone was hot and bothered under the ninety-degree sun. Merry resisted the urge to accelerate the collective mood when she found out the ticket prices. She had contemplated treating everyone until she added up the cost to nearly three hundred dollars, not including state tax. They agreed to pay their own way. Merry promised to buy everyone a cold drink once inside the park. Merry thought about Lew, the man she admired. He never seemed to be bothered about money. In fact, he didn't get bothered about much. A pang of worry suddenly came over her and she wondered if Lew should even be diving. He'd only recovered from the quadruple bypass the previous year and his cardiologist had warned him about scuba diving. Merry sighed as she walked through the turnstile. *Let it go.*

CHAPTER FIVE

11:30 a.m. Saturday

IT TOOK Merry an hour to realize she'd left her cell phone in the minivan, a major irritation. She took a few minutes to herself and found a pay phone. Lew and Merry seldom went very long without communication. That was how they operated. She dropped four or five dollars' worth of quarters into the slot during the course of the conversation. Lew picked up after four rings.

"This is Lew."

"Hey... how's it going with you?"

"Getting a little choppy, winds picking up, but the sun's still out and I have a Mountain Dew, so I'm happy."

"It's getting a little windy here as well, they've closed a couple of the rides. Where are the other guys?"

"Neal's in the water right now retrieving Bill's weight belt."

"Bill's not diving?"

"Nope! Believe me, he's none too happy about it. I think the waves and his equipment were not adjusted correctly. He'll be fine in Captiva; I feel bad for him though. He's coming around slowly. He has a beer now and some chips. How are the kids?"

Merry felt sad to hear that things hadn't worked out for Bill. She knew how much he had been looking forward to the dive. There would be better days. She didn't mean to hesitate to respond to Lew's question, but she needed a minute to let the information churn around. She was sure he picked up on the silence. No one could read her so well. "We're okay. I think Billy got heatstroke before we made it into the park. He threw up in the parking lot."

"That didn't take long. You don't sound happy Merry?"

"We had to mess around with the back door on the darn minivan. Anna's going to wring Bill's neck when we all get back. She wanted him to fix it before they left home."

The phone line became static filled for a few moments. "Merry, we're losing reception. We're thirteen miles out you know."

More static. "Love you, Lew, I didn't get a chance to say that this morning." She hesitated. I was more than happy to hear those words and it helped ease the bad feeling I'd been left with since that morning. She broke the silence. "All righty then, I'll let you go. We'll probably be later than you." She paused. "When is that front supposed to move in?"

"Not until tomorrow, no need to worry."

"Okay, love you… I know this isn't what you wanted to do today. I promise I'll make it up to you. We're not going to be here too long, and we'll have a nice Grouper dinner. A couple of scotch and waters will fix everything up."

"It might take more than a couple, Lewie."

"We'll see you soon." The connection ended.

***

Merry hung up the phone and walked back to where Anna and Jackie stood in a ridiculously long line, waiting to buy souvenirs. The kids were sitting under a tree eating ice cream bars.

Jackie spoke up. "How are the fellas?"

"Well, not exactly what I'd expected ... Neal's down in the water spear fishing and Lew's up top fixing Bill and himself a drink."

Jackie frowned. "Bill didn't go diving? That's surprising. It was Bill wanting to go diving that turned this day around."

Merry knew Jackie didn't mean it the way it came out. "It seems he had problems with his gear."

Jackie nodded, seeming to accept the excuse. "Oh! That's too bad. Hopefully, it will be a lot calmer when we head down to Captiva." She smiled, taking a deep breath. "I say we try to leave before dinner time." She looked at the kids. "Just a few more rides?"

Anna looked concerned. "Did Lew say Bill was okay? He's been so hyped about this… all he's talked about for months."

Merry knew Bill had been enjoying more than a before-dinner cocktail at home and how pleased Anna had been to see her husband take an interest in diving and away from the bars. "He's all right, honey. Lew said it's a little rough out there and it was Bill's decision to come out of the water. Lew said he's happy enough… he's enjoying a beer."

Anna rolled her eyes at Merry's last bit of information. "I know ... he's out there with his dad… a good chance to bond a little." She gave Merry a small smile.

Merry turned back to Jackie. "Sure, let's see how many rides we can get on before we leave." Merry was sure everyone was surprised by her change in attitude. The other two women seemed to pick up on the new plan and headed out to brave the long lines in the hot Florida sun. As far as Merry was concerned, she'd made up with her sweetheart; everything was good.

***

Around five o'clock, everyone had enough of *Busch Gardens*. Jackie once again sent Billy in through the minivan to unlock the back hatch from the inside. Everyone packed themselves in for the long ride back.

Merry found her phone under the front passenger's seat and dialed Lew's number. It rang several times before kicking into voice mail. She stopped the call but felt an odd zap of electrical worry snap up her spine. She didn't like it one bit but kept her concerns to herself. "Strange!"

"Something wrong with the phone, no charge, bad reception?" asked Jackie.

"Could be, I'll try again in half an hour. So, tell me, how are your parents and the Everglades gallery?"

Jackie smiled, eager to change the topic. While Jackie had let Merry and Lew go several years ago, Clyde had re-hired them a few years back to work at their Big Cypress Gallery. It had been an awkward time, but it had helped them out of a hard spot financially. "Niki and Clyde are doing great. We've just opened up a couple of cottages where people can stay and enjoy Everglade Swamp Walks. They enjoy sharing their backyard and showing folks the unique, one-of-a-kind ecosystem. It's a big thing with people looking to discover more about the Everglades--pretty cool. We had a couple who'd just done a Nile River Cruise and they commented how their stay with us beat the Egyptian Tour hands down. Clyde is still plodding around up to his knees in the water trying to find that perfect picture."

"How are you doing, Jackie? We haven't talked in a long time, not since before the baby."

Jackie smiled, eager to hear Merry's concern. Her response was upbeat. "Busy as all get out, kids, the galleries. Neal is thinking of coming on full-time with Dad. We have the dry-cleaning business and our real estate investments; they're doing really well… though I think he'd like a change."

"You okay with that? Not easy working with your husband."

"Sure, why not? We get along like two high-school kids. I love him to death and besides, he keeps to himself and doesn't talk a lot. He'll be doing the day-to-day stuff, more to do with the prints and photography."

Merry nodded, but she was not really paying close attention. That heat flashed up her spine was turning into a fireball of a headache. "Let me try Lew again." She hit the numbers of his cell carefully. It rang four times and clicked over to voicemail. "Still no answer... I'm a bit concerned." Merry swiped away sweat from her forehead even though the car's airflow was roaring cold.

Although Anna had put off incurring roaming charges, she now tried Bill's cell. Nothing! No connection, no voicemail. "I can't reach Bill either. Maybe they're hauling out, or Bill might not even have his phone with him."

Jackie shook her head, not knowing whether she felt mad or beginning to worry when she tried Neal's number. "It'll be a bit strange if all three don't answer." She said before her phone didn't connect with her husband's cell. Her mind rambled through all the viable explanations as to why all three of the men were not available. "What the devil? Maybe they've stopped off for a drink someplace noisy. You never know? I bet they're having a good old time. Now, I wanna find out where they're at ... We could meet up with them, no sense letting the boys have all the fun!"

Merry knew she could count on Lew to want to be back before they arrived home. He's considerate that way. "They're probably out back at your place, Jackie, left their phones in their bags or in the car."

Jackie shook her head. "A bit early for that, Neal likes to take his time cleaning that boat, flushing the engines out. Maybe they bagged some fish. He'd want to clean them at the marina. He doesn't like the guts sitting around the garage waiting for garbage day. I wouldn't expect them home until six." She gazed out the window looking towards the Gulf. The sky looked purplish black ... not a good sign. "I'm so happy they weren't going to be out there long. Look at those nasty clouds to the west.

The kids looked a bit cranky. "Let's stop for a bite-to-eat at Wendy's." Jackie figured the food might keep them quiet.

***

Merry tried Lew's phone one last time as they pulled off the highway at Venice. "Still NOTHING." Thoughts danced in her mind with so many ideas why they were not answering, but now her worry began to set in and quicken her heartbeat. All thoughts of the men having fun on the water or stopping for a drink faded away. Merry knew better. Her loving husband was too considerate not to have called her, even if the three of them were stopped someplace. Merry put her phone back into her purse.

The van became deathly quiet. Merry's fear for her husband must have shown on her face and that same fear made its way to both Jackie and Anna.

Anna started to cry.

Merry and Jackie knew she had been on the edge ... trying her best to hold back her worries. Merry placed her hand on Anna's knee, which only made things worse. Anna let out her pent-up anxiety with a wild-sounding wail.

Jackie turned around to look at the kids, their wide-eyed look-of-wonder stared back at her. The children didn't know how they were supposed to react or if they were supposed to be upset. Jackie only smiled. "Everything's all right. We're almost home! Who's gonna be first in the pool?" Her challenge seemed to keep them at bay for the moment.

Anna continued to wail uncontrollably, nearly driving off the road. "What am I going to do without him?" She swerved back into the middle of the highway.

Merry and Jackie looked each other in the eye, realizing they needed to get everyone out of the van and into the house so things could be kept calm. The kids didn't need to hear anymore.

Jackie spoke sternly to Anna. "Keep your eye on the road and remember what we're doing here. Let's get home safely... okay?"

Anna nodded, rocking forward and back in her seat as she navigated the road.

Merry tried to calm Anna. "Look honey, things happen. The men no doubt are busy. Neal and Lew know what they're doing. Maybe the boys are helping someone else out of a bad spot. Let's not jump to conclusions. We need to stay up." She nodded towards the kids in the back. "No more scary speculation."

Merry eyed Jackie in the backseat. Both women knew Kayla, Ashley, and Billy took in and understood everything being hinted at or said.

Anna sighed and shook her head. She put on her best fake smile. "You're right Merry, no sense jumping to conclusions." Her body language told a different story, her hands tightened on the steering wheel, her lips pulled back across her teeth.

***

It took ten more minutes to reach Jackie's house. All three wives knew they wouldn't see Neal's truck and boat parked in the driveway. As they passed the lake upon which Jackie and Neal's house was located, Merry could see at a distance how their women's intuition would prove to be correct ... the driveway was indeed empty, and the house looked dark and lonely.

The kids in the back began to sense there really was something wrong even though they seemed to be sitting in the back not paying attention.

Billy was the first to yell. "Where's Daddy?"

The other kids, Kayla and Ashley chimed in all looking for answers.

Merry's heart flipped in her chest. She could feel her face

Waiting for Morning Time

flushing red. She knew if she tried to speak, it would have come out gibberish -- gibberish was going through her head. Her hopes and desires were meshing with her doubts and fears.

Everyone else piled out of the car, except Anna. Merry blocked her in as Jackie took the kids inside. Staring up at Merry, she remained seated in the car with worry in her eyes. Anna appeared to be on the verge of panic. She kept her mouth drawn tight while opening and closing her fists. Still, when her tears flowed Anna managed to ask, "You okay, Merry?"

Merry was not okay and blurted out a feeble request. "Just give me a sec."

They both needed a moment to prepare for the ordeal ahead of them.

Merry worried her heart might stop as a pang of pain shot through her chest.

Anna stopped crying when she saw the physical distress on Merry's face. She put a hand on her shoulder. "I know I'm having a hard time but let me ask you again. ARE YOU OKAY, MERRY?"

Merry caught her breath finally and looked shocked by Anna's loud voice shouting at her. She placed her hand on top of Anna's and said, "I am., I didn't feel too good there for a moment. I'd been holding in my emotions, and they got the better of me."

Anna nodded. "It's okay to let them out. Bottled-up emotions can hurt you ... at least that's what my mother used to say."

"Anna, we can't go into that house looking a mess. Let's give ourselves a few minutes. I always feel better after I pray. Let's put our hopes out there in prayer."

Anna nodded.

When Merry began, the words flowed. "Jesus, bless our three men and bring them home safely. Bless these families and the children." She hugged Anna.

"That sure was a short prayer, Merry, you think we should make it longer?"

Christopher Bowron

Merry smiled. "We've said it all ... what more is there?"
Anna smiled and finished their prayer, "Amen!"

CHAPTER SIX

Nine p.m. Saturday Night – Venice Florida

JACKIE CAME out to the van to see what was keeping Merry and Anna. She poked her head in the van window and asked, "What's going on girls? We got a problem here?"

Anna spoke up. "Merry's... having a difficult time. I think she's all right now."

Jackie came closer to take a look at Merry. "You okay, girl?" Her eyes narrowed.

"Better now." With Jackie not being very religious, Merry didn't want to bother telling her how she'd encountered a few panicky moments and needed to speak to the Lord and ask for help in order to ground her feelings again.

"Glad to hear it. So, Neal's truck isn't here and it's after nine. They should've been back a long time ago. I tell you if there isn't a good reason why they haven't called and they are okay ... I'm gonna be really ticked off." She took a deep breath. "When I went into the house... first thing I saw was that the dogs hadn't been fed. There's no way Neal would have left the dogs alone for that long without feeding them. He dotes on those dogs as if they were his kids."

Merry nodded. "Good point. Is Snuggles okay in there?" Merry had left her dog at Jackie's house when they went to *Busch Gardens.*

"Yes. The kids are playing with her."

Merry asked, "Is there anywhere else you can think of where they might have stopped on the way back?"

"I was thinking the same thing. They might be at Neal's mother ... Cheryl's house. That's where Neal keeps the boat and she's a scotch drinker like Lew. Maybe they tied into a good bottle... or two and lost track of time. I'm going in now to give her a call."

Merry liked the fact that Jackie was coming up with ideas as to why the boys were not back. None of Jackie's ideas stopped the gnawing in the pit of Merry's stomach. She knew something went really wrong and when she shared her feelings with Anna, she agreed with Merry. If the boys were being negligent ... it was out of character for Lew. For that matter, it was out of character for Neal and Bill to frighten their wives without calling. Merry and Lew were tied at the hip and Merry knew he didn't like being away from her for too long. They had grown very dependent upon each other... maybe too much so, but neither of them complained. They enjoyed a late-in-life marriage, their connection solid. Each one could depend upon the other one *till death do they part.*

Jackie did call her mother-in-law's cell. It seemed to ring for a long time before she picked it up. "Hello?"

"Hi, Cheryl, it's Jackie."

"Jackie? Oh sorry, I'd fallen asleep on the couch."

"Sorry to wake you, but it's important."

Hearing Jackie's dialogue, Merry's heart leaped in her chest. She could see a similar look on Anna's face. Both women slid into more fear for their husband's safety as they listened. Their eyes flickered back to Jackie as she spoke with Neal's mother. They could both understand how Cheryl might also feel hearing the alarming news.

"Look, Neal went out fishing in the Gulf earlier today with Lew and Bill Lipsit. I'm sure he already told you this because he was going to park the boat back at your place?"

"Yes… he told me about his plans when he came to pick up the boat yesterday. What's wrong, Jackie?"

Jackie could hear the nervous waver in her voice. "We were hoping he was over there with you… dropping off the boat. But since you're asleep, it doesn't sound as if that's likely. We just got home from taking the kids to *Busch Gardens* and the fellas aren't home yet. We've had no contact from them since early this afternoon."

"There must be an explanation. Maybe they stopped off at a bayside bar. Or maybe engine problems. I'm sure there's been something unexpected. Neal and Lew are seasoned boaters… surely, they're safe, Jackie."

Jackie refused to let her mother-in-law's dismissal of her worry bother her. "Yes, I know Neal's an expert boater. He's my husband, but he's not back. The motors are brand new. We figured all this time maybe they stopped at your place after dropping off the boat."

"What are you saying? They haven't called?" Cheryl's voice raised a pitch. "Have you been to the boat launch to see if the truck and trailer are still there?"

"No, but calm down, Cheryl."

"Please don't tell me to calm down, I'm his mother and you're worrying me."

Jackie drew a deep breath. "Okay. I apologize. Yes. That's what I'm thinking. We're going to leave as soon as we can get the kids settled."

"You'll call me as soon as you get there?"

"Okay… yes, I'll give you a call right away." Jackie hung up.

The three women went directly to the kitchen where Merry said, "Jackie, I need a drink, do you have something strong?"

"Yes, we've got bourbon, it'll calm the nerves." She rummaged through the liquor cabinet finding a good bottle and poured each of them a long shot over ice.

Jackie sat down on one of the stools ringing the kitchen island.

"No sign of them at Cheryl's. You heard that ... and now, I think I may have stirred up too much with that call... but we had to find out and she deserves to know there might be trouble." Jackie sucked in another deep breath, sipping the strong liquor now warming her.

Merry nodded and remembered how Jackie once told her how Cheryl could be excitable. "I heard you mention going to the marina ... sounds like a plan."

She nodded. "Yeah, I'm going to the boat ramp. I wanna see if the truck and trailer are still there."

Merry said, "I'm going with you. If they're there, you'll want to drive them back."

"My thoughts exactly. Though I may think about that. What if they were to find their way back to the launch and it wasn't there? Neal would be mad at me. I'd appreciate your company nonetheless."

Merry glanced around the countertop. "Where do you keep your phone book? I'm going to look up the number for the Coast Guard Search and Rescue, just in case."

Jackie nodded. "Anna, you're going to have to watch the kids. We'll help you settle them down before we leave."

She nodded, on the edge of tears. "What could have happened?"

Jackie answered. "Who knows? It's an awfully big gulf out there. Whatever's going on, they're not able to make contact and that's what worries me the most. It could be they've experienced engine trouble. Both engines are brand new, but sometimes, crazy things happen with new motors, like electronics. They might have gone quite a way out and can't get cell reception. This is what I'm thinking." She paused for a moment. "I don't feel we should call this in, though, until we know for sure the truck and trailer are still at the launch."

Anna's eyes welled up again. "Let's get the kids settled, I don't mind watching them. I'll be honest... I'm too upset to be of help. I couldn't bear to go there right now."

Waiting for Morning Time

"Good girl." Jackie gave her a long hug, remembering Anna's recent hard times. "I'm sure everything's going to be fine. We'll be giving them hell soon enough for being so damn inconsiderate." She gave Anna a big smile, which seemed to console the woman enough to move forward.

***

Getting the kids tucked in was never Merry's thing. Instead, she made herself useful and ripped the emergency rescue numbers for the Police, Fire Department, and the Coast Guard out of the phone book.

Anna looked beat, perfectly understandable under the circumstances. "Call me as soon as you find out anything." While she was the best person to stay back with the children, her lack of not knowing what was going on left her in a fearful state. She waved to the two women pulling off the driveway in Jackie's car. Returning to the house, Anna began cleaning the kitchen. She needed to be busy and needed to keep her mind calm.

***

Jackie began to talk as soon as they slid into the front seats. "Poor soul, Anna looks like a deer caught in the headlights."

Merry nodded. "To be honest, I feel the same way. I hope it doesn't show."

"No. You've been pretty calm I'd have to say. I'll tell you though, while I might appear to be in control mode right now, I'm really in attack mode. But I'm scared to death. This is how I get when things aren't going well. Neal hates it when I get this way. He doesn't like confrontation."

Merry sighed. "People react in different ways. I pray and you go *Rambo*." They both chuckled, despite the ever-growing seriousness of the situation. "You know what we're going to find, don't you?"

"Come on, Merry, let's stay positive."

Jackie turned onto the main road as Merry sent a silent prayer for the men's safety. Prayer was the only thing she could do as they sped off towards Venice boat ramp.

***

Driving along, Jackie's thoughts went to Neal. They hadn't been together long enough for her to lose her husband. She'd met Neal months after having Kayla. Her beautiful baby girl was the product of a very short relationship. Her mother Niki stayed by her side and acted as her pregnancy partner. Niki became her best friend when she broke down and told her she was pregnant. She stood by her side and supported her to tell her father.

Jackie remembered being afraid to tell her father about the baby. She'd asked to see him, saying she had something to tell him. His face looked pale and worried when she walked in the door. She could see he feared bad news. When she revealed her secret and showed him how much she wanted the baby, he became overjoyed.

"This isn't death. This is a new life… this is a good thing, Jackie!" They had only recently dealt with the death of their son, Ted. Jackie's brother died in a car accident. Going forward was a good thing.

Her parents came from the cool generation of hippies, gypsies and free spirits. They raised Jackie and Ted while travelling the western seaboard of the United States. They lived in California and sometimes Mexico, but they never lived in a building. If it wasn't a camper, it was a sailboat. Clyde and Niki were excellent sailors. Jackie slept in close quarters with Ted for many years growing up. They had always been close. The Butchers had been lured to Florida by the promise of turquoise waters differing from the dark black waters of the Pacific. Their little family ultimately settled in Ft. Myers.

When Kayla was born, motherhood brought out the best in

Waiting for Morning Time

Jackie. Being grandparents did the same for Niki and Clyde. They all grew to love and cherish Kayla. While Jackie continued to run her business and be an active parent, she didn't know how she would ever be able to meet a man. One of her close friends suggested trying a dating service. Reluctant to meet a stranger on the internet, she also felt she couldn't see herself trotting around bars with a one-year-old. After putting her profile on the website, she went on four or five dates without a connection. When she received a call back from Neal, she smiled and remembered how they talked for hours, their common love of sailing being the theme of their conversation.

On her first date with Neal, Jackie had to bring Kayla. Neal did admit later that meeting someone with a kid hadn't been on his wish list. However, the bond with Kayla grew strong to the point where Kayla would know Neal as her *Daddy*. Neal adopted Kayla and became her father when she was three years old.

It was on their second date that Jackie knew Neal was the one and she wanted to marry him. While she had always dated tall blond men, Jackie knew the tall ... dark ... and handsome Neal was the catch of her life. However, she wouldn't wait forever for him to propose. She planned to give him until Christmas, roughly six months' time. When a wedding ring didn't appear, she gave Neal a little more time until Valentine's Day.

They were to go to a Valentine's Dinner/Commodore's ball at the Venice Yacht Club, where Neal's parents were members, and his dad, Robert, would be sworn in as Commodore that night. She pulled out all the stops, dressing in a sexy red dress, looking like Julia Roberts. Jackie kept her eyes on the road as she smiled. Remembering the conversation, it started out with small talk, leading up to more serious matters.

"*So, Neal, am I your Valentine?*"

Neal rubbed his jaw as he drove to the party. "*I'll think about that.*"

"You'll think about that? What the hell's that supposed to mean?"

"Just what I said," his low deadpan voice irritated her. He continued to drive past the Yacht Club, pulling into the parking lot next to one of the Jetties.

Jackie's heart began to beat, fearing he might be breaking up with her.

He parked and looked her in the eye, pulling a small black box out of his pocket.

Her heart skipped and her Rambo Anger brewed in her stomach. "So..."

Neal could be shy, to say the least. "I guess I'm asking to marry you."

"You guess? What about being my Valentine?"

"I was afraid you were going to say no to me... I mean about marrying me."

"You silly, man!" She kissed his lips hard and long. "Yes!"

Neal only smiled, being at a loss for words to show his happiness. Needless to say, they were the news of the dance.

Merry stopped her prayers to glance over at Jackie. "You're smiling?"

Jackie nodded. "I guess I am. I was thinking about Neal."

Merry shook her head. "I can't stop thinking about Lew. This is so hard."

Jackie nodded again, showing she understood, but trying to hold back her tears.

***

The boat launch lay on the outskirts of Venice. Jackie pulled off the ramp from the main road and turned into the parking lot. The moon and stars were very bright, which only made the reality clearer as they

Waiting for Morning Time

saw the lonely truck and trailer sitting pretty much smack dab in the middle of the tarmac without another vehicle around them.

Merry's heart sank. She looked over at Jackie to see her mouth pulled tight, chin on her chest as she looked down to her lap.

Jackie pulled up next to the truck and got out. Merry followed. They both made a circle of the vehicle. Not knowing what else to do, they kept looking at it as if it could shed some vital clue as to the disappearance of the three men. It didn't enlighten the two women. Instead, seeing the truck and trailer still parked there and not driven home made the fact crystal clear ... their three husbands were *missing*.

***

They must have circled and touched the truck and trailer parked there ten times until they both stood and cried. Hugging each other, they let their tears flow. Both suspected the truth but didn't want to face the truth. The wind began to whip around them. It felt much more violent than they both expected from the coming storm.

Merry's chest thumped hard with the thought of Lew out there in the terrible weather, moving in as predicted. Only a silent prayer could ease her fears and give her hope. *Please God give us your wisdom, and Jesus give us your strength, we are gonna need it.*

Looking at each other, both women felt icy desperation crawling up their spines. Their mouths were gaping open. Both were at a loss for words. Jackie broke the silence. "Give me the number for the Coast Guard. Something real bad happened to those men."

Merry nodded. "Do you want the Marine Patrol or the Coast Guard?"

"Coast Guard!" She snapped back. Not meaning to be abusive, Jackie was short-tempered, trying to stay focused. "And let's get into the car."

Merry read off the number for the Flotilla 8-6 Venice Auxiliary.

Jackie put her phone on speaker. They could hear the call being re-routed and connected. The Venice Auxiliary must have shut down for the night.

Finally, a female dispatch answered. "United States Coast Guard?"

Jackie spoke several decibels louder than her normal voice, needing to be understood. "I'd like to report a missing boat… three men on board."

"What waters are you calling about?"

"Venice, Florida."

"Hold on, I'll put you through to St. Pete's."

"Thank you."

Click. The women could hear the call being re-routed.

"St Pete's Coast Guard."

"Yes. My name is Jackie Obendorf, and I need to report a missing vessel with three men on board."

"When did they go missing?" The man's voice sounded bored—disengaged.

"Sometime later in the day ... I would guess."

"Do you know there's been a *small craft advisory* has just been issued for Collier, Lee, Sarasota, and Hillsborough Counties? He paused for a moment. "Were they out for a cruise, fishing?"

"Yes. Spearfishing off Venice, one of the man-made reefs ten or so miles out. They were supposed to be home four hours ago. They went out earlier in the day when the weather was perfectly fine."

"Let's hope that they're off the water now as it's getting pretty bad out on the Gulf— dangerous!"

"No." Jackie paused. "They would have called. I think something has happened to them and they're still out there. We just found our truck and trailer still parked at the Venice public boat launch. I'm looking at it as we speak. Two of the men are seasoned boaters, familiar with the waters and weather."

"Ma'am, we've not logged any distress calls from any craft this

Waiting for Morning Time

evening, nor this afternoon for that matter ... which is the prerequisite for an immediate call for a search and rescue. Happens all the time. They're probably in some marina bar and haven't called in yet. These days with technology, no one misses calling in a MAYDAY."

"Our husbands aren't in some bar. I guarantee, if they were on dry land, THEY-WOULD-HAVE-CALLED-US. This isn't like them ... do you understand?"

"Mrs. Oben...."

"Obendorf!"

"Sorry, Mrs. Obendorf, I understand your fear, and the Coast Guard is here to help, but it's a big ocean and we have to follow some protocol. I'd suggest you call back in the morning and file an official report when you know for sure that they are lost. We require time to make an assessment and search plan to start without a *distress call.* This takes time and manpower."

"You mean to say... we have to wait before we can make a report. Then you have to figure out whether it's legitimate or not?"

Silence.

Merry nodded to Jackie, proud she was not so eager to back down and give up.

The man spoke. "No, I can create your report right now. Is this what you would like to do?"

Jackie looked at Merry who nodded. "Yes, we would like to do that."

"Okay, but, there most likely won't be anyone going out until the morning. If we can find the manpower and my superiors give the okay, it might be sooner. The Doppler indicates the wind is going to continue to escalate through the night. The real brunt of the storm will be hitting tomorrow morning. I'll also tell you a plane went down in the Everglades this evening and our C-130s are down somewhere between Miami and Naples searching."

Jackie spoke. "I'd like to do the report now."

"Absolutely, but it will take some time."

It took at least an hour for the information to be given, the questions going into great detail above and beyond their names and the description of the boat. She also told him the last time they had made contact and the best guess as to where they might have been. Jackie had been to the dive sites before and cited the names and approximate locations of a few of the probable spots, M-16 and M-9 being two of them.

Jackie experienced a flash of panic when the dispatcher started to ask about hair and eye color. It somehow drove home the seriousness of the situation. They were not messing around, the reality that the men were in a life-threatening situation hit home.

"Can you give me a contact number, Mrs. Obendorf? We'll call you if and when we are able to start a search."

"Are you saying they won't be able to go up tonight? Don't you have infrared? Can't they at least take a pass on their way back from the Everglades?"

"We've discussed this. Be like looking for a needle in a haystack, ma'am. I'll promise you this. I'll pass the report on to my commanding officer right away. We'll call you when a decision is made. It's not up to me to decide where the manpower is sent. I'm a dispatcher. I stress the point... check in with some of the local bars and restaurants that have wharves or landings to harbor a boat."

"Local Bars in Venice shut down at 8 PM. If I don't get a call at the break of dawn, you know I'll be right on it."

"10-4, Mrs. Obendorf ... and like I say, I mean it in the best of ways, I hope your men are safe. I understand your fear. Most everyone who calls in is the same way. We'll check in, first thing in the morning—or sooner." *Click.*

"They don't seem to give a crap!" Jackie yelled.

"Sounds like a matter of protocol to me." Merry regretted the words.

"Sorry, Merry, protocol isn't good enough. What if they're out there in a goddamned situation... Lew's got heart problems? Time could be of the essence." Jackie made a move as if she wanted to throw the phone across the parking lot. "Are you gonna take *okay* as good enough when your man's life might be in peril? I'm not. We need to get focused here."

Merry nodded, feeling ashamed of her ability to take the easy answers of others as gospel. "As you said on the phone, Lew and especially Neal are very experienced. I can't see what might have happened. They were both raised on the water."

Jackie sighed in exasperation. "Yes. They were, but that doesn't give us answers." They both stood looking out at the Gulf. The strength of the wind kept increasing to the point where they both had a hard time standing upright. They now envisioned their men miles out on the Gulf in the wind, waves... and darkness. "No one should be out there", Jackie murmured more to herself than to Merry. After a few minutes of silence, Jackie spoke up, "Unbelievable... no, let me rephrase, possibly believable. That's not a normal sea. Bad things can happen to good boaters, even excellent boaters in weather like this and it's only going to get worse he said. Maybe the boat flipped over on the way in. That's a strong possibility. It could have happened in some unexpected fashion. This is why they call these things accidents; no one plans on them happening." She looked down at Merry who sagged lower into the seat, not wanting to stand anymore. Her head kept bobbing slightly. She didn't want to voice another concern—that of pirates. They did exist. It was not unheard of for a boat to be robbed in full daylight. She caught her breath with the thought. Jackie let the words get outta her mouth. "What if the guys are already gone?" She added in her own mind, *robbed and shot*. Both of their hearts took a flip.

Merry quickly tried to negate that notion. "No... I can't let my mind go there, neither of us can. We need to refocus on what to do next. I've had a gut feeling all day, and it's still simmering in the back of my head."

"I'll admit you haven't been yourself."

"Jackie, the feeling is intensifying as I stare out at the water and back at the empty trailer. I know they're not gone ... there's something's wrong, but they aren't gone... they are missing and in bad trouble. We need to get back to Anna and the kids."

As Jackie turned to agree, they spotted a car pull into the lot, eventually coming to a screeching stop next to where they had parked. Jackie stared at the car and mumbled, "Uh oh...."

Neal's mom Cheryl jumped out of her car. She looked frantic, her mascara smudged, her face pale. The look on her face when she saw the empty trailer said it all. She understood the men hadn't made it back. "Have you called anyone?"

Jackie answered, "Yes, of course." She tried to calm down her voice ... lower than when she spoke to Merry. "We called the Coast Guard."

"And?"

"They reluctantly took my report."

She cut Jackie off. "Reluctantly?"

"There was no distress call made by the boys. They cannot start a search until they've been missing for a certain period of time, and evidently, a plane went down in the Everglades. Their manpower is all down there."

Another car roared into the lot. Jackie only shook her head and rolled her eyes.

Neal's brother, Mark, and his wife Holly exited their vehicle. Mark, tall and lanky like Neal, shrugged holding his empty hands out to Jackie. "So, what's going on?"

Jackie reran the story from the beginning. When she finished, they all stood dumbfounded, looking out at the Gulf. Jackie took the words out of Merry's mouth. "We can all stand here wasting time or

Waiting for Morning Time

we can get on with things. They're not magically going to pull into the harbor now... let's all go back to my house where we can formulate some kind of plan. If we sit and wait for something to happen, I have a horrible feeling it ain't gonna happen. I'm not going to stand here waiting for the Coast Guard to rescue my husband. I think we need to take matters into our own hands. I won't be able to live with myself if they're lost out there and we haven't done everything possible to help them."

Jackie's word *lost* hung in the air while everyone took a deep breath. Finally, they all got back into their vehicles.

Jackie turned to Merry, sitting next to her, and squeezed her forearm. "We're gonna do this, girl. And we're gonna do this together. I know you're not doing well, but are you okay? You look like you might throw up. You look white as a sheet."

Merry nodded. "Stunned is a good word, Jackie. Yes, I feel a bit queasy. I'll be fine by the time we get back to your place. I need to come to grips with things that's all."

Jackie nodded, looking out of it in her own way. The realization their men were in trouble was taking its time to sink in. "You know this could get a bit crazy, right?"

"What do you mean?"

"The more who know they are missing the more personalities will get involved."

"Okay, I'm following."

"You and I have to keep things in control. We can't let things get messy. We are in charge ... right?"

Merry could see where Jackie was going, and she agreed. "They are our men."

CHAPTER SEVEN

NEAL SWAM slowly near the sea floor towards the far side of an old troop carrier. He had been following a black Grouper swimming from side to side, almost as a game until the old fish became weary of the much larger man. Neal decided to wait it out a few minutes, letting the big fish settle into his surroundings and forget Neal had been following. *Peeking around the back of the truck*, he smiled. The Grouper must have decided it was safe to resume its own hunt for smaller reef fish, which were plentiful.

If Neal dared to move out from behind the reef, the Grouper would spook. It would need to be a longish shot. When he aimed and pulled the trigger, the small spear jettisoned from the gun with the cord following. The sharp spear hit the twenty-pound fish just behind the head, causing it to turn back into the troop carrier and pull the line in with it. Neal strapped the gun to his dive belt and grabbed onto the line with all the strength he could muster. He had to plant his flippers on the rusty coral-covered vehicle to gain enough purchase to pull the fish out of its hole. It took a minute ... maybe two, but eventually he had the fish at his side and Neal smiled at his catch of the day. The big Grouper became docile with no fight left in him. Neal couldn't understand why people wasted their time with hook and line.

Spearfishing seemed so much more effective and so exciting in his estimation.

Neal took some time to have a bit of fun and checked out the old tanks. He found it amazing how quickly the coral had taken to the metal Junkers down on the seabed. He felt happy being down at the bottom of the Gulf. He never tired of exploring the reefs. Neal had been in the water all his life. Being an excellent swimmer, he naturally took to underwater diving. He and Jackie used to go on diving trips with friends regularly. Life's obligations have a habit of getting in the way and Neal missed his time under the waves. Quiet and serene, the undersea world was vastly different. It suited Neal, who enjoyed his own company. Not that he didn't look forward to diving with Bill ... he was anxious to share some underwater time with him. He would be lying if he didn't say he was angry with Bill. The day had been arranged around Bill's desire to get out on the water. Neal couldn't believe he never asked him to check his equipment before jumping into the water. Being an expert diver and the senior dive buddy, Neal would have gladly helped Bill and the problem would have been averted. He shrugged it off, deciding it was not worth the argument.

It was time to return to the surface. A couple of reef sharks seemed to be taking an interest in his Grouper still twisting and turning on his stringer as his blood sifted off into the blue water.

Taking his time going up, Neal followed the anchor's rope. As he neared the surface, things didn't look right. The boat looked too dark, the topside a stark contrast from the white hull. He could see two people swimming directly above him. *What the heck?*

He broke the surface of the water next to Lew and Bill. Spitting out his regulator, Neal couldn't help himself and blurted out his confusion and his anger. "What have you done to my boat? No really, what the hell...?" He swept his arm towards the boat aggressively while his face turned red and the veins in the side of his neck were bulging. He looked at his pride and joy now tipped over in the sea.

Pieces of equipment, loose papers, and clothing were floating close by.

Remembering the sharks down below, he knew they were not going to be able to do anything about the boat. Neal released the bleeding Grouper from his stringer. The Black Tips he had spied below would be on them in minutes. He didn't fear those sharks, but if they came after the Grouper, they could attract a Bull or a Hammer. It wouldn't take long to start a feeding frenzy especially when a storm was due above the water. Once the lone Grouper was eaten, Neal knew the three of them staying afloat would be their second course.

***

The three of us stayed quiet, bobbing like corks and looking as if they were in shock, while Neal took a few minutes to assess the situation.

I was the first to try and explain what happened to the boat. "Sorry, Neal, all of a sudden the back started filling up with water." I didn't know what else to say. I understood my friend's anger watching Neal roll up his eyes, flare his nostrils, and take in hard breaths like a bull bucking to get out of a rodeo shoot.

Neal only shook his head. "What the heck were you DOING? Don't you think you might have seen the water before it got to THAT point? Did you call in a DISTRESS?" He turned his head away, suspecting the truth and hiding his anger. Before turning back, Neal knew by the look on my face ... neither of us had called in a MAYDAY.

"It takes some time for a boat like this to start getting even close to LISTING. No damn SOS! What about the CELL PHONES?" He slammed his fist down into the water.

"The cells slipped into the water before we could get to them. Look, Neal, I'm sorry, but really… it all happened so fast."

"You couldn't start the *ENGINES* and run the PUMPS?" He kept

Waiting for Morning Time

holding his breath to stave back his anger. Neal took a long deep breath, trying to regain his control.

I sensed what was going on with Neal. He cursed the fact he'd been down below when the dirt hit the fan. I could see it in Neal's eyes. The man blamed himself for what happened. I couldn't blame Neal one little bit for feeling that way. I decided to let the man calm down before saying anything more.

Being a standup guy, Neal never said another word about it. No more blame. He disappeared in a cloud of bubbles.

I felt awful for him... *hell,* I felt terrible for all three of us. We were in the water with a whale of a storm heading our way. We were in deep trouble.

Neal returned in a few minutes with two adult-size life jackets, a bag of flares, a twenty-foot rope, and a can of something I didn't recognize. He went back down one last time and retrieved a new tank of oxygen and a couple of boat bumpers. I helped him switch over the tank strapped on his back, no words were spoken.

Neal handed me his dive hood and gloves. "You guys are going to need something to keep you warm. It's roughly seventy degrees this water. I'll be fine in my suit, but I'm a little worried about the two of you." He looked visibly calmer now, having been given time to digest the calamity. "You know we're going to be out here in the water for the night. No MAYDAY, they won't start a search right away; even if the girls call it in. And even then, someone's going to have to drive right over the top of us to be spotted." He nodded towards Bill, who now turned around and looked away from them.

I nodded. "Bill's more than a little frightened."

Neal's words explaining the horror facing the three of us... hit hard. We knew the cold hard facts to be true. Neal and I moved around Bill to look at his face. We both saw the vacant look in his eyes and how the corners of his mouth pulled down.

I tried on the gloves and handed the hood to Bill. When the gloves didn't fit either of us, I gave them back to Neal.

Neal took a few minutes to tie both ends of the rope he'd retrieved to the two boat bumpers which were still floating close to the boat and a couple of child-sized life jackets. The rope gave us something else to hold onto besides the bowline.

Bill finally spoke up and handed me the cap. "Dad, you take the cap. I'll be fine. I'm more worried about you." Bill spoke in a calm manner, looking almost serene.

The change made me worry. I could understand Bill's fear, but the sudden change. Reluctantly, I pulled the hood over my head, where most heat escaped from the body.

Bill turned to Neal. "What Dad's saying is correct; it happened too damned fast. I was of no help. We're sorry, Neal, about the boat ... about everything. The high waves made it difficult to get a bearing on how far she was sitting down in the water. It was as if the Scarab slid rear end first into the Gulf and there was NOTHING we could do."

Neal nodded. He held his hand over his mouth as if he was deep in thought. "Have you tried to get on top?"

I nodded. "It's hard to stay up there, too damned slippery. Bill even cut his leg up trying."

Neal nodded again. "Maybe the three of us will be able to manage it?"

The three of us tried several times to get up on top of the overturned boat. When we made it even halfway, the wind and waves attacked us. We tried several times while the strong winds battered us from above, the high waves and swirling water nudging the boat from below. In the end, trying to get up on the boat was an exercise in futility. Every time a giant wave hit it swung the boat around in the swirling waters while the three of us fought the down drafts beating on them from the sky. In the end, we kept being thrown into the ocean. While the water felt cold, the air felt even colder. The process of climbing up on the overturned boat only to be pushed off by the

Waiting for Morning Time

strong winds or pulled off by the high waves drained our energy. Heroic efforts left the three of us in the dark water exposed to whatever might be lurking below as the sun lowered in the sky.

Neal suggested, "Let's keep ourselves a few feet away from the boat. Instead, we can take hold of the bowline. His wisdom kept us from banging against the hull when we were caught up in the waves.

As the hour darkened, the Scarab began to go down in earnest. During the following hour, it sank stern first to the point where only a few feet of the bow remained above water.

Neal spoke up. "We need to stay with the boat as long as it's above water. When they start to look for us, the dive sites will be the most logical places to start a search. Some of my buddies know M-9 and 16 are my go-to-spots."

"Let's hope so." I shook my hooded head. "The sooner the better cause this water is darn cold."

Neal added, "The white hull will be a heck of a lot easier to spot in this surf than our heads. I know it's going to be tough with the hull pushing up and down in the waves, but it would be suicide to move away from it."

I agreed, slowly nodding my head.

Bill remained silent.

The three of us and the capsized boat rode the waves as nightfall and the storm approached.

***

COLD, COLD, COLD ... it was not just cold, it was freezing cold. The temperature of the water frightened me more than any shark attack where death would come quickly. Bill and I were more affected than Neal in his wet suit. We began to shake with chills. The truth of the matter crossed all of our minds: *How were they going to make it through the night?*

Hypothermia would become the dreaded enemy. An hour or so might be doable, but the whole night? I had been shaking for the past hour; taken a chill and couldn't seem to get over it. If I had been at home, I would have had a hot shower and tucked myself under a warm blanket.

Neal kept going over the events in his head. He kept asking himself what might have caused the boat to swamp. There were many possibilities. Glancing over at me, I could tell he felt bad for me looking so cold while Bill seemed to be faring a little better. Still, Bill had turned into himself, not looking or talking to either of us. Neal worried about Bill's silent behavior. While it would be hard to tell what normal might be under their circumstances, Bill didn't seem to be reacting in a normal way. The man looked as if he had turned off a switch in his head to escape what was going on around him.

**

During the next hour or two, few words were spoken, each doing our best to remain calm. Neither Neal nor I could say for sure when Bill made his decision. We were both lost in our own mental hell, busy exorcising fiery demons.

Bill disappeared.

We noticed his absence simultaneously and looked at each other before we both swam around the boat.

I yelled, "Did he go under?" I looked around to see if I could find Bill's life jacket floating on its own. I figured Bill may have wanted to simply give up and drown himself. An electric pang of shock and deep loss sizzled through my body, negating any cold I felt.

"No. Hey, there he is." Neal yelled and pointed. It took a few minutes searching the waves, but Neal eventually spotted him floating off on his own a hundred yards away bobbing up and down in the waves, his head difficult to spot in the rolling sea.

We both yelled to Bill to swim back. Either he couldn't hear us, or he chose to ignore the calls. Bill continued to do so, slowly drifting further away.

***

Bill could still see his dad and Neal. The two appeared to be so strong in the present set of circumstances. If the cold water didn't kill his father, the man would find the resolve to survive. The same went for Neal. Bill got the impression Neal would have started swimming for shore with the wet suit keeping him warm if he and Lew hadn't been stranded along with him.

Bill put on a brave face when the boat first started going down, but he was frightened ... maybe even terrified. The Scarab appeared modest in size when sitting in it, but now seemed massive as it crashed down into the water with every wave. More than anything, Bill feared being hit in the head as he held onto the rope still attached to the bow. His fear of being killed by the surging boat, the dark water, and what slithered beneath it kept mounting, beckoning him to his own death. Bill felt positive he wouldn't survive and decided to expedite the inevitable. Worse, he suspected the bleeding cuts on his legs were sure to attract sharks, which would put the other two men in peril. He didn't want to be a burden to Lew and Neal nor be remembered that way. All he had to do was let go of the rope and silently float off into the massive swells.

Bill didn't know what would happen as he drifted on his own. All he knew was his own terrifying fear and how he didn't want to burden them with his anxiety. Bill figured: *fate would take its course, the sea, the cold, or the sharks.*

Once he had decided to take matters into his own hands, drifting away, it seemed amazing how fast his fear dissipated. He became serene, suddenly able to think about Ashley, Billy, and Anna. How he loved to tease Ashley and see Billy's infectious smile when he came home from a hard day at work. And then there was Anna, the love of his life and mother of his children. Life would be tough for her being alone; he had looked after her since their marriage. Still, Anna would find her way, being a smart woman. Prior to Bill drifting away, he had to stop thinking about them. Their loss was a big part of what paralyzed him with fear. He couldn't bear the thought of never seeing them again. Now, it seemed strange how thinking of them didn't change his perspective, terror taking over reason. He knew he was most likely in shock.

His decision to drift off on his own did bring tears to his eyes. He sobbed quietly, shaking from the cold and from his fear as he said goodbyes to each of them. Their faces etched in his mind. Once he felt somewhat settled about what he had to do, things became quiet and almost comfortable. He had made the initiative and he could live with the decision. Once Bill accepted death, there was no longer any reason to hide from it. One fear, strangely enough, cancelled out the other fear. Two negatives making a positive, if that was even possible?

***

When Bill first decided to move away from the boat, it appeared as if he had drifted quickly, the current pulling him away from the anchorage. After several minutes, he turned to see if he could spot the Scarab. Surprisingly, he could. He had figured to be long gone at that point. Looking back again, the boat was still there. In fact, it seemed a little closer ... the white point of the hull bobbing up and down in the waves. He was not quite sure whether he was happy or upset with the revelation. Bill wondered if he had found a back eddy in the Gulf current. For whatever reason, the boat appeared to be moving towards him. He didn't try to swim away, nor float back to the boat. The choice was not his to make. He continued in his shock-ridden cocoon to follow wherever the waves took him.

***

Waiting for Morning Time

When Neal and I discovered Bill was floating away from us, I felt the dark terror of a parent whose child is lost and in danger. A memory popped into my head of a toddler, walking into a busy street back in Niagara Falls. I could still see the cars rushing towards him. I remember running into the traffic, grabbing him by the scruff of his neck before we were both run over. I channeled his new emotion into dealing with the present danger. "What's going through Bill's head?" I asked out loud.

"His eyes haven't looked right since I surfaced," said Neal.

"What do you mean?" Lew had noticed it too but hadn't taken it as anything other than being fearful in their predicament.

"He's like a gazelle when it knows the lion has him."

"What? How so?"

"I'm not a psychologist or anything, but I do like to hunt, and I've read about it, bits and pieces here and there. I'm trying to figure it out and been thinking about it myself." He became quiet for a moment. "Humans have what's called a fight or flight response. I've been taking this in for the past few minutes. I can see in your eyes, that you're not afraid."

"No. I'm not afraid. Well… I'm afraid for Bill."

"Exactly!"

"You don't look afraid either."

"I'm not really afraid, maybe I'll as this all settles. Right now, I'm concerned for both of you. See, that's how it works. My instincts are to protect right now. I've got on this wet suit and a tank full of air. I hate to say it, but if something happens to both of you, it may take me some time, but I think I might be able to make it to shore. Of course, that would depend upon which way the current is moving. Right now, it's pulling to the northeast, which would bring us closer to land if we let go of the boat."

"What were you saying about Bill?"

"I need you to promise me something, Lew. If we get to Bill somehow, I don't want you to hold this against him. He can't help it.

He's the cornered animal. He's gone past running from the hunter; in this case, the Gulf of Mexico. He's conceded to death. He's past normal fear. Bill's in shock, ready to roll over and let the lion tear out his throat."

"I think you're right. I'm really not afraid of dying. I went through all that a year ago with my heart attack." I looked out into the Gulf and stared at the mass of clouds, now moving slowly toward us. Then I looked back towards Bill still bobbing. "So, Neal, how do we save him?"

Neal frowned. "I really didn't want to do this, but I see no other choice. We'd be better off hanging around this spot, not drifting away. Eventually, the coast guard is going to come to the typical dive sites. Jackie knows that's where we went. If we swim out to get him, I doubt we'll be able to get back to the boat. He's several hundred yards away now. We can't swim faster than he's drifting. Do you follow?"

I nodded; the quandary as presented by Neal hit me like a brick.

"Let's cut the anchor line and drift towards him with the boat. Its mass below the water line will get picked up by this strong current faster than it can push one of our relatively smaller bodies. If he doesn't get gobbled up by something, we'll catch up to him given time. Then I'll drag him back to us. We'll still have the bow of the boat sticking out of the water. Search planes or boats will be able to see it… hopefully."

Once again, I looked out at the brewing storm, the waves now becoming big swells, the wind whipping spray off their crests, saltwater burning my tired eyes. Neal wore his goggles even out of the water as they were a needed prescription. "How long do you think before that storm hits?"

"It's held off longer than I'd have thought. Supposed to hit during the night, but my best guess would be sometime in the morning."

Waiting for Morning Time

"If what you're saying is true, our best chance at being found is tomorrow."

"Yes. We'll have been missing long enough by then to warrant a search. But who knows how far we'll have drifted through the night."

All of a sudden, I became mad at Bill. He'd put us in a bad spot. "If we stayed here, we'd have a better chance of being found in the morning? What the hell is Bill thinking?"

"Not quite academic, but yes, and we have to remember… Bill's not thinking anymore."

I looked out at Bill, not being able to pick him up anymore and save him from something that might come rushing at him. "I can't leave him on his own to die."

Neal put his hand on my shoulder. "I never expected you would, and neither would I. Let's cut this rope. It's a dumb thing to do, but I would rather die trying to save him than live with the guilt of knowing we might have saved him."

I nodded. "You're a good man, Neal."

Neal shrugged. "Either you are or you're not, I see no choice." Neal reached down to his lower leg and retrieved his dive knife. Within moments, he'd cut us free, and we soon started to flow with the current. Without tension on the anchor line, the boat heaved lower to the stern, the bow pointing directly towards the blue sky, our only connection to where rescuers might consider looking-- now severed.

CHAPTER EIGHT

ANNA SAT alone in the Obendorf's large sprawling bungalow. The two youngest children were settled in bed, the older ones watching television. She felt isolated. It would be one thing to deal with all of the emotions she was experiencing in a familiar place, like her own home. But she felt awkward here and not able to get comfortable in someone else's home, strangers to boot. As much as she wanted to stay and look after the kids, Anna wished she had gone with the other two women, the wait slowly killing her. Her nerves were frayed. Time seemed to move too slowly. Every time she glanced at the clock; it looked as if it had hardly budged.

By eleven o'clock, the older kids were sleeping. Before he had dropped off, she promised Billy that his daddy would be home in the morning. She couldn't help but feel bad lying to her son, no matter how much they all wanted it to be true. She somehow knew Bill wouldn't be back. She hated the fact she'd been having such a hard time dealing with her emotions, her mental state well beyond control. She felt stressed beyond all belief—unhealthy stress. Anna couldn't help but think Bill might be dead. She loved him dearly, but thoughts of what she would do without him started to flood her mind, stabbing her with the harsh realities. The death of her father and uncle, a month

Waiting for Morning Time

back was too much to bear… and now, this new horror. Anna was an emotional being and now, the men had gone missing. This was the straw that broke the camel's back. She could no longer control her outbursts; something inside her felt broken--the snap almost audible.

The damage occurred when they were driving back from Tampa. The possibility of losing Bill was emotional but much different than with her dad and uncle. Bill was the breadwinner in their family, and she'd never held down a serious job since they were married. Anna enjoyed being the quintessential stay-at-home mother. She could picture having to sell their house to pay for their children's upbringing. didn't What would she do? The whole scenario of being a widow with children to raise was a disturbing thought, and so foreign to her.

Since she was not a boater, Anna hadn't considered going out with the guys, even when they had planned for Captiva later in the week. She didn't think of the apparent dangers involved with being out on the ocean. She remembered Bill fawning over the Scarab, rubbing its sleek hull. She could hear his voice plain as day. 'It's the *Miami Vice* boat, Anna. It's made to run fast in the ocean, on top of the waves. We can get back before that storm even thinks about moving in on us.'

'Be careful out there.' The words seemed the right thing to say, not imagining for the life of her that they needed to be heeded.

"It's a safe boat." He had told her smugly.

How did he know that? "They're gone." She said out loud. Fear set in, hearing herself say the words. Nervous, she started wandering around the house, picking up things, and washing the countertops. She couldn't sit still. She didn't have any friends down in Florida, besides Lew and Merry. She felt terribly alone. To make matters worse, she left her good hearing aid back in Canada, and not being able to discern every word left her tired and frustrated in a haze all alone. She wished it was not so late. She would love to call her mom. She should have called her. Merry felt like a surrogate mother, sweet and their relationship stayed strong… but Merry was not her mom. Anna needed her real mother, the only woman who would know how to make Anna feel better.

Her heart thumped when the headlights appeared in the driveway. It flipped again when she noticed more than one car. *Did the girls find them?* She stood meekly in the kitchen, not wanting to get her hopes up. Still, Merry would have called if their husbands had shown up?

***

Jackie and Merry could tell by the look on Anna's face, that she was not taking things well. She looked pale even though her face was sunburned; her mouth drawn, and her eyelids swollen and hanging low.

"Did you find them?" Anna asked a cautious look on her face, her eyebrows raised.

Jackie knew they were idle words. Surely, she could read the look on their faces coming through the door and see they were not happy. Jackie didn't blame her … the poor woman looked terrified. Jackie turned away, not able to respond, doing her best to keep her own emotions in check.

Merry spoke up, trying her best to shed some hope to keep Anna calm. "We think something must have happened to the motors. They're probably stranded out there."

Anna retorted sharply. "What about the cell phones then? They all have one. Bill doesn't use his much, but he sure as heck owns one and wouldn't hesitate to use it if he needed help. The motors and the cell phones all at the same time? Come on, Merry. I'm very upset, but I'm not stupid. What about the radio? Don't boats need to have one … by law?"

Merry wished she could have taken back her words when Anna started to cry. "You have to stay calm, honey."

Waiting for Morning Time

They turned to see Neal's mom, Cheryl, along with his brother, Mark, and his wife, Holly, coming through the garage door into the kitchen. Besides low-level sobbing emanating from Anna, the room was quiet, and everyone stood dumbfounded.

If Merry was not so upset herself, she would have taken Anna aside and calmed her down. Instead, she gave her something to do, which seemed to placate her for the moment. "Anna, would you please make a large pot of coffee?"

She nodded, holding back her sobs.

Jackie spoke up. "Look at the bunch of us. Time is critical here. Neal, Lew, and Bill only have so much time. On the ride back from the marina, Merry and I decided we would be proactive. We can't leave matters in the hands of the Coast Guard. I'm sure when the time comes to rescue them, they will be on the spot, but they don't seem on task with the search. I can't believe they wouldn't send out a plane to at least have a look. How much longer do they have to be missing before someone will take this seriously?"

Merry shuddered, imagining Lew floating out there in the dark cold water. Eerily, she knew he would be thinking of her at this moment; her heart felt as if it might break. "I agree with you, Jackie, one hundred percent."

Jackie nodded to her. "There can be no doubt now ... something happened to them ... something is wrong."

Everyone nodded, mumbling they agreed.

"We need to do whatever we can to help them. I have this rotten feeling if we don't and leave it up to others, if they aren't already gone, they certainly will be gone. I don't know how else to say it." Jackie's hands shook gently, her nerves almost getting the best of her.

Merry cut in. "You're right, but can I say one thing? We need to focus on them being alive. We should think of nothing else until we are told differently. We owe this to our men. We cannot be deterred until we find them. God demands this of us. He will support us if we keep our faith in Him." She took a deep breath, "I know they are alive." Her premonition stayed strong in her mind and her heart.

Cheryl spoke, her words came slowly, and her voice sounded a notch below hysteria. "If something has happened... the boat has sunk... how long can they survive out there?"

Jackie answered, trying to keep Cheryl calm. "I'm sure the Coast Guard will have some idea. We'll have to ask the next time we talk to them. Okay, enough feeling sorry for ourselves. Let's make a list of the people we need to call."

All six sat around the kitchen table, drinking coffee and making notes. They took turns throwing out suggestions. After half an hour, they compiled a list two pages long, everyone being put on task.

Merry made the first call to the Sarasota Sheriff's department.

"Sarasota Sheriff's office, how may I help you?"

Merry tried to keep her voice as level and calm as possible. "I'd like to report three missing men."

"Yes ma'am," said the female on the line. "Can you tell me a little more? Have they been abducted?"

"No ma'am." Merry went on to describe their situation.

"Ma'am, you've already called the Coast Guard. They would be the most capable under these circumstances."

"CAPABLE! They've done nothing. They didn't want to take our report until the morning... they're not going to do anything until the morning ... for that matter. If our men are out there, we can't sit around waiting for them to die. Surely, there's something that can be done?"

"Ma'am, I'm a dispatcher. I don't make the decisions. I'll take your name and number and the names of the men. You said they've been missing since mid-day?"

"That's right."

"I'll pass it on to the Desk Sergeant, but as I said, there's not much we can do. Someone will call you back. I'll take your name and number."

Merry gave her information and hung up, thoroughly exasperated. She looked at Jackie and exclaimed. "Nobody wants to do anything."

Jackie finished up a call just as Merry hung up. She'd decided to call some of Neal's diving friends. It was late, but everyone was eager to help. In the end, Jackie was able to get the GPS coordinates of all of the potential dive sites.

Mark spoke up, his voice shaking. "I heard you talking about the guys maybe stopping in at a bar. I know where Neal would have set in ... I'll give them a call." Being a local, he knew them all. Everyone listened in, but after a dozen calls, he had no luck. No one held up much hope before he started, knowing that it would be a lost lead, but it was important they could relay their information to the Coast Guard the next time they contacted them. Plus, the word was out within the boating community: *three men were missing*. If the men were safe and sound somewhere, they would have tried their best to contact them. "No luck. No one's seen them."

Jackie voiced her thoughts, "They're in trouble. Those fellas are too considerate not to check in with us. They're not in some bar."

Merry called the Venice Police but received the same treatment as from the Sarasota Sheriff's Department, except to say that they were very compassionate. "Leave it to the Coast Guard."

Jackie called the Coast Guard again. She was routed through Venice to St Pete's, and lucky enough to speak to the same person. "St Pete's dispatch."

"Hello! This is Jackie Obendorf calling. I filed a missing person's report with you a few hours ago."

"Hello, Mrs. Obendorf, good speaking with you again. I'm sorry to report, I have nothing new to tell you."

"Yes sir. It's nice speaking with you again as well. I wanted to tell you we have followed your advice but have not heard from our husbands since we last spoke."

"There has been no contact?"

"No, sir. We haven't made contact with them. I would like to give you the coordinates of the possible dive sites they may have visited. Can I email them to you, it might be easier?"

"Yes. You can do that. I'll give you the e-mail address." Jackie could tell the man made his best efforts to placate her. Perhaps their emergency was receiving some push. "Are you able to get a plane out tonight?"

"No. Mrs. Obendorf, the planes are still down south of Naples."

"I can't believe they're still down there. Could you please at least send them over those spots on their way back north?" Jackie sighed in exasperation.

"Out of my hands, ma'am, I can only relay the information. I'll say it may be too rough to send planes over the Gulf."

"Okay, I understand it's getting too rough. Think about how my husband must feel." She put her hand on her hip.

"Ma'am, I'm only the dispatcher. I have been told we will get the C-130's out in the morning ... crack of dawn."

"Okay, first thing in the morning, thank you." She hung up.

***

Merry called Pastor Pat, her congregation's minister. She broke down as she told him of the day's events. He sounded sleepy, but soon woke up with the reality of her terrible news and hearing the sadness in her voice.

"How are you holding up, Merry?"

She had to catch her breath before responding. "I'm in and out of it. As long as I keep myself focused, I seem to be okay, but when I called you and described the situation and the hard reality of what might be going on ... I lost it."

"What do you expect?" His dry voice cracked as he spoke.

"These are a horrible set of circumstances. You are reacting strong and helping the others from what I can tell."

"Pat, we're doing everything we can do in a practical sense. We're trying to keep on top of the local authorities as best we can." While trying to find the right words she burst out. "We need prayer!"

"I couldn't agree with you more." He didn't hesitate to jump into the action. "Here's what we'll do. I'll start up a prayer chain through e-mail. By mid-day tomorrow, we should have thousands praying on Lew, Bill, and Neal's behalf. The chain will keep growing until we find them."

Merry's heart soared with the news of Pat's great idea. "Perfect!" We need the Lord's help to find our men. The prayer of thousands couldn't hurt."

"Look, I'll come up there after Church tomorrow to give you my support. Is there anything else I can do?"

"Yes, if you don't mind?"

"Anything!"

"Could you stop by the house and pick up some warm clothing and Lew's heart medicine? It's in the master bathroom. Just grab everything with his name on it. I'll sort it out when you get here. There's a key under the cement planter at the back door. Oh, lest I forget, Snuggles' food is in a green bag in the pantry."

"God bless, Merry. I'll say a special prayer once we get off the phone." He hung up after she gave him Jackie's address.

***

Merry decided to take a break and took Snuggles outside for a walk and a quick pee. She couldn't help but notice how the wind picked up since they arrived an hour ago. The thought of poor Lew out there in the terrible weather broke her heart. She prayed for God's Angels to be with their men, to protect them, and for them to place a hand around Lew's heart for extra strength and warmth.

***

As Merry returned, Jackie hung up from making a phone call. She smiled. "I just called Mom and Dad. They're heading up here right away."

"They won't get in till two or three a.m." Merry exclaimed.

Clyde and Niki Butcher lived behind their Big Cyprus Gallery, surrounded by a million acres of everglades wilderness halfway between Naples and Miami on Tamiami Trail ... highway 41.

"I told them to sleep in the camper, but I suspect Dad won't be in a mood for sleeping, nor mom for that matter."

Merry was genuinely happy to hear Clyde and Niki were on their way. She and Lew, used to work for them for a short time, well after Jackie knew them. Both were take-control kind of people--thinkers. They needed all the help they could get, smart people included.

Jackie leafed through her phone book until she noticed Merry looking over her shoulder. "I'm going to call our very good friend, Rich Godoy. He's a pilot. We need to get some more planes out there. When I'm done, I'm going to start calling friends, everyone I can think of who owns a boat."

Jackie and Neal were members of the Venice Yacht Club. The Commodore would be the first person she would call after Rich. Jackie felt sure the Town of Venice would rally for one of its own.

Merry nodded, "While you're doing that, I'm going to call our good friend, Bill Cameron. Bill's a Lieutenant with the Lee County Sheriff's department and lives across the canal from our house.

Jackie nodded, agreeing she had a good idea.

Merry hesitated before dialing as it was now: 12:45 a.m. late, but Bill picked up on the second ring, he'd been working until midnight and just arrived home.

"Bill Cameron."

"Bill, it's Merry."

Waiting for Morning Time

It took a couple of seconds to compute. "What's wrong. Merry? Is Lew okay? Someone rob you?" He knew Lew had suffered heart difficulties and it was past the witching hour.

"Lew's gone missing."

"What do you mean? He didn't come home? Has he been out drinking? I can get a car to go gather him up for you."

"No, Bill, I could only wish. Lew and his son, Bill, along with Neal Obendorf went diving today up here in Venice, which is where I am now. They haven't come back. No calls, nothing. We think something has happened to them out on the water."

Bill fell silent for a short moment. "Have you called the Coast Guard?"

She went on to explain what had happened thus far throughout the day, stating how the Coast Guard had done nothing to be proactive.

"Merry, I'm so sorry."

"I know you are." She could hear it in his voice.

"Listen, I'm going to help, but I have to make some calls. Now, of course, I'm going to try to organize a plane for the morning." He paused for a moment, thinking. "I know some people up in the St. Petersburg Coast Guard station, I'm going to try to pull some strings. In the meantime, I want you to call the Coast Guard again, and the Sarasota Sheriff. No more being rational, I want you to sound hysterical. They won't pay attention to you if you're calm. Believe me, I know. The squeaky wheel gets the grease."

Merry trusted Bill, his advice making her feel a bit better. "Thank you!"

"Now, let's keep in touch. As I said, I'm going to make some calls and get back to you soon. I want you to keep everyone calm." He hung up.

***

"Hello?" The groggy male answered his phone.

"Rich, it's Jackie."

"Jackie? What the hell? Someone die?" No one likes getting calls at this time in the night, and Jackie had never called Rich since it was Neal who was his friend.

"We're not sure about that."

"Meaning?" She could hear his irritation rising.

"Rich, Neal went out diving this morning, he hasn't come back."

"Did he stop in with some of the guys?"

"You know as well as I do, Neal wouldn't do that without calling." She proceeded to give Rich the details. "I need to call in a favor. Rich. Can you get a plane up over the Gulf tomorrow?"

Rich was shocked, but the question was redundant as he was about to say how he would do it. "Of course, Jackie, I'm going to call in a flight plan right away, but it might be tricky. They don't let you fly around in circles. If Neal is at one of the farther dive sites, I may not get approval to go out that far in a single prop plane."

Jackie sighed. "No one seems to be able to help. Don't get me wrong, I know you want to, but our guys are in trouble, and we seem to keep getting caught up in regulations and protocol."

"I get it, Jackie, but you don't mess with the FAA. I'll do whatever I can, don't worry. If I have to break the law to save Neal, you know I will."

"I don't want you to do that, but I appreciate the sentiment."

"Can Nicole help in any way?"

"I'll think on that. I appreciate this, Rich. We're desperate."

"I would be, too, Jackie. Neal's my friend, I am... you know what I mean."

"Of course, I do."

"I'll let you know how I make out first thing in the morning. I'm going to call a few more friends as well... pilots. We need as much help as we can get. We're not going to have much time if that storm is

Waiting for Morning Time

going to hit later in the morning. There's a lot of water to cover out there."

"Thank you, Rich." She hung up.

Merry came in as Jackie finished up her call. The two sat down and Jackie repeated, "Rich said he'd be able to go out first thing in the morning. He'll try to get a few of his pilot friends who have planes to go out as well. I'm going to make that call to the Coast Guard."

Merry nodded. "Bill Cameron our friend, said to sound frantic. They won't react to calm and collected."

Jackie let Merry's words churn in her head for a few moments. "I can do that." She tried calling 911 and asking for the Coast Guard and found herself connected almost right away. To this point, they had called directly. 911 seemed to be more proactive. She raised her eyebrows looking at Merry.

"United States Coast Guard, dispatch, how can I help you?"

She put on her best female upset-and-worried voice, which really was not put on at that time in the night. "Sir, I'd like to report th… th… three missing men. We've been expecting them back for six hours now."

"Have you made contact with them, ma'am?"

"At three o'clock. We've been trying ever since."

"What kind of boat and do you have the registration number"?"

She gave him the information. "Sir, this isn't like them. Two are very experienced boaters. If there wasn't something wrong, they would have called us. They were supposed to be making dinner. I don't know what I'm going to do!" Mark, Holly, Cheryl, and Anna came closer to hear Jackie's side of the conversation.

"Calm down, ma'am. Can you give us some names and descriptions of the men?"

She pretended to lose it for a few moments, sobbing into her arm. "I have the coordinates for several of the possible dive sites they may have been at. We gave a report earlier." She gave him her phone number, address, and particulars.

"Hang on for a few minutes." He left her hanging for what seemed an age. "Ma'am, your incident has just been given priority. We're going to send out a plane ASAP. It's equipped with infrared. We'll contact you at this number if we find them."

Jackie thanked him profusely and hung up. "They're sending out a plane!" Everyone in the kitchen whooped it up and exchanged high-fives. Finally, someone committed to having something done.

Merry called 911 and asked for the Sarasota Sheriff. Using the same ploy as Jackie with the Coast Guard, she gained their attention quickly. They granted the situation emergency status." She hung up, putting her hand up in the air for some more high-fives. She shook her head. "It's amazing how sounding out of control got us what we needed. Being rational, and calling the correct numbers did nothing for us. Sarasota agreed to send out a chopper within the next half hour on the outside of the inter-coastal waterway."

Merry tried her luck with 911 and the Venice Police and was similarly rewarded with a chopper on the inside of the inter-coastal. The ball certainly appeared to be rolling. Bill Cameron called shortly after her last call, happy to hear the success Jackie had achieved. He indicated he too had contacted the Coast Guard and he was working on lining up a plane through the Lee County Sherriff's office to go out first thing in the morning.

Jackie told Mark, Holly, and Cheryl to go home, and she would call them first thing to let them know what was going on.

Mark said, "I'll get our boat ready at sunup. I'm not going to be able to sit tight doing nothing. I'll call some friends, I'm sure they'll be willing to help."

Jackie and Merry both smiled. Jackie said, "I'm going to make some calls for the next hour, see if we can get some boats lined up for the morning. See you tomorrow." Soon after they left, everyone except Jackie, who remained busy on the phone, went to bed and tried

Waiting for Morning Time

to catch a catnap.

***

Jackie and Merry lay on her big king-sized bed, once Jackie finished with the calls, trying to get some rest before what looked to be a big morning. Anna went to get some sleep in the spare room with Billy.

Jackie talked while staring at the ceiling fan as it slowly spun around over the bed. "I can't figure out in my head what could have happened. We've been out on that boat a hundred times and in some pretty rough weather. I hope they are simply stranded with no power. They could have taken on some water and fried the batteries. Maybe the new engines fouled up?"

Merry let the words spin around in her head for a few moments before she said, "That would explain why they're stuck and can't use the radio. What about the cell phones?"

"They could be too far out to receive cell service?"

"Then how was I able to call Lew earlier in the afternoon?"

"I don't know... Maybe they went further out after that call... maybe the oncoming storm is messing with the signal?"

"I don't know, Jackie. Three separate phones, different coverage plans. I think somehow the boat sank ... went down quickly before they could get to their phones. It's the only scenario that makes sense."

"God, I hope not. The Scarab is designed *not to sink*, at least that's what Neal has told me over the years. There are many air pockets in separate compartments. If it went down, at least they could stay with the boat. If that's the case, someone will spot them in the morning. I know it's horrible they have to stay out there all night. It must be awful, but we'll get them back when the sun comes up."

"Then we have to give them the benefit of the doubt through our positive thoughts and prayers."

"I can agree with that, but you know I'm not much for praying, Merry."

"Okay, I can handle the prayers, you can work on the positive thoughts."

"Deal!" Jackie dropped off to sleep after an exhausting day.

Merry prayed most of the night. "Dear Lord. Bless our three men. Keep them warm and away from the dangers of nature. I know you will do your best to keep them safe and alive long enough to be found." After a time, she fell into a semi-dream-like state, where she saw three angels with their wings touching, forming a circle with their men inside the ring. She could hear the wind and sea spray hitting their feathers. She could see their strong arms and hands helping them keep their heads above the water when needed. The image came across as so real to Merry, that she nearly swooned. She could see the ripples of the Angels' muscles, their unkempt flowing hair wild in the heavy wind. She smiled, knowing they were alive and for the time being, they were safe in God's hands.

CHAPTER NINE

AT THE TIME of the incident at sea, Bill Cameron was a Lieutenant with the Lee County Sheriff's Office, used to that kind of situation being presented to him. However, this calamity was close to home and the timing was more than urgent.

Lew and Merry lived opposite him on one the many inland canals which crisscrossed the landscape of southwest Florida. He and his wife, Canda were close friends with the Lipsits. There was always a party in the Lipsit backyard and Bill and Canda were always invited, welcome regardless of the circumstances.

Bill was shocked to hear the news, as was Canda as she listened in on the phone conversation with Merry. When Bill hung up, Canda immediately sat up in bed to ask, "What the hell's going on?"

He relayed what he had been told and she let the words sink in for a minute. "There's something wrong. Lew knows what he's doing out there and he would never stand up Merry... just wouldn't happen."

Bill nodded as he slipped a t-shirt over his head. "I agree. Those two are lovebirds, even after being married for fifteen years. If Lew didn't call in, or make it home on time, there's a problem."

"Were they out on a friend's boat? I think I remember Lew's boat parked behind the house in the canal."

"Yes. I took a look... first thing I did. It's still there." The large thirty-plus foot cabin cruiser was hard to miss, even in the relative darkness. "If he'd been out on his boat, I don't think there would have been a problem. His friend Neal's boat is a cigarette boat... a smaller model. It's made for skimming across the tops of waves and going fast. I don't think it was designed to stop in open seas to fish; especially in the weather that's coming in now. The transom is real low and susceptible to taking on water. The twin engines drag the back end into the waves when it's not flying across them. If I remember correctly, that's the one design flaw with the Scarab, those boats have their purpose. Sitting out in the Gulf in rough weather isn't one of them. I bet they took on some water, fried the batteries making the VHF useless."

"What about their cell phones?"

"Twenty miles out at sea ... with that storm moving in, I doubt they'd have cell service."

Canda shook her head in disbelief. "Can't the Coast Guard go out there? Surely three men in the water would be easy to spot?"

"No MAYDAY called in. Coast guard won't go out for at least twelve hours of them going missing, and if what Merry says is correct, a plane has gone down in the Everglades. All manpower down there... makes sense. I have to make a few calls, Honey." Bill finished dressing and went to the kitchen. Grabbing a glass of water, he looked out over the canal at the Lipsits house illuminated by a single light on the back of the building. He saw the boat moored on the dock, directly behind their house. It sent a shot of panic running through his veins picturing where Lew might be now. Being a cop for many years, he had seen some terrible things happen. How something so innocent could turn into a tragedy. Not for the first time, he thought how the ocean shows no mercy for those caught in its grip. Bill had a bad feeling. Rarely did bad situations like this one turn out for the

Waiting for Morning Time

better. On top of everything, that nasty storm was brewing and said to hit in the morning.

Bill had a few contacts up at St Pete's Coast Guard Station. While it might be highly uncommon for a Sheriff's office to contact the Coast Guard ... two counties away. He punched the auto dial.

"St. Pete's dispatch."

"Good morning. This is Bill Cameron from the Lee County Sheriff's Office."

"Good morning Mr. Cameron, how can we help?"

Bill recounted the events of the past day to Cortez as best he could, also mentioning the names of his contacts at Cortez.

"Thank you, Mr. Cameron. You'll have to wait until 8 a.m. to speak to one of your contacts. I'll mention you called. Can you give me your return number?"

Bill could feel his blood beginning to boil, but he couldn't blame the dispatcher, protocol is protocol. "I'd like to speak to the ranking officer on duty."

"Sir...?"

Bill cut him off. "I'll have Rod Shoap; Lee County Sheriff call you within five minutes if you do not put me through." Bill was good friends with his Boss. The fact that Rod was an acquaintance of the Lipsits, gave him the confidence to make the threat."

After a short silence, where Bill knew the dispatcher relayed the request, he came back online. "Hold a moment, I'll put you through to the ranking officer."

"Chief Warrant Officer Banks. What seems to be the issue, Mr. Cameron?"

"Lieutenant Bill Cameron, Lee County Sheriff's Office," he corrected him. "I'm not making this call Officer Banks to pull rank or ask for any special favors. I'm sure you aren't aware of why I'm calling. One of the men believed to be in harm's way is a good friend and a very experienced boater. His friend, Neal, is also extremely seasoned having grown up on these waters. Thus far, all we've heard from the Coast Guard is protocol. I understand that. We have our own sets of protocol, but we also rely upon common sense. Something happened to these three men. I've been on boating trips with Lew Lipsit, to the Keys and many day trips in the same waters we're talking about. He wouldn't be out there if things didn't look right. If Lew said he was going to be back by two p.m. That man would have been back by two p.m. Now let's give him a little leeway… it's now nearly two a.m. I'll bet my next year's wages these three men are in trouble. You know the stats better than I do. The longer they remain out on open water, the greater the chance something serious might happen to them. A Scarab is susceptible to water coming in through the transom. I believe they've fried their batteries and haven't been able to make the call. Who knows what might have happened to their cell phones. They could be out of range, or if… God forbid, the boat has gone down. They could be floating out there, their phones dead in the water."

Banks stayed silent for a few moments. "I'll contact the Lieutenant and voice your concerns, sir. We do have a few birds out there at present and I'll see if they can't swing past the coast a few times on their way back. By the time they are ready to go back up, your case should be priority."

Bill let out a deep breath. "Thank you. It's also my intent to get one of the Lee County planes up in the morning."

"Lieutenant Cameron, you know this is not practice. I doubt you will get a flight plan to fly past the line."

"I'll look into that. Just wanted to give you a heads up cause I'll have the Lee County Sheriff's department contact Sarasota County Sheriff's Department."

"I'll leave that to your discretion. Sarasota won't be happy ... you're stepping on their toes."

"Officer Banks. If you were in my shoes, would you do any

different?"

"I can't comment on that, sir,"

Bill sensed a small degree of empathy in the man's voice. "Thank you, again."

"We'll do our best, Lieutenant."

Bill hung up. His next call was to the Lee County Sheriff.

Seeing the caller's name, Rod Shoap picked up on the second ring. "Bill, it's nearly two-thirty in the morning. What the hell's up?"

Rod was a good friend and Bill wouldn't take advantage of their friendship if it wasn't important. They'd played music together in their twenties and Rod had been moving through the ranks of the Lee County Police force ever since.

Bill explained what had transpired over the past twelve hours.

"Dammit Bill! Whaddaya need?"

"I want to get a plane up there before dawn breaks. I wanted to call Cameron McKinney, tell him to get one of the twin-engine Cesna Skymasters ready." Technically, you need a twin engine to get access to a flight plan over the Gulf. Carman was Captain with Lee County Sheriff in charge of aviation.

"Take whatever you need for as long as you need it and God bless. I'll coordinate with Sarasota and Hillsborough if you need it."

"They won't be too happy about a Lee County plane coming up there, Rod?"

"Not your problem now, I'll look after it. I'll try to get you a flight plan ASAP."

CHAPTER TEN

I SLID INTO a semi-comatose state. My body moved involuntarily to somehow keep my head above water. It almost became a routine except when the odd rogue wave rolled though and demanded more attention. Still, my mind drifted back to my life with Merry. A smile formed on my lips as I recalled when we first met. Both of us were going through a divorce and I had just sold my dry-cleaning business.

During the divorce process with Janet, I bought a motorcycle to ease what I guess was a midlife crisis. It was a beautiful machine called an *Aspencade*. I traveled everywhere on it: the east coast of Canada, Nova Scotia, Florida. Though free again, I became lost... with no purpose.

A friend of mine, Bob Sentinel, called one day. Bob possessed a keen mind for business and knowing I was a hard worker with cash to invest ... Bob reeled me in on both accounts and I was not disappointed. I couldn't continue driving the eastern seaboard forever. Bob could see more than the investment. We were good friends back then and Bob worried about the state of my soul.

"Lew, you've spent the last year chasing your tail. I wish I could have done it with you, but you need to get some damned focus in your

life. You can't ride that motorcycle forever. It's time to get yourself back into a rut. I don't mean a bad rut, but a rut that gets you into some purposeful routine. Once you're there, things will fall back into place. I know you. You're a survivor and a person who needs to be busy."

I was knuckling my forehead with my right hand. "Okay, what's your darn point? What do you expect me to do?"

"I'm looking to buy another business. Why don't we do it together?"

Bob was the type who could turn a lump of coal into a gold nugget, and I didn't want to give up the opportunity, even if it meant parking the Aspencade in the garage for a while.

"There's a trade show next week up in Toronto."

"Okay, what are we looking at?" I had been to dozens of trade shows in my day.

"Health food is the way of the future. There's going to come a day when we all start looking at ourselves and say: What the heck have we been feeding our bodies? Why are we so damned fat? People are going to spend money to get healthy. We need to get in on the ground floor."

That was the 1980s. No one was talking about heath food in a big way back then, and it struck a chord with me, I come from a family of very large people. I had always struggled to keep my weight down; some healthy food in this life of mine one way or another couldn't hurt and if I could make some money at the same time—all-the better.

"It's at the Constellation, we'll do a couple days a piece, see what we come up with. What do you say?"

"Okay Bob, sounds good." I remembered hanging up the phone with a feeling of purpose, which at the time seemed to be exactly what was needed.

***

Bob took the first day at the conference and at the end called his new partner.

"This is Lew."

"*Hey, Lipsit, I think I've found something, a product called Herbal Life. When you get there tomorrow, have a look. I think it's a winner. Let me know your thoughts. The margins look really good and once we get into the swing of things, it should look after itself.*"

The next day, I found the booth and let them know I was Bob's business partner. I really liked what the Herbal Life people were saying, pretty much selling me on the idea after an hour or so listening to the pitch. Needing some time to think, I decided to take a walk around the conference center to see if I might discover a nugget of gold on my own. Little did I know, the nugget wouldn't come in the form of a business opportunity.

I was nearly through the place when I stumbled across a booth sponsored by Jack Lalanne Health Shakes. The program seemed decent enough, but what caught my eye was not the benefits of the shake, but the female training the sales staff. When I locked eyes with her for a short second, she smiled until her attention dragged back to her work. My feet became rooted to the floor, they didn't want to move, nor did I want to leave. Still, I felt foolish standing there staring at her. Finally, I had to and walked away finding a booth serving chilidogs and ordered a couple—maybe three. Finding a dark corner, I grabbed a table just in case the Herbal Life people caught sight of me and what I planned on eating ... as if it really mattered.

Wandering around for another hour, trying to forget the woman, I focused on finding the next big deal. I spied a line of people in front of some kind of big black dispensing machine. Getting closer, I could see it was not a dispenser, but rather a fortune-telling device. Choosing ten colors in the order in which they came up told a story. I paid fifty cents to retrieve my story. Walking to the side of the machine to examine my paper fortune, I bumped into a person being so intent to find my future. I looked up to see the pretty female from the shake booth.

She smiled, eyes locking with mine once again.

"This is kind of neat!" I looked down at his fortune and her eyes followed.

She frowned. "That's weird, let me have a look."

I handed it to her, and she put it side by side with hers. The colors and their order were identical. She nudged a lady standing next to her, examining her strip of paper. "Do you mind if I take a quick look at yours?"

The lady smiled and handed over her machine fortune. The papers were vastly different. After checking a couple of others, who had purchased a fortune from the machine, we both saw how every one of the fortunes differed.

What spooked me the most after closer examination was the last color: black. It signified a recent loss or divorce of some kind. I looked straight in her eyes and asked, "Are you getting or going through a divorce?"

She slowly nodded. "I am." She didn't need to say another word.

Still staring at her, I couldn't hide a smile from forming on my full round face. "Hey, I'm being rude. I'm Lew. Lew Lipsit." He extended his hand.

She accepted his hand, holding on a little longer than customary. "Merry Tartar."

It took some time for me to learn that her name was spelled M e r y instead of the biblical, Mary. All the while I kept thinking it a quirk of her Ohioan accent. Not wanting to let the opportunity slip away, I asked. "Can I buy you a drink?"

When she hesitated, the pause caused a slight blip to my heartbeat.

"I'd like that, Lew. I have to finish up with the crew. It'll take me a half hour. Can we meet upstairs in the Constellation lounge?"

"Good idea, I'll be there."

***

I became restless as I waited for the wonderful woman. If there might be such a thing as love at first sight, my chance meeting felt like it. I'd been hit by the proverbial thunderbolt. Ordering a gin and tonic, I sat back on a plush couch in the swank lounge and waited.

Merry kept me waiting. An hour and two drinks later, she sauntered into the lounge causing the pang in my heart to beat heavier. I felt like an idiot school kid.

When she sat down on the couch beside me, not up against, but within inches, I picked up on her aroma. She smelled really good. Funny how people have their own aromas. It was not just her perfume that was now labeled *MERRY!* It was truly the fragrant presence of Merry. At first, I would have to say that I liked it, but as seconds ticked by, I became intoxicated by the aroma. Taking deep breaths of her scent, it frightened me to realize her aroma was only available to me by sitting close to this woman. I didn't want to move away.

"What'll you have?" my voice cracked between long breaths.

"Gin and Tonic," she answered without noticing his drink.

When the waitress came by, I ordered *two more of the same ... how strange... we like the same drink ... another coincidence?* By this time, the chilidogs were not cutting it anymore, and I needed to eat a full meal. Halfway through her first drink I asked her. "Would you let me buy you dinner?"

She hesitated obviously pondering the invitation for whatever reason until she finally smiled and said, "Lew, that's the second best offer I've received today."

I felt the hair stand up on the back of my neck for all the wrong reasons, pang of jealousy coursing through my veins. *Had someone beaten me to invite her for dinner?*

Curious to know I asked, "Second best?"

Merry smiled coyly, letting the tension linger for a few more

Waiting for Morning Time

seconds. "Don't worry, Lew, the first best happened when you asked me out for a drink."

I exhaled, having held my breath for her answer. I started to laugh and so did Merry. In fact, we couldn't stop laughing together. When the waitress came around, we ordered dinner, not taking our eyes off each other showing each other how happy we were to be together.

"Tartar? Such an unusual last name ... where is it from?"

"It's Hungarian."

I could see what looked to be an Eastern European influence in her features. She got comfortable. "I've got all night."

Merry took a deep breath. "It's a bit of a story."

I indicated with a flourish of hand I'd be okay with however long it took.

"I married my brother's best friend, which in itself makes my situation more difficult. There are certain expectations which go along with that kind of arrangement."

"I can imagine." I nodded for her to continue.

"How should I say it? Paul is...?"

I saw a tear in her eye. "Let me guess, *abusive*?"

The mounting anxiety left her face quickly replaced by her smile. "You are a very intuitive man, Lew Lipsit." She hesitated, her face flushing again. "It began verbally when we were first married, and then it became more physical. I won't get into the details except to tell you...." Merry paused. "He frightens me!"

"That's a terrible way to live ... being afraid. How does Paul frighten you?"

She nodded. "He's a strong man for one thing and then there's his guns."

I could do nothing other than raise my brows while waiting to hear more, but not liking the direction her conversation was headed.

"He likes to shoot guns in the basement, especially when he's mad."

Nice. "Has he ever threatened you with a gun?"

"Not point blank, but he threatened to kill me if I ever left him."

"So… are you leaving him?" I couldn't help but raise my voice before giving the room a quick once over.

She nodded. "I told my brother about it months ago and he more or less forced me to move out. I thought he would be upset. Why do we do things to make other people happy, when things are so damned upsetting?" She took a sip from her drink. "He went over and talked to Paul. My brother told him he knew what went on and he had contacted the police and now they knew of his threats to me. So yes, I've moved out, but I still don't feel safe. I don't know what he'll do when asked to sign divorce papers."

"Is it clean cut?"

"Divorce ... it never is Lew, you should know that. He wants alimony. I'm the breadwinner. I've got a pretty good wholesale business."

I sighed and looked down, feeling bad for the woman. I possess a soft spot for abused people and furry creatures. I didn't like bullies and had been in more than one fight straightening one or two out.

"Tell me something about yourself, Lew, something to take my mind off all that stuff. I find it terribly depressing." She moved a little closer, her elbows on the table holding up her chin as her sparkling eyes gazed up at him.

I didn't know where to start, so I began to ramble. "I've been a lost soul since my separation. I've put forty-thousand Kilometers on my bike, been all over the eastern seaboard."

She smiled coyly. "Has it helped you to find what you've been looking for?"

"Well…?" I took a moment to find the right words. "It may have taken a while, but I'm feeling pretty right, just sitting here, I mean with you."

She didn't seem taken back by the brash words, but I could feel my face flush with the bold proclamation.

We finished dinner with lighter conversation, and I could remember being distraught when the time came for us to leave. "Can I call you?"

"Of course, you can. I think I've met a new best friend. Call me anytime."

It wasn't exactly the answer I had been looking for, but gladly accepted her business card. I wrote my home number on a table napkin and asked, "Can I call you tomorrow?" I needed something to hold onto and didn't want to walk out without it.

"I'll call you. I'm here for another day ... maybe at dinnertime, how's that?"

When I moved to give her a goodbye kiss, she offered her cheek. I gave her a slightly more than cordial cheek press, taking whatever one could get.

***

The drive back to Niagara Falls seemed to take forever. I was resolved to the fact that while Merry seemed like a great gal, she was not interested in me in a romantic way. We had enjoyed a nice evening. I should feel blessed to have had the time I did with her. I decided to think about the business at hand. Herbal Magic would be a winner and would go fifty-fifty with Bob.

***

I made sure to sit close to the phone so I wouldn't miss Merry's call ... if, or when it rang. I had his doubts whether she would call. I took his time looking over the Herbal Magic's numbers and projections, which seemed like a no-brainer. If the sales mounted to what their people indicated, there wouldn't be too much of an initial cash outlay, allowing for a quick start up.

The phone rang... one of those old black phones with a rotary dial, old even in the 1980s. I answered, sounding sophisticated. "This is Lew."

"Why hello, this-is-Lew!"

Her voice sounded grand. While never at a loss for words, I didn't know what to say back after her cute witticism.

"Lew?"

"Yep, I'm here... I have to tell you, it's sure good to hear your voice again."

She didn't respond. Instead, she said, "Say, are you hungry? I'm finished early and I could drive down there. How long is it?"

"I'm always hungry, so yes! It's a little over an hour." I gave her the address and waited... very impatiently for her to arrive.

***

I took her *over the river*, as those who lived in Niagara say, meaning they crossed the Niagara River to the States. We went to my favorite place in Lewiston, New York. Apple Grannies was a casual family restaurant, serving cheap drinks and great food. That great combination kept the business open all these years.

We talked, ate, and drank for hours, ending up being the last patrons of the night. I couldn't specifically remember what we talked about except for one thing, neither would forget. She put her hand on top of mine while staring into my eyes.

"Lew, I don't know how ... maybe we will just be great friends, maybe more? But we will be part of each other's lives forever. I just know it."

I had never *truly* talked with a woman before… the way we honestly talked with each other. We didn't step on the other person's words, nor did either one monopolize the conversation. We were just two people being happy to be alone together and listening to each other's voice.

Waiting for Morning Time

We made it back to my apartment sometime after midnight. I remembered wanting her to stay but would admit being a bit of an old fashioned guy, and perhaps she was an old fashioned girl. Merry drove back to Toronto that night, but not before we shared our first kiss. Not too drawn out, but there was something very romantic there.

As another wave rolled over my head, I remembered being sad with the thought of that first kiss lingering in my mind. She would be driving back to Columbus the next day. At the time, I didn't know if we would see each other again.

***

Neal nudged Lew on the shoulder. "Hey, you okay?"

I popped out of my daydream, mad at myself for slipping off to sleep.

Since we cut the anchor line, the boat started to sink faster now that it was allowed to float stern down. The water slowly kept creeping into the air-filled cavities. If it had remained anchored, Neal believed it probably would have remained afloat at least until the following day. The angle at which it lay in the water did allow for the various air pockets to remain filled. Now, only three feet of bow remained above water.

Neal pointed to Bill's bobbing head, only a dozen yards away. "It's time. I'm going to go and get him. Keep hold of the rope whatever you do."

"I was afraid of the state in which we might find my son. I understood what Neal meant by Bill's willingness to give in to the ocean, but still found it odd it happened so quickly. *Would I be able to change him back into Bill, or would he be lost to despair*? A pang of worry overtook me. *Did Bill want to come back to the boat?* I prepared myself for what might occur and watched as Neal swam over to nudge him. My heart soared as I could see Bill nodding and then they both turned back towards the boat. It took a minute or two for them to return. I didn't know exactly what I saw in my son's eyes as Neal put Bill's hand onto the rope. *Could it be shame?* I didn't think Bill planned on ever having to look his father in the eye again. This realization shook me to the core. Maybe we would…maybe we wouldn't make it out of the present mess, but I had nearly lost my son. I inhaled quickly once involuntarily, then moved closer and gave him a hug, feeling Bill shudder with sobs as he returned the embrace.

After a few minutes, I took Bill's face in between my hands and looked my son straight in the eyes. "Bill… you need a damn attitude adjustment." Being a little more than gentle, I slapped his cheek. "You're being selfish… think about your family. Anna ... she's not held a job in years. Your kids, Billy and Ashley. You've got a young family and you need to work this out now so you can support them. They need you. Don't you ever do that AGAIN!"

As the reality of how hard it would be to survive entered Bill's mind, I could see the vestiges of childlike fear creeping back into his eyes again.

"I'm sorry, Dad. I don't know why I let go and floated away. I felt overwhelmed with fear. I don't know even now whether I want to do this."

"Nobody wants to do ... THIS!" I slapped his cheek again. "But here we are, and right now, we don't have a choice but to try and survive. If we stay alive long enough, we will be found. You can count on it. Are you with us?"

Bill sheepishly nodded.

Neal pulled a canister out of the bag he had brought with him from the boat. "This'll make us feel a bit better. He opened the valve on the canister's top and inhaled. Closing the valve he said, "Nitrox."

Bill asked. "What the heck's that?"

"Enriched air that'll relive fatigue… make you think clearer. We use it after a long dive ... gets more oxygen to your muscles." Neal extended the can towards us.

Bill and I inhaled the gas. Bill spoke up. "I'll admit, it's cleared my head instantly, though the cold air reminds me of how dry my throat is. Man am I thirsty. I could drink this ocean if it didn't taste so salty."

Neal frowned. "Don't even think about it, buddy, salt will mess with your head."

***

The waves started to build higher, not so high as to spill over our heads, but high enough to lift us up and down a dozen or so feet with each one passing below. The Scarab kept sinking below the water line ... then popping back up like a large behemoth. Only minutes of fading light remained. We could no longer see the sun as it now sank below the massive storm closing in on us.

All three of us must have been looking in the same direction seeing the boat at the same moment: a pleasure craft appearing on the horizon. We all raised an arm, waving frantically, excited by the emergence of the boat, thinking this would be our rescue. At its closest point, it would pass by a half mile away.

When it was at the closest distance, Neal fired off a flare. They waited for the boat to turn, but to their mutual dismay, it remained on course, disappearing over the horizon. Maybe the boat's operator had his eye on the impending storm or perhaps his eye on the waves, which would be tricky to navigate. As quickly as our spirits rose, they sank, leaving each man's resolve at an all-time low.

As we floated, the air became cooler by the minute. We watched solemnly as the sun's glow disappeared, shrouding the edges of the storm clouds in brilliant reddish orange hues with a slight tinge of purple. The three of us stayed to ourselves and keeping our eyes open, but not looking at each other. Any man would fear darkness we now faced out in the ocean. The mutual dread we felt couldn't accurately be explained.

A few words popped into my mind: helplessness, dread, tired, cold and what swims below us?

Neal's thoughts, he would later say, were more practical. He worried for the two of us and our lack of protection from the cold. His wet suit proved to be a godsend. Without it he wouldn't have made it half as long as us larger men.

Bill could only think about sharks. He kept recounting a movie he once watched. People were caught in the ocean and the sharks kept nipping at them as they floated in open water. The sharks slowly wore down the resolve of the floating people until they ended up dying from loss of blood.

The sun had been a blessing during the day as we were able to find some comfort from its heat, but now in the dark that luxury would be gone. It became bitter cold. Bill and I could sense our body temps dropping and nothing could be done about it. As night set in, we knew it would only get worse.

Bill broke the silence. "When this boat finally goes down, we could get sucked down with it… like when big ships go down. I've heard you can be pulled under?"

Neal shook his head. "No way! Even when this baby goes under, there's still too much air inside it. It's gonna float for a while underwater. At that point, it'll no longer be in the waves, it'll drift for miles like that. The gas tank alone is only a quarter full. There's enough air in there to keep it suspended."

The waves were continuing to build as a cold front began, the storm being pulled in with it. I didn't think the boat would pull us down with it either. It was not big enough; but something else concerned me.

"Whether that's going to happen or not, I'm not feeling good about being this close to the boat when these waves kick up and these swells start turning over. We run the risk of being bashed up against

Waiting for Morning Time

the boat. It's already taking all the strength I have to stay far enough away holding onto this darn rope." We all looked over at the Scarab as it sunk down to the bottom of a swell, then lifted up at the top, sort of spinning. At times, we were above the point of the bow, looking down at it. "I can imagine myself, or any one of us slamming down onto that point. If we were going to die out here, I don't want it to happen by being stupid." I looked over at Neal for confirmation of my worry and could tell my friend didn't agree.

Neal shook his head. "You guys are crazy. We don't want to let go of the boat. It's the only thing that's gonna be seen when or if they send planes out to find us. We're gonna be three little black heads floating in a massive turned-up sea. It's a death wish to leave the boat. I'd rather take my chances with it."

As Neal gave his sermon, the boat lifted up out of the water three or four feet, nearly picking Bill out of the surf with it. I looked over at Bill, his face nearly invisible in the near darkness. "What do you say, Bill?"

"I'm with you... whatever you think."

I looked back at Neal and read the determined look on his face, but Neal was able to stay buoyant with his personal buoyancy device; it was harder for Bill and I to keep above the waves. "Neal, you can stay if you want, but we're leaving the boat. I don't feel good about being near it... it's the waves, and I'm having a hard time seeing the boat as it comes out of the water in the dark."

Knowing Neal would be able to stay buoyant, I grabbed the two boat bumpers tied together with rope. "I hope you don't mind if I take these. Our life vests are getting soggy, and this rope is the only thing keeping us on top of the water and... with a lot of personal effort. We won't survive without them."

Neal shook his head again. "It's a death wish leaving the boat! I've been hanging in here with you two, when I could've been swimming for shore hours ago." Neal regretted his last words as soon as he said them.

I felt many emotions: sadness, hopelessness and anger. I knew that Neal meant the best, but I'll admit, it became hard to remain rational this close to death's door. I held back any snide comments I was harboring, they would accomplish nothing.

Bill spoke up. "The hardest part about staying with the boat ... I can't keep riding up with every wave ... I'm becoming exhausted. I'm going to drown if I stay here… I know it."

So… the decision was made, at least for Bill and I. We needed to be careful letting go of the rope so that we didn't get sucked up against the Scarab. Several kicks and some strong swimming, we were free from any danger, slowly drifting away. I felt helpless, but not scared. Bill's fear radiated from him like electricity. I felt what a predator must feal when on the hunt. I feared that whatever lurked below us would sense it as well.

***

Neal kept hold of the bowline. He couldn't believe that we were not willing to suffer through the night, fending off the boat in order to stay near the beacon that could easily be spotted. It would get picked up on radar in the morning, and possibly even tonight if the Coast Guard started a search. Neal felt he had kept his head so far. Anyone who dared to go out on the ocean knew they had to keep their wits out on the water. The sea didn't make exceptions for mistakes. It was logical to Neal for all of us to stay together-- with the boat.

He watched the two of us, floating away to try and make it on our own. Neal knew he couldn't let them go. They wouldn't make it through the night. He thought about Jackie, Kayla and their new baby. He could have tough it out, but could he live with himself if he was rescued, knowing he may have been able to keep me and Bill safe through the dark night?

His mind was made up, but when he tried to let go it seemed as if

Waiting for Morning Time

the bowline became stuck to his hand and he couldn't let go. His fingers had become claw like from holding the thick twine. He needed to concentrate harder. Finally, Neal's hand opened to let go and his body started drifting in the same direction as Bill and I. Neal floated for a time, keeping us in sight. We were only a dozen yards away, but we were so concentrated on where we were headed, we didn't turn around to notice him yet. It was Neal's first chance to relax his mind while he caught up to us. He needed to concentrate on happier things to keep him alive in the present. He kept sight of his friends as his thoughts drifted.

***

Neal met Jackie a few years back. They were a perfect match; Jackie outspoken and confident, Neal quiet and practical. The two had been out on the Gulf a hundred times together and never came close to having a problem. Jackie would know they were in trouble. He hoped she would try her hardest to get a search started. Government agencies were never easy to push, and it would take a lot to get the Coast Guard out there that night. He knew his wife and Jackie would stop at nothing until she got her own way. He almost chuckled thinking about her ... *you didn't want to confront Jackie when she became focused on something.*

He knew his mom would freak out. She had always been uneasy with the latitude Neal's father gave him when it came to boating and the water. Still, Neal had never given her reason to truly worry in his thirty plus years. She would know something was very wrong. He didn't have a doubt in his mind that his family would know something was wrong—they would come looking for him.

He knew giving up the Scarab to float away with the current, took logic and probability out of the rescue equation. We were now at the mercy of the powerful Gulf currents changing frequently, especially with a front moving in, which would mess with the probabilities. There would be a degree of predictability, but that was about it. We could end up off Tampa by the next morning, while the search could be taking place south near Venice. He allowed himself one expletive before swimming to reunite with the us. "DAMMIT ALL!"

***

He paddled in between the two of us, trying not to startle us especially with Bill's shark phobia. He grabbed on to the boat bumper, giving us both a dirty look. "I couldn't let the two of you drift off alone."

His appearance didn't feel like an admission that either course of action was right or wrong. Not for the first time, I got the feeling Neal thought we were not able to look after themselves. I would have to admit the notion got under my skin-- just a little. Still, I was very glad Neal joined up with the two of us.

***

Darkness overcame us as the last vestiges of sunset faded away. We were blessed with light from the moon and stars. Bill discovered if he waved his hands in the water they glowed.

Neal spoke up for the first time in a while. "Bioluminescent. It's caused by a chemical reaction in microscopic plankton. When you stir it up and bring it to the surface exposing it to oxygen, it glows like that."

Bill became agitated at the notion. "So, we're floating around out here like beacons to the sharks below us. Nice."

Neal shrugged. "Not much we can do about it."

From that point on, Bill did his best to not move very much, holding onto the rope as close to the one bumper as he could to keep himself afloat as still as possible.

***

A short time later, we noticed planes taking off in the east, their lights easy to distinguish in the starry sky. Neal exclaimed. "I hope they're coming to find us. I'll keep a flare ready if one comes close."

Bill made a suggestion. "Maybe we've drifted closer to shore. I can almost see where they are taking off. Maybe we should start trying to swim in that direction?" We all agreed and gently began to push towards the east. The act of swimming seemed to help moderate our body temperature, or at least it felt that way. If nothing else, it kept our minds in the present.

Neal watched as one of the large planes, probably a Coast Guard C-130 passed them to the southwest, close to where the Scarab went down, but too far to risk using up a flare. Neal said, "Hey, look at that."

I could see the expression on Neal's face ... an *I-told-you-so scowl*. Both of us turned our attention back to swimming.

The rest of the planes did indeed look to be searching along the coast, but much closer to shore. "A lot of good that does us," chided Bill. However, it did give a glimmer of hope that someone might be looking. We tilted our heads back and watched the ineffective search that came nowhere close to our actual location.

Christopher Bowron

CHAPTER ELEVEN

THE GULF OF MEXICO ecosystem is an ever-changing creature, similar to most large bodies of water except for the fact that it is comparatively shallow for the massive area it covers. The water is continually churned up from the bottom due to seasonal temperature changes, currents, tropical storms and varying algae blooms; positive and negative.

One constant remains, if the algae are present, there will be a vibrant food chain existing. The Sun feeds Phytoplankton, small micro biotic organisms. The organisms provide a harvest for the next in line, Zoo Plankton, which are made up of jellyfish and omnivorous fish like Mullet. Next in the chain are Herring, Shrimp, Pinfish and squid followed by more omnivorous carnivores like Catfish, Jack Crevalle, Sea Trout, Mackerel, Snook, Tuna, small sharks and Bottle Nosed Dolphins. At the apex, sit the large sharks; Bulls, Hammerheads, Great White's and Tigers.

If one wanted to find a great example of the Gulf Food Chain, they could follow a shrimp boat. Over decades, the captains of these boats follow a learned path, traversing the nutrient rich currents, which flow through the coastal waters of the Gulf. More often than not these days, the boat's navigation would be programmed to follow

Waiting for Morning Time

a code of pre-plotted GPS instructions, the crew sound asleep through the night.

The massive female Tiger Shark, nineteen feet long, over 2000 pounds, cruised behind the boat as she had learned to do for decades. She lived in the deep channel of the Boca Grand Pass picking up the shrimp boats as they left Charlotte Harbor. The large predator was greedy and learned over the years to chase off smaller sharks, often chewing them in half with one powerful bite to fend them off her almost endless banquet of Mackerel, Jack and Tuna, which were caught in the boats netting, or chasing the abundant shrimp. Like a whale, she would slowly rise to the surface where her four-foot wide mouth cut swaths through the abundant prey so she could gorge herself.

***

Neal spotted the boat first. Watching its lights for a few minutes indicating it was heading almost straight at them. "Hey!" He didn't need to say much more. Bill and I were in a semi-comatose state, not sleeping, existing under the radar of freezing to death and distilled panic. I swished my hands around to get the blood flowing, soon elated by the fact a boat was nearing, but also cognizant that shrimp boats often ran on autopilot.

Bill's eyes were still glazed over with fear, something Neal and I grew accustomed to seeing. Neal appeared okay, excited with the possibility of a rescue. "We've got one more flare, handheld!"

I had been out enough at night shark fishing on my own boat to know you got out of the way of the shrimp boats. Chances are they might not see you. "They could be sleeping." It is the middle of the night. We need to swim away from the boat. If they don't see us, we'll get swept up in her nets, dead within minutes."

Neal said. "I'm going to let off the flair as we get really close."

Heads were nodding in agreement, each of us, our eyes wide open in anticipation of the rescue. Neal grabbed the rope between the two bumpers and started pulling us out of the trawler's way. Bill and I joined in.

Soon we reached a safe distance, roughly a hundred yards of the starboard side of the shrimper, well away from her nets. Neal fired the flare as the boat neared, holding it up in the air waving it from side to side.

The shrimper continued on its course, straight ahead, with no signs of life on deck. We yelled as loud as we could as it passed. A multitude of emotions passed through each man's head and heart. Excitement, hope, disappointment, loss and then… terror as the boat appeared to be passing us unnoticed. Someone appeared on the deck. All three men knew the fisherman wouldn't be able to hear them, but we yelled none-the-less, as loud as our parched throats would allow. The person shone a flashlight out onto the water, narrowly missing us as we waved our hands, but the waves were too big and hid us from view every time the beam of light came close. The man must have turned in unison with the heavy surf as the flare sunk into the bottom of a trough.

"WE'ER RIGHT HERE!" Neal yelled. He waved the flare viciously from side to side. Bill and I looked on in disbelief as the trawler edged away from them… traveling into the night, it's lights becoming smaller and smaller, eventually disappearing.

***

The large shark caught a different scent, sensors on the end of her snout feeling the movement from the side of the boat… panic… larger food, less work. She turned to the side, slipping under the large side netting, which over the years she had learned to avoid.

From about fifty feet below the new prey, she turned upwards. Tiger sharks are different from other apex predators like the Bull, White or the Hammer. They liked to check out their prey first, unlike the other species, the Tigers were scavengers, not necessarily hunters; opportunists… would be a better way of describing them—lazy another. As the massive fish passed under the rapidly moving target, or targets, she couldn't tell if it was one large prey or many. She came close to the one on the end, moving near to nudge it, to see if it might be edible, or in fact was another Shark which she needed to chase away. She didn't like the smell of the rubber on the fish. She turned around with a massive swish or her tail, disappearing into the dark Gulf.

She could still sense the rapidly moving forms, which were more than intriguing to her, a much more efficient way to feed, unlike the many small fish she would consume behind the hulking mass of the boat and its nets. Maybe the other end would taste better. She sculled her tail back and forth returning to her quarry, coming in on the thrashing object on the other end. She would need to have a taste of her prey to see if it would warrant attacking. She opened her massive jaws, which would engulf one of the strange-looking fish in one bite.

Before she could eat her prey, a bright light erupted on top of the surface of the water. The light frightened her, her Tiger Shark senses telling her to move back to her less aggressive prey behind the trawler. Her eyes stinging from the light, she turned away with one massive push of her tail, abandoning her attack, hurrying to get back to the smaller, but much more docile fish now following the slow-moving Shrimp Boat.

***

"Did you feel that?" Yelled Bill as he frantically waved towards the boat as it passed.

Neal yelled at him. "What?"

"Something passed below me, I felt a push of water. It didn't feel like the current."

Bill had been griping about sharks since the beginning. Both Neal and I knew many fish followed those boats. Neal didn't want to discount Bill's statement, but at the same time, he knew they needed to remain calm. "Don't splash around if you can help it." He didn't want to tell him that he too thought he had seen the tip of a tailfin just under the surface of the water, and it was not that of a small Blacktip shark... it was something much bigger. "Sharks can follow these boats." Neal said calmly.

"Great." Bill started to shiver.

I put my hands on my son's shoulders. "If they're gonna get us, they're gonna get us. Sharks can sense panic. Let's try to stay as calm and as still as we can."

***

The three of us… castaways, stared at the boat as it passed on into the darkness of night. Still, we had continued to holler at the disappearing craft. Neal held onto the flare until it sputtered and fizzled its last gasps of light. "How come that guy didn't see the flare, he must have seen it originally?" Neal continued. "Perhaps it was just bad luck, and he was looking the wrong way when we appeared at the top of a wave, blocked from his sight when we were in a trough."

We looked at each other, hugely discouraged. No one spoke for several hours, drifting in silence, rising up and down on the waves, too tired to think of anything but our immediate survival.

***

As the night wore on, the moon dropped over the horizon, and the stars slowly faded away, replaced by clouds. It became very dark. Soon we couldn't see each other's faces. All that Neal and I could hope for would be that Bill wouldn't decide to let go of the rope. We focused our worry on him constantly, but neither of us were in a state to be able to do anything if it needed to be done… if we could see what needed to be done.

Waiting for Morning Time

Neal bobbed up and down on one end of the rope, Bill and I on the other.

I couldn't see Neal, yet I could feel his weight on the line. For the first time since the boat went down, I wondered about how the boat could have sunk so quickly? The Scarab would have been dry when we left Jackie and Neal's place. Whatever happened occurred once on the water. The bilge would have been run dry by the time we arrived at the dive site. So... in the time it took Neal to make four or five dives, the boat flooding to a critical point where there was no stopping her from swamping. I blamed myself and to be honest with myself, I was sure Neal did, too. I couldn't blame Bill; He had been too focused on the events of the day not a boater like his myself.

For the first time in several hours, I called out to my friend. "Neal?"

Lost in his thoughts, it took him a moment to respond. "Yeah, Lew?"

"What would have made the Scarab take on so much water... so quickly?"

Neal thought for a while before he responded. "I've been thinking about that. I thought it could've been a split in the hull. It was a fairly rough ride going out. The boat was airborne a few times, hitting the waves pretty hard. But I took a good look at the bottom when we were trying to get up on top of it—couldn't see anything."

I nodded, though it wouldn't be seen. "That could happen and you're right, we would have spied that. What if there was water getting in by the boot for the motors? We were slamming down pretty hard stern first into the waves while you were down there; the current kept pulling us sideways, sometimes almost backwards into the waves."

"No... I just had those motors put on a few weeks ago, all of the work done by the dealer. Unless they screwed something up, there shouldn't have been a problem. They're bigger motors than the old ones, but it shouldn't have mattered ... they were supposed to be lighter than the old ones. It could have been a through hole that popped out, but that would have taken a real long time."

"I, Suppose. Ultimately, we'll never know, unless they somehow find her… soon."

Neal went quiet for a few minutes, rising up and down with the waves. "There wasn't enough fuel in the boat. If we had a full tank, I could see the Coast Guard looking for her. They would be concerned about the environment. The cost of searching for the boat would more than offset whatever it's worth. I'm lucky we just paid the insurance the other day. Crazy, you never expect anything to happen. Jackie just received the notice of coverage yesterday."

Bill's voice sounded hoarse from thirst. "You're lucky."

Neal half laughed. "I suppose. I hope I'm lucky enough to be lucky."

We all laughed nervously at the attempt at humor.

Bill couldn't help himself. "What about sharks? We haven't seen any… well, except when the shrimper passed us bye."

Neal answered quickly. "They're down there, but they don't like the waves. Something would have to draw them to the surface. We're pretty lucky that it is so rough. They'd be after us for sure. But then again, someone might have found us by now… and, we probably wouldn't have sunk without the waves in the first place."

Bill said. "Pretty sure I saw one when the shrimp boat passed, something big."

Neal spoke. "There you go. The chum from the boat drew them up."

Bill could still see the size of the tail fin in his mind. "Them? What I saw was pretty damn big."

Neal jumped right in. "I'll be honest. I saw it too. I think I got bumped but didn't want to say anything."

Bill spoke up. "Okay, you don't have to say it. You didn't want

Waiting for Morning Time

to scare me."

I said. "I'm just trying to put it out of my mind. No use thinking about it. Let's face it. If that fish wanted to eat us, we'd be dead now. I think Neal scared it away when he set the flare off."

They were quiet for a time until Bill broke the silence. "I watched *Jaws* about a month ago."

I couldn't help it. "You know if you keep this up, your mind will start playing games. Bill, I've heard enough about the sharks. Put it out of your head."

"No sorry Dad, I don't mean what happened in the movie. I know there aren't any Great Whites out here."

Neal contradicted Bill's statement. "There are, but further out."

Bill said. "Thanks, Neal. I wasn't worried about Great Whites. I was thinking about the part where Brody, Hooper, and Quint are sitting in the fishing boat talking about their wounds. Quint pulls his pant leg up and points to his leg and says, 'US Indianapolis, 1945.' I can't remember the specific words, but he says something like '800 went into the water, 300 came out. We floated waiting to be the next one to be taken.' I kinda feel like that right now. I've been waiting to be bit for the past five hours."

Neal spoke. "That was different. I watched a documentary on the Indianapolis. The explosion would have drawn sharks from dozens of miles away. There would have been blood in the water from hundreds of dead sailors. Different kind of sharks… Oceanic White Tips. We don't have them here. Mostly Bulls and Black Tips."

"So, you're saying we're okay? Bulls?"

"Not really, this isn't very good at all. I'm just saying, put the sharks out of your head like Lew says. We're gonna get picked up in the morning. Worrying about what could happen won't help us. Think about your kids, your wife, what you'd like to do to her when you get back to shore. Think about them naked, waiting in bed for us."

"Now there's a thought to hang onto." I said.

For the rest of the night, we didn't say much. We thought about our lives, our wives and their kids. Neal's words were wise. Not thinking about the bad things which could happen, made the night pass without too much fretting. What became a concern was the true reality and present danger, the exposure to the cold water. I no longer shivered. I could feel my breathing getting shallow, my mind drifting uncontrollably; the same thing happened to Bill. Shock sets in when your body temperature begins to drop. Neal was in a slightly better place, the wet suit paying dividends, keeping him relatively warm.

Though I'm a devout Christian, I'm not normally a preachy soul, but I decided to take the moment to say a prayer out loud. "Dear God, let us see the rising sun in the morning and that our women have found the strength and will to believe we still live."

Bill followed with an "Amen!"

Neal chimed in, "Amen. All I can think of is waiting for morning time. I can't wait to see the glow of the sun rising."

Neal's words held true as we put positive thoughts in our head.

CHAPTER TWELVE

CLYDE BUTCHER put down the receiver after talking to his daughter, Jackie. Clyde had been anxiously picking up the phone at twelve midnight. He let it ring several times before getting out of bed, but the caller was relentless. Clyde's memories were brought back to the night he received the call that his son, Ted, had been killed in a car accident.

He stood silently in shock listening to his daughter. After a time, he slowly walked down the hall of their Everglades cottage to the dark bedroom. His wife, Niki sat up in bed and turned on the light. She could tell something was wrong by Clyde's body language: his shoulders slumped; his gait slower than usual.

"What is it?" Niki asked as her heart climbed up her throat.

"Neal isn't home yet." He watched Niki fall back on her pillows, her face pale.

"What do you mean? Is he out at a bar?"

Clyde stared at Niki. "You know Neal's not like that."

"Like what?"

"A bar guy ... a drinker. Neal is with Lou Lipsit and his son, Billy. They went diving today, but they didn't make it back."

"What do you mean?" Niki needed more information.

"Jackie says they haven't received any contact from the men. They left first thing in the morning, supposed to be back by mid-afternoon. The truck and trailer's still at the launch."

"How's Jackie?"

"On the edge ... I tried to calm her down. Merry and Bill's wife, Anna, are also at Neal and Jackie's house, along with the kids. Jackie's trying to be the strong one."

"We need to get up there."

"I said we were coming ASAP."

Niki nodded, trying to remain calm. She packed a small suitcase for them and got dressed. Within fifteen minutes, they were on their way. It would take just over two hours to get to Venice.

■■

Clyde's artistic work carved out a niche as a photographer who uses an 8 x 10 large format camera and only prints black-and-white images. His main focus was the Everglades and Florida. His photographs are exhibited in museums throughout the United States and owned by people from all over the world. He believes the earth is a sacred gift and he will always be known as an environmentalist, speaking around the country.

Jackie's father would give his daughter support in her stressful time, but he would also offer his brain and clear thinking. He believed all situations happen for a reason, usually with a degree of predictability. His mind churned as he drove up I-75 towards Venice. It didn't surprise him that the Coast Guard hadn't offered help off the hop. No MAYDAY, no search. Like his daughter, he knew that they needed to augment the efforts of the authorities. He couldn't sit on his hands and watch. He needed to get to where things were happening in order to put the pieces of the puzzle together.

He looked over at Niki. He knew he could count on her to be strong, but at that moment... his wife, Jackie's mother, looked vulnerable. Niki looked as awful as he felt. Emotions are raw when

Waiting for Morning Time

you are fresh to bad news. He didn't have time to come to grips with the reality of the situation just yet. Neither did Niki. He said the words out loud: "Neal could be dead."

Niki looked over at Clyde, putting her hand on his. "He could be. But there is no sense in going to that place until there's proof. In the meantime, as far as I'm concerned, he's alive."

Clyde smiled, bolstered by his wife's encouragement.

Clyde and Niki pulled off the highway at approximately 2:30 am and immediately headed out to the Gulf of Mexico in order to get a feeling for the direction and the force of the wind. He pulled up as close to the Gulf as he could. As they stepped out of the car, they were assaulted by the heavy wind blowing hard off the Gulf. The surf was extremely rough; powerful waves crashed against the break wall, spraying briny mist up into the air.

Both Clyde and Niki couldn't help but think ... *if Neal is out in that water, they prayed he stayed alive until someone could get to him.*

It looked pretty bleak in Clyde's estimation. Neal needed to stay focused and think of his family, his wife, daughter and baby boy in order to survive.

Niki said the words aloud, which she would use as her mantra over the next few days. "Stay alive NEAL ... Survive!"

Clyde nodded and walked over to a police car that happened to be in the area. Seeing Clyde approach, two officers stepped out and greeted him. "Good evening, sir," said a female officer.

"Can you tell me how hard the wind is blowing?"

"It's roughly thirty miles-per-hour. You mind me asking what you're doing here at three in the morning, looking out into the Gulf?"

Clyde nodded. "My son-in-law is out there."

"Who's your son-in-law?"

"Neal Obendorf."

"Oh… that's a coincidence, we're on our way to the boat launch to monitor the car and trailer, just in case his boat comes back in," an empathetic look softened her stern features.

Clyde nodded. "So, you're on to it, now. It's good to know that you are on top of things."

"Why don't you head home now, we'll be keeping an eye on the trailer. We have your daughter's phone number, if they show up, you'll be the first to hear."

"Thanks." Clyde could see the wind, blowing straight from the southwest, which meant Neal's boat would be drifting to the northeast. "Do you know what time the big storm's supposed to hit?"

"Mid to late morning, so we hear from dispatch."

Clyde nodded and ambled his large body back to the car. Niki had waited there for him and slipped into the passenger seat. "Could they survive out there?"

Clyde nodded slowly. "I don't know for how long. Lew had a quadruple bypass a year ago. The water's pretty cold this time of year. I don't know, in the water ... maybe a day? The boat must have gone down quickly, or they would have made contact. We must assume they are floating out there… somewhere. Neal and Bill may have on their wet suits, which would be a godsend. I doubt Lew would, he didn't dive today. Jackie says they have the coordinates to a few of the dive sites where they might have been. I want to get on the Internet and see if I can find out a little more about the currents. I'm not going to be able to sleep, may as well be proactive."

She nodded, expecting no less. Clyde like Jackie could be relentless once on task.

"Let's get some coffee and then we'll head over to Jackie's. I'm sure they're not sleeping." Clyde sifted through the contacts on his phone and zeroed in on Marshall. He pressed the button, not worried he would wake his college buddy. Marshall seldom slept. The phone rang several times with no answer. *Strange?* Marshall always answered.

CHAPTER THIRTEEN

Sunday Morning, March 4th Venice

NO ONE slept much ... a catnap at best. Before the sun came up at roughly 5 a.m. The house was greeted to the sounds of Clyde and Niki banging around in the kitchen. Merry lay on the bed, waking after a short sleep. She remained there because it seemed the thing to do. She thought about Lew and the boys floating out there in the Gulf. Since they were not sleeping, why should she?

Jackie and Merry both popped out of bed at the same time, hearing the clamor from the kitchen. They didn't need any encouragement.

Anna experienced a rough night with the kids. She existed in a semi-weepy state, always on the verge of tears. A sad mother didn't make things easy for her son, Billy, who knew exactly what was going on around him. Jackie and Merry had decided there would be no fooling the clever boy and shared the facts with him as they came up. They appeared in the kitchen at the same time as Jackie and Merry.

Merry made a suggestion to Jackie while they were still in the

Waiting for Morning Time

bedroom. "We gotta cut Anna some slack."

Jackie spoke up. "Slack? She's been a basket case. What more can we do?"

"She's having a real hard time following what's going on with her hearing problem. She feels isolated and out of her comfort zone on top of everything else. I told you about her father last night."

"Jeez, you're right. I'll try my best."

Merry smiled. "I know ... you are already ... just wanted to remind you." Merry knew Jackie was on edge. Trying to remember someone else's emotions was not her top priority. Jackie focused on getting Neal back, nothing else. Bringing him back meant bringing back Lew and Bill, which was all part of the equation. The more distractions they endured, the more it would hurt their chances of being helpful.

Merry, throughout her life was naturally cognoscente of other peoples' emotions and feeling for others and knew it her job to hold things together ... whether it be Jackie, Anna, or the kids. She wanted to make sure enough prayers were being said. Merry saw the great strength in Jackie, which had grown over the years, which sometimes needed to be channeled. Jackie was a loving and caring person by Merry's estimation, but right then she had become Momma Bear protecting her cubs and her family. Merry let any of Jackie's brashness slide off her back.

Merry and Jackie walked into the kitchen and were greeted by the solemn-faced Butchers, who offered no hugs, nor condolences. The two seemed to be ready strictly for business, which seemed exactly what was needed. Clyde bounced around the kitchen as if his feet were on hot coals. "Can you get me onto the computer, Jackie? I want to search the web. I need to find out about the currents out there, and maybe get some charts and weather patterns." He looked over at Merry. "How are you keeping up, Merry?" He came forward to give her a hug.

"I'm holding up. Thank you for both for coming. We need your help." Merry turned to Jackie, trading questioning looks.

Jackie exclaimed, "You wanna get on the Web?"

"Oh, come on, just fire up your computer and I'll do the rest." Jackie followed orders. Clyde soon became frustrated with the slowness of the device. "Don't you delete the junk from this thing? They'll have drowned by the time I can attain anything useful." He took a heavy breath. "Well, this isn't working, so what are we going to do now to help the rescue?" He looked at everyone's face in turn, making sure they possessed the intestinal fortitude that would be needed.

Merry and Jackie were resolved to do what needed to be done, but up until now, they'd been far too emotional to really get after things. They had done some good work, but now they needed more backbone. Clyde and Niki possessed it and made sure that the girls did as well. The kitchen felt a much calmer place.

Jackie spoke up. "Dad, why don't we go over everything we've done so far?"

Clyde nodded, his Santa Claus beard bouncing up and down off his thick chest.

Everyone stood around the kitchen counter going over the phone calls placed last night and the responses they received: the Coast Guard, Neal's Dive Buddy, the Police – both Sarasota and Venice and finally, the Pilots.

Clyde dissected the information before he spoke. "We can't do any more with the Coast Guard. They're going to do their thing, same with the Police. The best we can do is to keep in touch with them. Cheryl, Neal's mom has a decent sized boat if I remember correctly—forty plus foot. Jackie, can you get on the phone with her and ask if we can take it out? Ask her if she has any charts."

"Neal's brother, Mark, said he'd be taking it out. I'm sure you could go along."

"Perfect."

Jackie made a short call to her mother-in-law, Cheryl. She looked up at her father hovering over her. "Cheryl says to go over to her place. She's going to look for charts in the garage. Mark and Holly will take you out and he has more friends who want to help."

"Okay. I'll head over to her house right away. Can you give me the pilot's cell numbers? I wanna make some calculations. Once I'm done, I'd like to talk to them."

Jackie gave Clyde the cell numbers, and he disappeared through the garage door like Santa up the chimney.

***

Jackie's kitchen became communications central. From that point on, there would be at least one person on a phone constantly. One of the first calls that morning went to one of Jackie's friends, Denise. She asked Denise if she could take care of the kids for the day. Once she explained the situation, Jackie's friend would be more than happy to help. It was amazing how the people contacted that day reacted the same way and were extremely helpful. Denise ended up taking Kayla and Ashley, leaving Billy and Robbie at the house.

The storm was slated to touch land around eleven a.m. meaning it would hit the men sooner. A consensus among the searchers decided the three needed to be found before the storm hit, or their chances were grim. Surviving in the cold open water that long would be bad enough, let alone trying to hang on through a massive northerly storm system, which is going to collide with a tropical warm air mass—it would be nasty.

Jackie's mother, Niki, made a nice breakfast, but no one seemed to want to eat. They all nibbled on the food, including Anna who reappeared from the bedroom with her son in tow. Billy was the only one who managed to eat what Niki put in front of him.

When Jackie called the Coast Guard again, they relayed her to St. Pete's.

"Hello! This is Jackie Obendorf."

"Good morning Mrs. Obendorf," a female voice said, registering some knowledge of the events surrounding Jackie's last name. "We were just about to contact you."

Jackie's heart leapt in her chest. "That's correct. We were in touch with you several times last night about the three men who are missing."

"Mr. Obendorf, Mr. Lipsit and Mr. Lipsit's son ... their search is now Priority One. We've already scrambled two planes, a chopper, and two search and rescue craft. We will be in touch, if we have any news."

Jackie's fast heartbeat started to calm down. It looked as if things were progressing. "That's wonderful news! I'm so glad we're being taken seriously."

The woman's voice lost its friendliness and she now sounded official. "We take every call seriously, Mrs. Obendorf."

"No, ma'am, I am grateful and want to thank everyone for their efforts." Jackie paused. "Please understand, we were beside ourselves last night."

"That's usually the case, but I do understand."

Jackie took a deep breath. "We've contacted a few pilots on our own. They will be going up at sunrise. We are hoping they might be able to coordinate with you?"

"Mrs. Obendorf. I would advise you to tell any of those pilots to stay clear of the search area as it is now blocked to all flight patterns. We aren't in any way allowed to coordinate with civilian efforts."

"What! That seems ridiculous!"

"Liability, Mrs. Obendorf, the Coast Guard doesn't want to be sued for any mishaps or malpractice from contact with civilian efforts."

Jackie could feel her heartbeat rising again. Looking around the room, she could see several others showing concern. "I don't care

Waiting for Morning Time

about liability ... I want my husband back!"

"Tell the pilots to stay away from the search area, though I'm sure they haven't been cleared to fly-- they should understand."

Jackie hesitated ... careful with her next words. "Okay. We'll tell them to stay clear of you. Hypothetically, what if we were able to attain flight permission? What if we find something? Can we call you?"

"You are free to call anytime, and as I've told you ... we will contact you immediately if we find your men."

"Can the pilots reach you?"

With agitation in her voice, the dispatcher responded. "There can be no contact with other pilots, it's against regulations. I hope you understand."

"No. I don't understand. We're busting ourselves here to help find those men, doing whatever we can."

The dispatcher cut her off. "If by any chance you do come across anything, call us immediately." She sounded well trained as to when to stop the conversation ... as if she knew the chances of recovery were slim.

"Yes. I can do that." Jackie sighed. "Thank you for your efforts."

"You're welcome, Mrs. Obendorf. Please leave this to professionals."

"Yes. I understand." She hung up.

Everyone in the kitchen stood on their feet, staring at her, waiting to hear news from her conversation. Merry couldn't help, but ask ... "WELL?"

Jackie showed the smallest of grins forming on the corner of her mouth. "There is an official search underway."

Everyone whooped it up for what seemed like a minute.

Once they calmed, she continued. "They are sending up two planes and some choppers at sunup, which is probably in the next fifteen minutes."

Niki frowned. "What's the argument all about?"

"Not really an argument, Mom. The woman explained due to liability reasons, they aren't allowed to coordinate with civilian efforts. If something became botched up because of ... let's say Rich Godoy and his plane. They don't want to be sued over it. They don't even want to talk directly with them. All volunteers are to stay clear, and if we find anything, we can only relay these findings or any info through a third party."

Anna shook her head. "Ridiculous! They should want all the help they can get."

"It seems like it, but they said to call whenever I wanted. I plan on doing it every fifteen minutes and the Dispatch promised to tell us how things were going."

Niki spoke up. "So that's it, we call off our efforts?"

Jackie pondered the female's words. "On the surface what they're saying makes sense, but my instincts say no. We should be doubling our efforts, if possible. We have several dozen boats going out, but my mind tells me the planes are most important. The process seems inefficient, and I really don't care what they say!"

Jackie's words were followed by a chorus of yay's and high fives all around the room.

From that point on, either Jackie or Merry were in touch with the Coast Guard every fifteen to twenty minutes, the Dispatch becoming their new best friends.

***

Clyde arrived at Cheryl's house, greeted by some very anxious faces. Cheryl looked as if she had put in a hard night. Her eyes were ringed, sunken and dark.

Mark spoke. "I tore the garage apart and couldn't find any charts. The ship's store over at the marina won't be open yet." He paused looking nervous, panic creeping into his voice. "I'm sure they have charts there."

Clyde clenched his teeth. The quandary presented felt to him like fighting blindfolded. "Then we'll have to do our best. We have the GPS coordinates for the dive sites," he said pensively. "Do you know which sites they would have gone to?"

"Depends, the ones closer to shore might have been busy with guys fishing. It's an unwritten rule ... you don't dive where someone's fishing."

"So... how far out are the closest sites?"

"Some are pretty tight, four to five miles. Neal would have taken them to one eight to nine miles out. They could have reached there in twenty or so minutes in the Scarab. But that's a busy spot. It would have been no skin off his teeth to ride out to the next site fifteen or so miles out. After that, we're talking twenty-five to thirty miles. I'd have to wonder if they would have gone out that far knowing bad weather was coming. Other than that, they would have had to go north or south along the coast."

Clyde cursed. "Darn, I wish they would have gone to a closer site. It would be a heck of a lot easier to plot out where they might have drifted. Six to seven miles further out could change things dramatically. The currents out there don't just go north or south, they eddy ... swirling towards the shore and sometimes away from the shore. The predominant current is north to south ... the Gulf Loop and the wind is pushing the opposite direction. So, we do have some logic to follow. They'll drift north ... if they're not still with the boat. Now what I'm not sure about is how the south wind will affect the men as it hits the Gulf Loop. Will it eddy towards shore or out into the Gulf? It's possible that they may not move very far at all—everything canceling each other out."

Mark raised his hand to stop Clyde. "What if they're still anchored at the dive site, and the boat's half sunk? There are a lot of air pockets on that boat, it's not designed to sink?"

"No ... Jackie told us that the Coast Guard flew over several of the possible dive sites last night. They found nothing. Besides, if that's the case we're heading to the dive site you think is most likely first. If they're there, we'll find them. Then we're going to hedge our bets and try to determine which direction they headed. But they'll be like finding a needle in a haystack in this weather. Jackie says there should be several dozen more craft searching this morning. Nearly all the boats big enough to handle the seas will be out, which is a comfort. It looks like the Town of Venice is getting behind this!"

Clyde stood thinking for a minute. "Nonetheless, we have to do all we can. I'll be darned if I'm going to stand on shore. If they die out there, I won't be able to live with myself!"

Again, his thoughts flashed back to the night his son was killed in a car crash and the paralyzing helplessness he felt. No. He would move forward if those men were alive, he believed they would find them. If they didn't, he wouldn't leave one stone unturned.

Mark nodded. "If they're near shore, they'll be found … where most of the smaller boats will be concentrated."

"That's what I'm thinking. But what if they're not? The odds are increasingly against them. The search grid has grown exponentially." Clyde pulled out his phone and called Jackie. "Hi, it's Dad."

"Just gonna call you. Did they find any charts?"

"No. They couldn't find any. Can you give me the cell number for your friend Rich, the pilot? I wouldn't mind having a word with him. Merry mentioned the cop from Lee County. Maybe you could get that cell number for me as well. I have a few ideas I want to go over with them."

Jackie cut him off and relayed to him the information given to her by the Coast Guard. "They won't let them fly."

Clyde thought for a short moment before he said, "We'll see what we can do about that. Thanks, darlin'. Let me know if you hear anything."

Waiting for Morning Time

"Will do, and here's the numbers for the pilots."

He jotted them down in a notebook he carried in his breast pocket and hung up. Cheryl and Mark both moved as if to speak. Clyde put his hand up to stop them. "Hang on, I need to call in a favor."

Clyde dialed the Governor's office, surprised to find someone there this time of the morning.

"Florida Governor's office." The female voice appeared cheery and alert.

"Clyde Butcher here, ma'am. I've met the Governor on a few occasions, he'll recognize my name."

"Mr. Butcher, I recognize the name. We have some of your prints in the office. I'm sorry but The Governor is not in."

"Ma'am, I've got a life-or-death situation on my hands and I'd like to call in a big favor." Clyde explained the problem with the flight plans and what was happening with the men."

"Mr. Butcher I'm so sorry to hear about your… situation. I know that the Governor will be more than eager to lend a hand. Could you please give me the airport and pilots' names and we will see what we can do? I'll give him a call ASAP.

"Thank you. It would also be helpful if we could give the Coast Guard a push."

"I'll have someone on staff give them a call as soon as I'm off the phone. Best of luck, Mr. Butcher, my prayers are with you. Please keep us appraised."

"Will do, thank you and thank the Governor."

Both Mark and Cheryl looked at Clyde wide eyed. Mark still pointed at the phone.

"Yes, that was the Governor's office."

Clyde followed up and called Bill Cameron ... the Lee County Sheriff's Dept.

"Bill Cameron."

Clyde could hear the wind whistling through the cell. "Yes, Bill, thanks for taking my call so early. It's Neal Obendorf's father-in-law

... Clyde Butcher,"

"Good morning, Mr. Butcher, I'm a big fan."

"Thanks, I appreciate you being a fan, but we have a real problem here."

"We met a few years ago."

"That's right, we met at Merry and Lew's. I understand you'll be helping us out."

"I'm still stunned this is happening. I know Neal and Lew as excellent boaters."

"Yes. It's a shock. Do you know the other pilot Jackie's been in touch with?"

"We haven't met, though I know he's a good friend of Jackie and Neal."

"I'm giving you his cell number. He's a good guy and I hear, an excellent pilot."

"He'll need to be in this weather."

"He's heading out there at the break of dawn."

"I'm planning to do the same."

"Yes, good … Can I tell you what I'm thinking?"

"Shoot."

"Okay. Do you have GPS on your plane?"

"Yes, of course."

"I'll give you the coordinates for the dive site we think they were at. They will have drifted north, to northeast. I'm going to suggest you search inshore, I'll tell Rich what you're doing. Between you two, I'd like to see you keep to a grid as best you can."

"I'd planned on doing the same thing. I'll stay east of the furthest dive site, if he'll stay to the west. Thank you for your help."

"You're welcome, please call Rich. Good luck and I'm glad we think alike ... it's only logical."

When Clyde hung up, he got the feeling Bill was trying to be nice to him. Clyde called Rich.

"Rich Godoy?"

"Yes, Rich, it's Clyde Butcher."

"We met at Jackie's, how are you?"

"I've been better as you can fully understand."

"Mr. Butcher, Jackie said you might call. It looked like we might have had couple of planes going up, but no clearance. It's just my crew now. We're waiting for our flight plan to be approved, but it doesn't look good. It's against FAA regulations to repeat a flight plan beyond the line, without permission and I'm sure that the Coast Guard will have their say."

"Check your clearance in fifteen, twenty minutes." He took a minute to explain his call to the Governor's office. "I just spoke to Bill Cameron of the Lee County Sheriff's department. He's taking a plane up there as soon as it's light. I asked him to call you." Clyde went over their conversation.

Rich cut in. "Yes, it's important we coordinate ... especially in this weather and with the Coast Guard up there as well, could be tricky. I'll have one eye on the horizon and the other on the altimeter."

"Safe flying, son! Yes. I know the Coast Guard's going up, but they do not know what we know. They basically told Jackie to shut up and let them do their thing."

"They're trained in this stuff. I thought we might lend another couple of eyes."

"Understood! I know they're trained in this sort of thing, but I couldn't live with myself, as I'm sure you, being a good friend of Jackie and Neal, feel the same. We need to do whatever we can to help those poor souls."

"I'm with you there."

"Please let me know how you're doing. We're going to head straight out in Mark's boat and pass through the most likely dive sites. Then we're going to zigzag northwards as far as we dare before that storm gets close. If you spot them, hopefully we will be close enough to pull them out."

"Ten four, Mr. Butcher, let's stay in touch and I appreciate what you've done to hopefully get the flight plan approved."

"Let's hope there's no problems with that. If there is, give me a call." He hung up.

Clyde helped Mark and his mother pack their things into his SUV before he made the next call. They needed to get to the boat.

As they pulled out of the driveway, he hesitated before dialing. His college roommate, Marshall, lived in California. It would still be the middle of the night there, but he hadn't been able to reach him earlier. He knew Marshall wouldn't mind ... the man was a paradox: extremely bright with an IQ off the charts. Some would say he was way out there, but Clyde didn't see it that way. In college, Marshall developed a following as a visionary.

Clyde kept in touch and considered Marshall to be a dear friend, one whom he wouldn't exclude from the present calamity. All help would be considered and appreciated, no matter where it might come from.

After college and a career in the tech industry, Marshall pushed away from society and became a Shaman ... a spiritual healer. Clyde, being a lateral thinker, didn't dismiss the fact that whether it worked or not, Marshall's input into the ensuing situation would be most welcome.

Marshall didn't sleep much. His sleep was interrupted a lot because he had the uncanny ability to know *when other people were thinking of him.*

When Clyde called him, Marshall was not surprised to hear from his old friend.

Click ... "Clyde, why did you wait so long to call?"

"I tried earlier." He said, still amazed at his old friend's psychic ability.

"Hmmm? My phone has been glitchy. The wonders of modern technology once again let us down when we need them the most."

Clyde acknowledged that Marshall being reclusive, often ignored his phone. And, with Marshall's ability to deduce the reasons why people call him. A lot of what people called magic, in fact is the ability of people with high intelligence to use it to its utmost.

I've only just come to grips with the situation as it's been presented to me. There were no formalities, there never were with Marshall. "My son-in-law, Neal, has gone missing in the Gulf… along with two friends."

"Oh dear. I'll be honest. I wasn't sure who it might have been ... I mean, who it is that's in trouble. How can I help?"

"We need to know where the three of them are located." Clyde went on to explain what had happened and what he knew thus far.

There was a silence for a time, which is Marshall's way. He would speak once he had digested all of the information and then make his proclamations. Again, his insights were most likely based upon probability. "Can you give me a bit of time, Clyde? I'd like to talk with the spirits, perform an augury."

"Of course, Marshall, I do understand. Call me as soon as you think you have something. Clyde knew Marshall would search for scientific fact first before making a guess based upon his feelings or what most call hocus pocus."

"I'm glad you've blessed me with your confidence, Clyde."

"I know you are my friend. We'll talk soon."

Clyde looked at the others, who had also been listening. "Okay, let's get to that boat of yours, Mark. Time's wasting."

CHAPTER FOURTEEN

IT WAS AMAZING to see the turnaround in attitude on Sunday morning. Saturday night's shock and worry replaced with hope. Worry still pervaded, but Clyde and Niki showed everyone involved how if they were going to help the men. They needed to gather their strength and not fall prey to weakness. There could be no room for tears. From Merry's point of view, Jackie showed herself to be the strongest of the three wives ... at least on the outside. She transformed her house into a battle hub. Anyone who wanted to know, or knew of anything of the ensuing events, called the Obendorfs.

While Niki took care of Robbie, Anna did her best to keep Billy under control. She seemed the only one who couldn't maintain functionality, too upset by the events to be of any real help except cleaning and watching over the kids. It by no means diminished her value, she took the disastrous events hard and no one blamed her. She was in a strange home, didn't know anyone, except for Merry. Watching over the kids and keeping the place clean was a huge burden off Jackie's shoulders.

Jackie kept in constant contact with the Coast Guard, the pilots, and the small armada of boaters she managed to round up. Unable to talk directly to the Coast Guard planes, she did talk to the Dispatch, who were more than happy to appease her questions. Rich and Bill, even though they could see the whites of each other's eyes when passing each other, didn't attempt to talk to the Coast Guard C-130s. Progress would be relayed to them through Jackie. Those involved on the civilian side, couldn't believe the process, but they weren't going to let it be a hindrance no matter how inefficient it seemed.

***

Niki Butcher decided it wouldn't be her role to organize and put forth agendas for the rescue of the three men. She put her efforts towards supporting Jackie; by keeping a strong outer shell and to make sure everyone had food and drink. No one ate very much, but it was a comfort. Everyone needed their energy, especially if they were not getting much sleep. She was a mom. When Jackie seemed ready to crumble, Niki picked her up and encouraged her, which helped Merry and Anna along as well. She didn't go to bed and busying herself in the kitchen preparing food. Like Anna, who found that cleaning helped her keep her mind off the events. Niki needed to stay busy as well.

Anna stared up at her as she finished wiping down the granite countertops. "You need to keep busy as well?"

"We all have to cope in our own ways, my dear."

Anna nodded. She was the only one who saw the car pulling up the driveway. She went to the front window, not being able to identify the vehicle until it pulled to a stop in front of the dark house, the sun still below the horizon. Once she could see it clearly, her heart skipped. She exclaimed in a shaky voice. "There's a Sheriff's cruiser in the driveway?" Everyone feared the possibility of ominous news.

Jackie, Merry, and Niki joined Anna at the front of the house. Jackie waited for the knock on the door before opening it. She brushed the front of her shirt down before opening the door and was greeted by two officers, one male, the other female.

"Jackie Obendorf?" said the female officer.

"That's me." said Jackie, her mouth drawn tight, expecting the worst.

"I'm Deputy Carter, Venice police." She pointed to the badge on her chest. "Mrs. Obendorf, somebody filed a missing person's report." She took out a notebook and read the names. "Neal Obendorf, Lewis Lipsit and William Lipsit. Did you file this?"

Jackie's voice went up a few decibels. "We did, but that was... let me see... eight or nine hours ago. You mean to tell me you're just starting the search?"

The woman looked embarrassed, her cheeks reddening. "Mrs. Obendorf, I'm sorry, but this was just called in." Everyone listened with keen interest, a touch of anger filling their hearts, replacing their dread.

Jackie pointed to Merry. "This is Mrs. Lipsit, she's the one who called it in. Tell me if I'm wrong, Merry, but didn't the Venice Police say they were sending up a chopper LAST NIGHT?"

"Yes, they did." Merry felt a release of anger as the words left her lips. She took a big breath to calm herself.

"I'm sorry, officer, but this isn't making any sense?" Jackie placed her hands on her hips.

Deputy Carter looked a shade brighter now as she backed out of the doorway. "I'm sorry to have bothered you, Ma'am. I really am. I'll have to look into this."

Jackie was on her, following her out the door. "And by the way, they're still missing. I hope by your exit, it doesn't mean the search for them is OFF?"

"No ma'am, someone will get back to you soon." She turned and walked stiffly back to her car.

Jackie returned to the house and slammed the door behind her. "What the heck was that all about?"

Niki put her hand on Jackie's shoulder. "It must have been a

Waiting for Morning Time

second Dispatch. You said that Merry called twice."

Merry spoke up. "Kinda makes sense. My first call, I was matter-of-fact, the second one I sounded panicked, distressed ... I got an immediate response from that call. This must have been from the first call nine hours ago. That's terrible!"

Everyone put the strange encounter out of their minds and got back to the matter at hand.

***

Before Merry did anything else, she prayed. "Lord Jesus, help us to find our lost husbands before the storm hits us. Keep them safe and, Lord, please ask your Angels to put a warm hand around Lew's heart. I know they have been watching over them. Please keep them alive."

Merry's next job would be to call Pastor Holmes, the preacher at Anna and Bill's church in Niagara Falls. The phone rang several times before Holmes picked up. "Good morning?"

"Pastor Holmes, this is Merry Lipsit from Ft Myers. Bill and Anna's stepmother."

"Hello, Merry. It's nice to talk to you. Anna's mentioned your name from time to time. Is everything okay?" He thought he could detect angst in her voice.

"I'm calling because Anna and Bill need your support." She explained what had happened. "Anna would have made the call, but she's too distressed to do it and Anna fears she might lose it if she talks to you."

"This is terrible news, Merry, but I'm glad you called, the poor soul. Are you sure she won't take the phone?"

Merry looked over at Anna and could see she was barely keeping it together. "I'm sorry, but I'm sure of that. I would ask that you please contact Anna's mother Geraldine, Lew's daughter Debbie and her mother Janet. I'll be honest... I'm barely functioning myself and I don't think that I could bear to make that call at this point in time. I'll give you their numbers and trust that you will do your best to handle the situation."

"We seldom get asked to do what we are here for anymore, Merry. I'd be happy to. I'm sure that they will want to contact you. What would you like me to tell them?"

Merry wasn't sure what to say. "Debbie can call me in the mid-afternoon. I'll have my cell on."

"Okay, that's good of you."

"Pastor Pat, our Minister down in Ft. Myers, has started up an email prayer chain. Could I ask you to do the same in Canada?"

"That's a wonderful idea, Merry. Could I ask you to give me Pat's phone number?"

"Absolutely!" She thanked him and hung up, pleased to get things rolling north of the border. After that, Merry began to call as many friends as she could, members of their church, and anyone she thought might be able to help, even if only for moral support.

***

An hour later, the doorbell rang. Again, a Venice Police cruiser sat in the driveway.

Jackie answered the door. This time, two male officers stood on the porch.

"Mrs. Obendorf?"

"Please call me Jackie."

"Okay, Jackie. We're sorry about the confusion earlier. I'm Deputy Sherriff Roy Car."

She cut him off. "Two separate dispatches, right?"

"Ahh ... yes. The one was cancelled when the second one came in. Somehow it didn't register. It has since been shut down and entered the system again."

"Something like that, right?" Jackie said sarcastically.

He shrugged the comment off. "I wanted to let you know that a chopper and a plane went up from the department last night and they didn't find anything. We've been working in conjunction with the Coast Guard."

"I'm glad someone is." She didn't mean to take things out on the man, Jackie normally a very calm person, but lack of sleep and the incredulousness of the entire search and rescue process pushed her to the limit of her patience.

He frowned.

"What I mean is, we have friends who are pilots and they're out there now. They aren't allowed to contact the other planes or boats directly… the Coast Guard I mean."

He corrected her. "The Guard aren't allowed to talk with civilians."

She nodded. "Thank you, you're right."

"I'd like to let you know that I'll personally be keeping you up to date on anything we find. The Venice Police Department is one hundred percent behind you. If you need anything or want to know anything, give me a call." He handed Jackie his card.

Jackie softened somewhat, seeing the sincerity in the man's face. "I appreciate that, Deputy Car."

"I'd like to make one more suggestion. If I were you, I'd contact the media. They'll pick this up like a hotcake. I warn you, though, they will hound you until you find resolution one way or another. Still, it will get the information out to the public. You never know who might be out there, having some valuable piece of insight. I've seen it work before, mostly on land, but I can see the desperation in your face. You look like you are trying shake every tree; most people do, and they don't think to take this step."

"Okay, I appreciate everything you've said, and I'll call a good friend of mine. Heidi Goldman. She works for ABC as a news anchor in Sarasota."

"I've been interviewed by Heidi on a few occasions. She'd be a good place to start. I'd contact the newspapers as well." He turned to leave. They got the feeling that the man had been told to tread carefully after the mishap, his expression somber his actions sharp and uncomfortable looking. He had done this before. "I'll keep in touch."

She took the officer's hand in hers. "I appreciate you coming here and clearing this up." She smiled as he turned away. She had the feeling the man had their back. After Jackie closed the door, she was on the phone with Heidi.

CHAPTER FIFTEEN

RICH GODOY, the first person contacted Saturday evening, was a personal friend of the Obendorfs. His wife Nicole babysat their kids, as well as having gone on a few diving trips with Jackie and Neal. Rich, a hobby pilot, didn't hesitate to offer his help when Jackie called him.

He put his cell back into his pocket after talking to Bill Cameron. He was glad to know there was a central brain thrust behind their mission today. He knew Clyde to be a noted environmentalist and one who studied the natural occurrences of south Florida; mainly as they pertained to the Everglades. Rich never thought he knew more than Clyde when it came to tides and currents. Rich knew how to fly a plane and that was what he was going to do.

When talking to Clyde and Bill, he mentioned how he would need to fly at around 500 feet of altitude in order to spot the men. Flying that low was a dangerous task, which would require special permission. Bill Cameron, being with the Lee County Sheriff's Office, would have a better chance to attain clearance for the flight pattern for himself, but Rich doubted he would be able to get a clearance for him.

Rich couldn't help but chuckle at Clyde's comment: "I'm a friend of the Governor. Don't you worry ... I'll get you that ticket."

Sure enough, when he arrived at the Venice Island Municipal

Airport, permission had been granted for the flight plan, but warned him to stay clear of the Coast Guard and to be cognizant of Bill Cameron's plane and any others. No one wanted an air catastrophe on top of the present situation occurring at sea. He would need to be on the ground no later than 10:30 a.m. as the oncoming storm would be a hazard to any flight plan, approved or not approved.

As Rich pulled up to the rental plane, he was pleased to see his friend, Dave, who was also a pilot. Dave stood waiting along with their good friend, Shane, who agreed to be their spotter. The plane, a Cessna 172 –High wing sat fueled and ready to depart. They loaded up and waited for their cue to taxi.

***

The wind howled from the south with strong gusts. It was a bumpy ride out to the possible dive sites. As they flew out over the Gulf, they spotted a Coast Guard chopper passing low, a mile or so from the shore.

As they reached the first dive site, they could see the Obendorf's large forty-foot boat. It looked like a rough ride. He flew low over top, able to see their waving hands. He banked against the wind and doubled back towards the North. He tuned into the radio channel he and Bill agreed to use. Clyde would be locked onto it as well.

"Rich Godoy ... checking in."

Bill came right back. "Rich, I saw you pass to the west of me a few minutes ago. I've made a pass two miles closer to shore due north to Anna Maria Island. I haven't seen a thing ... except maybe a Hammerhead Shark and a few dolphins. It's gonna be darn hard to spot anything in that water. It's black as coal."

"I agree." Rich thought the same thing. "We're gonna have to fly right over top of them to have any chance of finding them."

"Ten four ... you're right. It might be a task at that. You won't

Waiting for Morning Time

see em' from directly above either. Gotta be at an angle ... the waves are too big. My spotter's having a heck of a time."

Clyde listened in. "Butcher here ... there's nothing at the dive site where Mark figured they'd gone to ... M-16. Not even a marker, and this sea is getting too rough even for Neptune himself. Between the Coast Guard and our efforts, we would have found them if they were simply stranded with a malfunction. We must assume they're floating, and the boat has sunk. We're going to take a course northeast, 15 degrees, towards Anna Maria Island. They may have drifted as far as twenty miles at this point, maybe further. If you spot them, we won't be too far away. I think we'll take harbor in Sarasota after 10:30."

Rich spoke up, "Yes. I have to have this plane back by then. I'll look to the west, and I'd suggest Bill, you keep on doing what you're doing to the east. Any news from the Coast Guard, Clyde?"

"Nada. Jackie's been calling every fifteen minutes. Do your best men, I know you will. It's getting awfully rough out here. Those poor men are in for a heck of a ride-- if they're still with us. We're heading back in after a few more sweeps."

Everyone seemed to be in agreement and the search continued a little while longer with the massive storm looming like a giant black monolith and rolling towards shore.

***

Rich made a big circle pass twenty miles to the north and then back towards M-16. Shane spotted something about ten miles north which at first, he thought might be a whale. He became sure as they made a closer pass it appeared to be the silhouette of a submerged hull; possibly that of the Scarab. He took an approximate GPS reading and asked Clyde to call it in to St. Pete's Coast Guard Station.

***

The rest of the morning yielded nothing for Bill's crew, his pilot Carman felt the strain from the dangerous flight. It was nervy flying, keeping one eye on the altimeter and one on the horizon. He made a final pass along the edge of the fast-approaching storm clouds, flying in and out of them. It soon became too dangerous, but it was easier to fly through the calm before the storm. At 10 am, he called it quits and headed back towards Page Field in Ft. Myers. They were on the tarmac by 10:25 am.

As they unloaded the plane and signed off for the fuel, he couldn't help but sense a degree of impending doom. If Lew and the other two men were out there, there would be no way they would survive the storm, now upgraded to being dangerous for even those on land. With a more sustained eye and twenty or so miles per hour, the storm might have been classified a Hurricane.

***

Rich and his crew similarly called off their efforts and returned to Venice Airport at roughly the same time as Bill. He also felt deep impending doom. One only needed to see the storm from their high vantage point to truly understand how massive and powerful it was. Rich only shook his head. No words were spoken as he and his crew cleaned up the Cessna. Rich felt deeply concerned for his friend.

CHAPTER SIXTEEN

4 a.m. Sunday Morning

I CAUGHT MYSELF nodding off as the side of my face received a spray of salty brine whipped off the crest of a menacing wave. I shook my head trying to wake up. *Stay focused*. No one was going to find us in today's weather… impossible. If I was going to survive, I needed to keep my mind focused and occupied. I put my thoughts back to happier times. It was all I had left to hang onto as the monotony of our dire situation wore on with no hope in sight.

My first phone bill after meeting Merry totaled over $650. Merry claimed her phone bill surpassed this amount. *Could it be love?* Merry would later call it puppy love, like we were in public school; it felt that way to me. Hour-long conversations for the most part, were about nothing, simply enjoying each other's voice, while our deep connection formed. We took turns calling each other, day after day and night after night.

Bob Sentinel and I moved forward as partners, structuring an Herbal Magic campaign. Between the two of us, it would be more of a part-time gig ... something we could manage remotely if need be. My feelings for Merry kept growing stronger and he was thankful to have Bob as a partner. During the two-month telephone correspondence, I managed to sort out my divorce, possibly spurred on by the new infatuation. It was an infatuation needing to be more than a long-distance tryst.

I went down to visit Merry that spring. Needless to say, the love affair would be consummated, and I didn't want to leave. I knew that I wanted to be with this amazing woman. I remembered the conversation vividly as I did my best to evade another rogue wave now threatening to toss me end-over-end.

"Lew... This isn't realistic." I could almost hear her say again.

"I'm not going. There's nothing for me back there," I responded like a stubborn child telling his parent how he didn't want to come inside after the streetlights came on.

"That's not true. You have kids... Herbal Magic... you are Canadian!"

I chuckled, leaning against the open car door. "Merry, Herbal Magic is of no consequence. Bob said as much. He's doing it more for me than as a strong business plan. Bob said he could see the magic in my eye... and to follow my gut."

"And what does your gut tell you?" She shifted back and forth on her feet.

I didn't feel bashful or nervous when I said it, as it came from the heart. "That I'm in love." I smiled as Merry's face looked so beautiful.

Her eyes stared at me hard, the way she looked when faced with a difficult question or proposition. "Are you?" She asked, biting her bottom lip.

I put my hand behind her head, pulling her face close, kissing her... hard. There's a difference between kissing with passion and kissing with real emotion; a kiss that was for real. No one can come back from that kind of passionate kiss. Before I would continue, I looked into Merry's eyes. "What do you think?"

She glanced at the ground. "What are we gonna do... you silly man?"

I smiled. "The only thing that can be done."

"Okay?"

"I don't have much back home… yes, there's the kids, but they'll be fine. Besides, I can't afford these phone bills. I'm going to go back for a week or so and tie up some loose ends. Then I'd like to come back... I can help you."

Merry didn't hesitate, smiling broadly as she felt the same. Still, she kept her desires to herself, not wanting to be selfish. "I'd like that!"

"Then it's settled, I'll be back soon as I can."

That moment would be the beginning of a special union. We rarely left each other's side… ever…always glued to the hip.

***

I moved to Columbus, Ohio later that spring and tried my best to help Merry in her wholesale business, excelling at the trade shows. I was a natural at promotion. It looked as if we would be a good team. However, after a year the American Government caught up with me and threatened deportation.

It would be a good news, bad news sort of thing. Though I didn't want to go back to Canada, Merry was still going through her divorce, and it had become quite messy. The presiding judge upon hearing of their plight encouraged Merry to go with me north of the border for a time, fearing for her safety. Life has a funny way of turning the table. We took the high road and looked at it as fate.

That winter, January 1982, we moved back to Canada. I remembered it being darn cold. We rented a room in Falls Manor, in Niagara Falls for a short time before finding a cute little house in Niagara on the Lake.

We benefited residually from the income Merry had earned and my present holdings. Herbal Magic was still a going concern and we managed to live in relative comfort. Merry's creative mind came up with an idea for a new product and she called it *Country Folk Art*. She had me cut wood into different shapes, ducks, chickens, produce, whatever we could think of that might fit the mold, making them into napkin holders, key holders or wall decorations with a purpose. We painted them colorfully and were off to the races. The business grew quickly, and the profit margins were terrific. Before too long, we'd purchased a barn on Niagara Stone Road across from Hunter Road that had been an old Massey Ferguson dealership and nowadays it's a Brewery.

***

I smiled remembering the day they were married in 1988. It would be one of the happiest days of our lives. We decided to visit our good friends while on honeymoon; Helen and Alan Bowron who were staying on Sanibel Island at the time. I remembered the moment when we drove our motor home over the bridge at Mantanza's pass onto Ft. Myers Beach. It would be a life-changing happenchance.

"This is it, Lewie!" Merry couldn't hold back her excitement.

I didn't have to ask her what she meant. I felt the same tug. We were *home*.

As much as we loved Niagara on the lake, it didn't have the allure of the tropical barrier islands of southwest Florida. When the time came to leave for home, we'd decided to move to Ft. Myers. Now that we were married, it would be easy for me to get a Green Card.

We sold everything we owned in Canada: the real estate earned a good return, but the sale of the business didn't do as well. While we made some money, it was difficult to sell a Ma and Pa type business. As I liked to say ... *That's life!*

We were off on a new adventure and a new life in Ft Myers, Florida. I remember bouncing around selling this and that, working with Jackie for a time, but eventually we found their niche selling real estate.

Waiting for Morning Time

While we made some money, it was not enough to get by without dipping into savings. I remember the day things turned around. We needed a farm... in Real Estate terms it is an area in which you focus your efforts, like a particular subdivision or small town. We looked into buying into a development called Heritage Palms a few weeks back. It seemed like a nice place to transplant with two world-class golf courses and clay courts for tennis. The place seemed to fit to a tee. I felt a strong urge to tell Merry why we should buy in the place. It seldom took that much time to make up our minds. I decided to call her. I'd tell her they were buying the condo.

The phone booth beckoned me. I tried his best to move towards it, walking across the driveway, opening up the plastic flaps that protected the inside. It seemed strange though, looking like the telephone booths in Canada, B E L L clearly etched across the top. I picked up the receiver and attempted to call Merry. I wanted to go home. I didn't want to be here anymore. I placed the receiver to my mouth, I could smell the molded plastic with a hint of stale cigarette from its last caller. "Merry...can you please come and get me." *Why didn't she come pick me up?*

I felt a tug... on the back of my life preserver. "Get back here," I heard Neal's voice. Snapping out of it, Neal dragged me back to the rope. "What are you doing?"

I shook my head, realizing what had occurred. "I wanted to call Merry." Both Bill and Neal looked concerned. I felt a pang of shock at what happened. The hallucination seemed so real. I could still see the phone booth clear in my mind's eye. I had even walked to it. I could feel the gravel mixed with shells under my feet as I plodded through a driveway to get to the booth.

Neal put his hand on my arm. "The cold, lack of sleep and salt water you've ingested is playing tricks with your mind." He looked at Bill and me. "This isn't going to get any better, boys, and if we don't get picked up soon ... we're gonna have to keep a close look on each other."

I grabbed onto the rope and settled back into the steady rise and fall of the waves… but I couldn't get used to the debilitating cold of the water. The realization that what I had envisioned was a hallucination cleared my head for the time being.

It was still dark ... probably four or five in the morning. Bill spoke up. "Dad, you were hallucinating. One minute you were here, the next minute you were floating off. I thought you'd given up life like I did. Like Neal said, we need to keep an eye on each other. If it's happened once, it will happen again. I pray to the Lord it doesn't happen to us all at once."

Neal agreed, "Let's try to keep in the present. I know it's hard. It'll be light soon and a lot easier to keep an eye on each other. Both of your body temperatures must be getting pretty low. Maybe that's what's doing it. I feel fine, but the wet suit's keeping me warm. Don't drink the salt water. I've heard that will mess with your head."

Bill half chuckled. "Easier said than done, you know?"

"I do know." Neal shook his head.

***

Every now and again, we got caught on a rising wave and had to tumble back down. Breathing through our mouths, it was inevitable that salt water found its way inside. After a time, throats became raw from coughing and fighting to breathe. We knew we should not swallow the water. Still, you couldn't help swallowing the saltwater, which made the whole process frightening. Bill couldn't help, but wonder aloud. "It's a crazy thing. All that water out here and you can't drink it, and yet you are so damned thirsty… really thirsty… impossible to explain thirsty."

Neal and I were glad to see how Bill appeared to be more involved with us. I thought Bill looked as if he was doing better than me. I could feel my body slowing down, age and inherent weaknesses taking their toll. I needed to think about moving my hands to remain buoyant. No longer did the motion of swimming work automatically. It was not like me to ever give up, but I didn't know how much longer I could go on like this. I hadn't taken my heart medicine in a day, but so far, I didn't feel anything abnormal. Still, my body was recovering from major surgery and reserves of energy were waning. I didn't want to become a burden to Neal and Bill.

It saddened me beyond belief, but I made a pact with myself, right there ... right then, I would ditch the life preserver and drop down into the sea if it came to the point where I couldn't fight to stay alive any longer. I knew it wouldn't take long. I would simply breathe in the ocean water when too far down to return to the surface, supposedly a peaceful way to die. Merry's face flashed across my mind. I felt foolish and prayed I wouldn't need to make such a decision. I wondered if the other men thought about the same thing. I am a fighter, but also a realist. I would go as far as I possibly could... being sure I would recognize when the time came to let go. It wouldn't be suicide... more like a self-imposed escape to heaven. I prayed ... *the pearly gates would open for me. I knew in my heart that I would also be aided by my wife's prayers.*

***

As the three of us drifted through the night, at one point we found ourselves caught up inside a flock of sea birds; mostly seagulls and the odd pelican sitting on top of the water. We could hear the squawking half a mile away and they must have been drifting faster than the birds. We soon found ourselves in the middle of the flock. It felt like comic relief with the noise and activity keeping the three of us alert and awake.

Bill yelled over the racket. "Can we eat these?"

Neal responded. "Just try and catch one. I bet you can't."

Bill tried to get close to a couple, but when he made his big move, it scattered the flock. Bill conceded he was no match for the bird's quickness. Faster than they drifted into the birds, they once again found themselves in relative silence except for the sound of the wind whipping across the tops of the waves.

Without warning, we drifted close to a large moving object. Bill and I prepared to defend ourselves with the boat bumpers. Neal huddled close beside Bill, finding it hard to see exactly what it was until it was on top of them. The beast decided to jump at Neal. Its loud screeching voice catching us off guard. It looked to be the biggest seagull anyone had ever seen. Maybe it was some other kind of bird ... it was still very dark.

Neal held out the extra air tank he'd been dragging along with him. The bird attacked it. The sound of its beak kept hitting the metal canister reverberating over the howling wind. If it had been someone's arm or face, they would have been seriously hurt. The bird bounced back and into the water right in front of Neal.

Frightened and angry, Neal yelled at the seagull. "You son of a gun, watch this!" He opened up the valve on the top of the air tank and sprayed pressurized air and water at it. The beast of a bird lifted itself up into the air with a flurry of slapping wings to disappear into the black night in a series of angry squawks.

Neal and Bill high fived. Neal pulled the rope, bringing me close to the two of them. He reached into the bag, which had held the flares and brought out the can of Nitrox. He motioned for me to put my numb lips to the nozzle. As I did, Neal released the valve, the oxygen enriched air, hitting me right away. After we all received a shot of it, everyone felt better for a time. When the effects dissipated within the hour, the three of us were left again to the monotony of survival.

***

We had been drifting off in our own little worlds for a time when Bill's voice pulled Neal and I back to the present.

"We're getting closer to them, aren't they beautiful?"

"What do you mean?" Neal said.

"The buildings along the shore ... we've been getting closer and closer. Can't you see them? I think we're close enough to swim for it. We must be only a few hundred yards now. I've not seen architecture like that in Florida ... it's almost Arabic…and it's so beautiful."

I pulled up close, hauling on the rope, placing hands on either side of my son's face. "Bill… its pitch black out. We can't see anything."

"Dad, they are right there, I can't believe you're saying this. I'm swimming for it."

"You are hallucinating ... just like I did an hour or so ago."

Neal pulled in close. He patted Bill on the shoulder. "Your dad's right, pal. Open your eyes. Look!"

They could see Bill's mood deflate. He shook his head trying to clear it. We both knew Bill was trying hard to keep up his spirits. We also worried he might fall back into a funk. When Bill slowly spun away, Neal waved behind Bill's back to get my attention. Neal put two fingers up to his own eyes, and then pointed to Bill as if to say: *Let's keep an eye on him."*

I nodded.

"They looked so real. It's like I could have reached out and touched them." He continued talking about his mind creating illusions more to himself than to the other two.

Neal spoke. "Okay, boys, let's try and keep it together here. That's the definition of a hallucination … at least I think it is. Everything looks so lifelike ... so real."

I interrupted. "You haven't been seeing things. I've been trying to knock them from my mind as they appear. I swore I saw the shoreline. It was still dark, not like Bill's hallucination. I needed to focus really hard to make it go away… no that's not the right word. I had to try really hard to ignore it. I closed my eyes a few times and it slowly disappeared. I'll also admit there were a few minutes where I saw a beautiful church, made of pure white alabaster. There were angels standing on the steps leading up the place. They beckoned to me. I got the sense if I walked up onto those white steps, they would look after me. I would find warmth there. I snapped out of it on my own, but it sure was beautiful. I wanted to walk up the stairs and hug the angels. If I hadn't experienced that hallucination an hour ago, this one might have done me in, gut wrenching pulling my eyes away from the beautiful scene, but I forced myself to do it."

Neal pulled the Nitrox out of his bag again, shaking his head. "I think we need another shot of this. The longer we're out here, the more our brains are going to start playing tricks on us and the harder it's gonna be to do what you just described. I haven't experienced what you guys are seeing yet. I'm sure it will happen. It is the effect of salt water. Enough salt will mess your head up. It's not good for your ticker either."

Neal turned to me. "How are you feeling?"

"I feel a lot better after the air. I'll be truthful, I don't feel any different with my heart, but this is starting to wear me down. I'm getting old you know. It's becoming harder and harder to move my arms and legs."

Both Neal and Bill nodded. Neal put his hand on the top of my head, covered by the dive cap. "I know how old you are, buddy. That's why I'm asking. Look, we need to be a little more alert. This is impossibly difficult. If we are going to make it, we need to support each other. We know hallucinations are going to occur, so let's keep an eye on each other. If it's any consolation, it'll be a heck of a lot easier when the sun comes up."

Bill chuckled, "I give both of you permission to slap me upside the head if I get stupid like that again."

Though the situation was dire, we laughed before once again settling in to the up and down roll of the waves, trying to get into a groove, as Bill would describe it.

***

We had never been happier to see the sun rise than that morning. It colored the sky bright pink and purple off to the east. An old seafaring rhyme popped into my head.

Red sky at night, sailors delight. Red sky in the morning, sailors take warning.

I often wondered about the validity of the old folk tale, but it seemed to be proving correct. As I looked out to the northwest, I could see the storm, looking more than just a menace. It looked like an impending wall of doom. A veil of darkness slowly moved towards land, threatening to swallow up the three of us tied together by a rope and two boat fenders.

Neal glanced over at me. He appeared to be trying to use prayer to keep his mind out of a stupor. Neal wasn't religious, but I thought *whatever works*.

After a time, I decided it was time to pull out all the stops... I had made snippets of prayer halfheartedly since the Scarab went down. Now, I really prayed asking God to have mercy upon us and to help find shelter before the storm gobbled us up. I shared my prayers to include Neal and Bill. I knew that I would be the first one to go down and it could happen soon. The storm scared me more than the water. I could tell it scared the other two men as well. With the new day's sun, it would be the first time we would be able to see each other in a dozen hours. I was not sure what my face looked like, probably paler than Bill and Neal. Bill didn't look great, but his youth seemed to be keeping him in the ballgame. Neal looked fine. His wetsuit took care of him.

Bill and my bare limbs were unprotected from the biting salt and cold causing them constant pain. I didn't know about the other two, but I began to develop salt rashes under my arms and throughout my crotch area. Every swim stroke with my arms and push with the legs became increasingly more painful.

The wind really began to pick up causing the waves to become nastier; no longer were they the deep rollers they been through the night. For the first time, the three of us began to tumble down the waves instead of rising up and down with them. There was nothing that could be done besides keeping our backs to the surf, so as not to take in a mouthful of it. One really big roller came at us, a massive wave which would break as it passed into us.

Neal yelled. "Here's a big one, look for each other once it's gone!"

Bill and I met eyes, motioning as if to say ... *Holy Smokes!*

The wave picked up our bodies and threw us forward down into the trough. I went feet first but caught sight of Bill flying headfirst into the water. Near silence ... the quiet of being submerged under water; each man sinking four or five feet under without much breath. Then the wave crashed overtop, spinning us around. If not for the soggy life vests, both Bill and I would have drowned. As the buoyant devices slowly pulled us to the surface, we gasped for air as our chapped faces broke the surface… where the noise of the wind became once again omnipresent. Neal popped up before Bill and I, his buoyancy much better due to the BC.

We looked at each other shaking the salt from our faces and hair. Everyone scrambled back to the rope ... the only thing we could do.

Neal lifted the extra tank he'd strapped to his belt. "Gonna have to lose this. Nearly knocked me out when I hit the water." He undid the Velcro strap and let the canister drift away. If one of us took a hit to the head from the can, it could kill.

We started counting the waves. Every seventh one would topple us into the trough below. So now, we began to prepare for the tumble each time it came. Neal, being a bit of a fish dove into the bottom, flipping himself under the wave and coming up for air in a relatively short period of time. Bill and I being heavier and a little out of shape, took the brunt of the waves each and every time they hit; sometimes able to control the descent ... sometimes not.

Bill wondered yelled. "How in heck are we going to survive this?"

All three of us were slowly becoming exhausted. I knew that I would be the first one to die from exhaustion.

Neal pointed. "Look over there."

It took a few seconds to see what caught Neal's eye. Several shrimp boats were on the horizon, probably five or six miles away. Neal rolled his eyes. He yelled to Bill and I. "The only place with a fleet of shrimp boats up this way is Anna Maria Island. We must've drifted a good ten, or so miles." His face dropped in despair. "How are they ever gonna find us here? We're too far from the dive site." He paused, spitting water from his lips. "Someone's gonna have to do some serious figuring to guess where we have ended up."

I nodded. "We have the girls. I know they won't rest until we're found, or it becomes unrealistic that we're still alive. We have to have faith."

***

As the morning wore on, the wall of the storm kept making its way closer. We saw a large boat pass by to the west ... between them and the storm clouds. I noticed it first. I was not sure if it was another one of the illusions. We did the only thing we could and waved to the boat. We knew it would have been next to impossible for those on board to spot us, unless they were right on top of our position in the waves. Neal yelled over the wind. "Who else would be out here in such horrendous conditions? Gotta be looking!"

It turned into a very discouraging moment for our shipwrecked trio. Now that the wind howled off the tops of the waves, soon we couldn't have any sort of a conversation besides shouting the odd couple of words to each other. The only thought each of us had was being rescued. *What would to take for anyone to find us?*

We could see a search effort happening. No one would be out in these conditions for a pleasure cruise. There were planes. We saw a few of them. Except for one, they were too far away to have any hope of spotting our little pinheads in the dark ocean. The only respite we could gather was the fact there were search and rescue operations looking. Even though, it would be a one in a million chance any of us would be spotted. It became a discouraging thought.

An hour before the storm hit, a small white plane flew along the edge of the oncoming wall of clouds. As it veered away from the storm, it passed nearly over them. We waved frantically, but the plane slowly flew away to the north without seeing us. Neal yelled. "It's a Cesena. I can see the darn spotter looking out the window. They cannot see us. What the heck!"

Bill started slapping the water in panicked futility and yelling. "They flew right over us! I…I can't believe it." He looked as if he might cry, but Bill managed to get a grip on his emotions. We stayed quiet. No one bothered to communicate. With heavy hearts, we turned our attention back to wave tossing, each of us somber as a black wall of cloud moved towards us. The air mass closing in became indistinguishable from the water. The wind dropped suddenly. It became almost quiet.

Lightning balls danced across the water behind the storm wall. Bolts, streaking from the water to the top of the air mass, made the storm seem like a living entity. It rolled over the three of us in the water like a massive black steam roller. We could feel the threat of death was upon us. Before it hit, Neal spoke in his low rumbling voice. "Boys, even if that plane spotted us Ain't no way they could've called it in quick enough to save us."

We gathered together in a tight circle. We could do nothing but look up in terror, it seemed as if Poseidon's wrath readied to fire

Waiting for Morning Time

down. No one said a word as we prepared to die. Death presents itself in differing ways ... whether slow and drawn out, or instantaneous presenting only a flash of recognition before total darkness. Birth and death are most personal experiences shared by all human beings. We come into the world and go out alone. No one can share the experience with you. Though I didn't choose death, I prepared for it. During endless hours of monotony and being tossed from wave to wave, I began to recognize death as a probability for all of us. My acceptance of the probability along with his faith in *God's Will* was the benefit helping me to carry on. My inner revelation, that life or death was out of our hands, brought a sense of calm. I looked at the other two, who seemed to be preparing themselves for the worst as well. I was proud to be with Bill and Neal at that moment. No one opined about our fate, all three of us met it with a brave heart. I nodded to myself and smiled for the first time in a long while.

CHAPTER SEVENTEEN

Break of dawn Sunday Morning

CLYDE PULLED the car into the Venice Yacht Club parking lot. The sunlight crept over the edges of the palm trees lining the border of the property. Mark escorted Clyde, Holly, Cheryl and Cheryl's friend, Nick, down to the Obendorf's forty-foot yacht.

It didn't take long to stow away the various bags that had been brought along. All Clyde carried were his wits and a borrowed pair of binoculars. With a holler, Mark indicated the boat was ready to sail. Everyone clambered aboard. Clyde looked happy to see Nick. It would be a rough ride and they could use an extra set of eyes and hands.

The wind whipped through the masts on sailboats creating a whistling sound; the gusts threatening to rip off canvas canopies and anything not battened down. The true onslaught of the wind shocked Clyde as the boat passed the protective jetty. Waves being pushed by nearly fifty mile-an-hour gusts, crashed over the long jut of cement and stone. Mark gave the boat a little more gas as the bow passed into the torrent of brown rollers threatening to turn the craft into the other jetty on the starboard side.

"By the hand of Almighty!" Clyde immediately wished he could take back his blasphemy as Cheryl began to wail. No doubt, his words added fuel to her fire.

"Neal's dead! No one can survive out there." She pointed a shaking finger towards the middle of the Gulf. "We're not going to find him out here!"

Clyde didn't bother trying to console her. He hated to admit it, but he thought the same thing. There were matters to be taken care of, namely trying their best to attempt a search. They owed it to the men. Others on the boat did their best to placate Cheryl, though it did little good. Clyde understood how she felt. Some people held back their feelings, a dangerous thing to do. He left her alone to grieve and worry in her own way, while he tried his best to block out the outpouring of his own emotion. Clyde could see how Mark felt for his mother, taking a deep breath before he pushed the throttle down. The large boat heaved forward into the massive brown waves with the froth off the top of them whipping their faces with salty brine. There was not any real fear the boat couldn't take the seas, but it would take some time to reach the first dive site as Mark couldn't open the engines up much past half throttle. They would search M-16 first. He heard his brother talking a few weeks ago about it, how he'd seen a pile of Grouper there in the late fall.

It took the better part of an hour to reach the site. As they passed deeper into the Gulf, the water changed from a churned-up brown color to a deep foreboding black. Clyde fought off the vestiges of seasickness as the craft pitched up and down through the swells. His biggest fear realized; it would be impossible to spot the men from the boat unless they ran right over the top of them. Then, how the devil would they get them up out of the water without killing them in the waves?

After the brief conversation with the pilots, they took a hitch out to one of the diver sites further out M-9. The second dive site yielded nothing. He turned to Mark. "Can you fire up the radio again? I want to talk to the pilots."

Mark nodded and dialed to the agreed upon channel.

Clyde took the mic. "This is the Nautilus, Clyde Butcher. Come in, Rich, come in Bill…."

There were a few moments of static before a voice rang out, "Bill Cameron here. Where are you Nautilus?"

"Dive site M-9 ... decided to have a look out this way before we drift towards Anna Marie."

"I was there twenty minutes ago, heading back your way now, one mile closer to shore."

Another voice checked in, "Rich here. I've had my eye on you Bill since we last talked. I'm due west of you, heading in the same direction."

"Ten Four. I can see you now. The darn water is so black. It'll be next to impossible to spot anything down there. We might have already flown over top of them."

Clyde cut in. "We've discussed this." He said sharply. "We've got to keep trying. They are down there. I guarantee it. Neal's Scarab has experienced something out of the norm. It sunk fast. The three men are probably floating with life jackets; some possibly in dive suits which are black. It'll be tough. All I can ask is ... we will keep trying until this storm passes through. If we don't find them, we'll come back out, we will regroup. We can't leave those poor souls out here without doing our absolute best."

"I'm with you." Bill said back.

"Ditto." Rich agreed.

***

Clyde and Mark continued for as long as they dared. In the end, they decided to drift where they thought the men might be, factoring in how far they may have moved, hoping they might luck into finding them.

Clyde turned to Mark, now trying to ignore the sobs and hysteria coming from his mother. "We're closer to Sarasota than we are to Venice. I say we hold down there until the storm passes. Judging by how far we've drifted, I think we will be closer to them there than if we headed back."

Mark nodded. "I'll call in for a birth. We stop in there all the time and our club has a reciprocal."

Cheryl hadn't stopped bursting out her sorrow since they left Venice.

Clyde motioned towards Cheryl. "I hate to say it, Mark, but I think we need to get someone up here to pick her up. I can't think let alone try to help the boys."

Mark nodded. "You gotta understand. Neal's her son."

"Got it, but we can't help him with her out on the boat."

Mark nodded. "If I can't get someone to come here, I'll send her back in a cab."

"Thank you. I know how hard that is for you to say."

"No, you are right, Mr. Butcher. She's out of her head. I feel like I'm out of my head, but I'm just pushing forward, dealing with it in a different way."

"That's all we can do son ... all we can do." He looked out at the fast-approaching front, slowly shaking his head. "Those poor men ... the longer this goes on, the less chance we have of finding them. They'll keep on drifting ... hypothermia ... sharks."

Mark nodded. No words needed to be spoken. He plugged in the GPS coordinates for Sarasota Harbor, fired up the engine and turned the boat to shore.

CHAPTER EIGHTEEN

THE OBENDORF house buzzed as the morning wore on. Niki Butcher put herself to work making more coffee and snacks, which at best, were only picked at. No one seemed hungry. No one seemed to have an appetite. However, the coffee went quickly.

Anna looked as if she hadn't slept at all. Her son, Billy, looked frightened. He had the sense to not make matters any worse with his mom by asking questions, which might feed into her fragile mood. He didn't say much but sat quietly taking everything in like a sponge, as kids will do. Anna smiled at her son and showed how extremely proud she was of how grown-up he acted. He showed no fear, but rather a keen sense of what was going on and Bill pitched in to help wherever he could.

Jackie kept checking in with the Coast Guard. She called every twenty minutes or so, making friends with each new dispatcher. Between calls, Merry and Jackie would check in with the two pilots, Bill and Rich, who were not having much luck. Though she acknowledged the fact several times now, it still seemed crazy the pilots couldn't contact the Coast Guard directly. At roughly ten am, the Coast Guard called. Jackie's heart jumped into her throat as she looked at the call display.

Waiting for Morning Time

"Mrs. Obendorf."

"Yes. Have you found something?"

"No. We are suspending the search until this storm front passes through. I know you don't want to hear this, but the conditions are no longer safe. We would advise you to call in the planes you have out there and any boats. They need to get into a safe harbor."

"Okay. I understand. Thank you."

Jackie called Clyde. "Dad, … nothing?

"No. I'm sorry."

"I know you're sorry. You don't need to say that. You're heading in, right? The Coast Guard just called, said it's pretty bad."

"You got that right. We're heading into Sarasota until this front passes through. We're doing our best under difficult conditions." He paused. Clyde didn't want to tell Jackie how bad the weather and sea was becoming, as he didn't want to worry her. "We need to get someone up here to pick up Cheryl. She's not handling the situation very well and understandably so. I'm afraid we can't think straight because of it." Clyde was cognizant of the fact that Cheryl's husband Robert, passed away less than a year ago to pancreatic cancer. She'd been a wreck since his death. The thought of Neal dying became too much for her to bear.

"Sarasota. Okay … we'll find somebody to come there and get her. You're going back out after the storm passes through?"

"We'd like to, we have to bring the boat back down to Venice."

"Okay, you guys be careful. Love you!"

Jackie put down the receiver. "Nothing!" She looked worried. "And, I haven't had one call from the other half of Venice who are out in their boats." She said this figuratively, but she'd been blown away with the support which arose within the town. One of their own is missing and the community quickly pulled together to help in any way they could. Jackie needed to revert to using Merry's cell as the phone calls were coming in nonstop on both of her lines.

Merry looked at Jackie as she watched the strong woman will

herself forward. She appeared maniacal and hyper focused to the point of almost bitchy, but she knew that was not the case. Jackie is a sweetheart, on the warpath to fight for her husband's life. Merry could only wish she possessed the will of that beautiful young woman who she had watched grow up from a teenager to a woman she respected. Merry changed the topic. "What about going public? We talked about it last night, like the Sheriff's department suggested."

Jackie nodded, thinking for a few moments. "I'm surprised Heidi Godman hasn't called me back. I'm going to call her again now. She's the news anchor at ABC News 40. Our kids went to daycare together, which is why I have her personal cell number. I think it's time we pushed a little harder. The police might be right, but we want to do this in a controlled way. We'll do one interview. You never know, someone may have seen something, maybe it will drum up some more help, we can only hope." Jackie began dialing Heidi's number.

Niki put up her hand and spoke before Jackie could complete the call. "You know you're opening up a can of worms? Once the media gets a hold of this, things could get out of control. It'll be big news. Those reporters are sharks and will do anything for a story."

"I feel I can trust her, Mom."

Merry spoke up. "I'm happy to be making a positive step. Sitting and waiting is becoming more difficult by the hour. I can't get rid of the vision of my poor Lew floating out there somewhere, counting on us to do something to help … Neal and Bill. As the hours pass, their chance of survival gets slimmer. We all know this, so let's get this going. The water looked so cold and unforgiving when we'd been down at the boat launch. No one deserves to be out there, especially with the storm coming."

Everyone turned their attention to Jackie as she reached out to her friend. "Heidi, it's Jackie Obendorf."

"Jackie, darling, how are things, and the kids?"

"Not so well I'm afraid. Neal and a couple of his friends have gone missing."

"What do you mean?"

"They're out in the Gulf. We fear something went wrong with our boat."

"How long have they been missing?"

"Since yesterday."

"Holy smokes, Jackie, have you called the Police... the Coast Guard?"

"Yes. We've called both and been in constant contact with the Coast Guard. There's a full-on search going on. And... actually the Venice Police are the ones who suggested we contact the press. The more eyes you have looking ... the better your chances of finding it."

"This is true ... sometimes, but for missing people on land. Were they out for a cruise?"

"No. They were spear fishing and supposed to be back mid-afternoon."

"Jackie... you should think twice about doing this."

"Why? I don't understand."

"What I'm going to say might seem heavy, but I'm going to tell you straight. When I post this news, it will be a field day ... you will get bombarded."

"Heidi, we want as much coverage as we can get."

Silence ... Heidi waited for a time.

"I don't get it, Heidi, don't you want this?"

"Normally I would, but this is close for me, and you are a dear friend. How long has Neal been missing?"

"It will be a day in a few hours?"

"Jackie, I don't have the stats on this sort of thing, but we get a few of these stories every year. How should I say this ... I've never seen a happy ending to one. You're going to open this thing up and I tell you, there will be news vans parked in your front yard. I know you're hopeful, those waiting for their loved ones to return always are. What's going to happen when they find their bodies? The story won't go away. You girls are going to have to deal with your grief. It will be devastating and you're going to have the hounds on your doorstep for a week. Like I said, I've seen it. I don't want to diminish your enthusiasm. In good conscience, I have to point this out to you."

Jackie deflated, her face drooped and her eyes looked sad.

Merry saw her mood swing and put her hand out, demanding the receiver.

Jackie pulled it back, shaking her head.

"No. I do think it's something we want to do. I feel strongly about it. I understand your reasoning." She put her hand over the phone and looked at Merry. "She doesn't think it's a good idea ... said it twice." She frowned not knowing what to say.

Merry said, "I just know it's the right thing to do. Can I speak to her?" She gestured towards the phone again.

Jackie shook her head and continued talking on the phone. "No. It's fine. Heidi, we've made up our minds to go ahead with it."

"I'm only saying this because we're friends." Heidi tried to console her.

"Yes. I know we're friends. That's why I'm asking for your help. I didn't know who to call, but if you're not willing ... I'll call someone else."

Silence. "Okay, Jackie, I've read you the riot act. If you want to do this thing, I'll handle it as best I can. I'd suggest meeting with one of our reporters ASAP. You said the boat and trailer are still at the boat ramp?"

"Yes. We left it there just in case they showed up."

"Sure... hang on I want to check with one of our weather people."

Jackie held on.

"Jackie, one of our guys says the storm will pass through by the evening. I'll have one of our reporters … probably from the Sarasota Herald meet you at seven ... by the trailer. If there's any change, I'll call you."

"Okay, great, if you don't call, we'll be there at seven."

Heidi spoke. "Do you mind if we do a short interview before we hang up?"

"No, of course."

Heidi spent ten minutes asking as many questions as she thought pertinent. Once finished, she hung up.

Anna spoke up. "Well? Are they going to help us?"

Jackie put her hand on Anna's shoulder. "She's going to arrange something. She said we have to be careful. Too many people get a hold of this and it could get out of control. They're like sharks and will go into a feeding frenzy. Heidi said she'd call a reporter at the Sarasota Herald."

Everyone nodded, nothing else to be done.

Within minutes the phone rang. Jackie picked it up. "Jackie speaking… yes, Heidi said someone from the Herald might call… More than twenty-four hours now… Yes. We know that. Six pm… Merry Lipsit and I'll meet you at the boat launch then… Neal Obendorf, Lewis Lipsit and William Lipsit… yes. We'll see you then."

Christopher Bowron

CHAPTER NINETEEN

I REMEMBERED being caught in a rowboat during storms on Lake Erie. You got wet and shivered under the thunder and lightning, but you felt invincible... being a kid. I knew better being older, no longer buoyed by youthful ignorance ... the storm we were caught in now was a killer. The squall looked like a massive grey and black steam roller threatening to squash us three castaways like pancakes. Lightning flashing up from the water leaving craters in the waves, steam hissing. Three of us clenched arms waiting for death to take us. I looked up into the sky and prayed silently for Merry. I prayed she would be okay without me and for God to take us into his hands and to take make it as quick as possible... so none would suffer.

With the lightning strikes getting closer and closer Bill yelled, "Get inside, we're gonna get fried." We looked at each other and started kicking into the black wall that threatened to gobble us up like a whale sucking microscopic plankton.

The edge of the massive storm sky passed within seconds taking the lightning with it, but the thunder continued to boom sounding like a great war drum threatening to drive one to deafness. The wind and the waves hammered with all the ferocity the storm could muster. It didn't get any worse than what we had experienced at this point in time, but we managed to move past the lightening that could kill us in a flash. We were tossed like ragdolls for what seemed like an hour. I continued with what I thought might be my last prayer between breaths of air. I couldn't see where Bill and Neal were located. All I could do was try my best to catch my wind after each wave. If the onslaught lasted much longer, once again, I felt I might have to give up. I had used what seemed like the last reserves of strength managing to barely keep my head above water. I had the urge to vomit, but my guts were entirely empty. Catching sight of Bill gave me hope. While I couldn't see my son's face, I did see Bill's head hunched over on his chin with saltwater spewing from his mouth. I yelled, "Billy!" But the call fell on deaf ears. I dropped down the next wave in a full cartwheel, once again losing sight of Bill. I poked my head above water after holding my breath for what seemed like dozens of seconds ... barely enough time to grab another deep breath before the next wave hit hard. I couldn't take much more. I resolved to accept his death by drowning. Fighting the behemoth waves simply took too much to endure.

My thoughts turned to Neal. Somehow, I felt he would be okay. He could swim like a fish. If their predicament hadn't been a life-threatening event, I thought how Neal looked earlier ... purposefully playing in the massive waves and enjoying the fun. I knew better now. Neal was trying his best to survive.

***

The three of us were mercilessly battered around by the storm, rising with the powerful waves and being thrown back into the swirling sea. Then the ocean calmed as we drifted into the silent eye of the storm. My feelings went from desperation to vast relief, from not being able to last much longer to enjoying a temporary reprieve. I grabbed the surge of energy I now felt, thinking how bizarre? I could go from the edge of giving up to now feeling ready to fight again and stay alive. I sensed we all felt renewed to keep fighting, because that was what we were doing ... fighting for our lives. A few more minutes of torment and I knew I would have given up.

The wind slowed significantly, almost taunting us to keep going. Bill still hung onto the bumper rope at the opposite end from mine. I paddled to him. Neal surfaced suddenly between us. The waves calmed even more, and we were blessed with cool rain pouring down, torrents of it. We leaned back trying to catch the sweet unsalted water in our mouths.

Bill was first to notice the zipping of fish fins along the smoother surface. They were not sharks, but we all knew those predators were not far below. Our sudden moment of reprieve quickly turned to dread as far as Bill was concerned. He had forgotten about the gashes on his legs. The waves probably saved them from attacks by the ocean's predators. Now, with the sudden calm, worry filled him once again. "Neal, can I borrow your goggles for a moment?"

Neal handed them to Bill. "They're prescription, don't drop em' or I won't be able to see."

Bill nodded and put them on and experienced difficulty seeing through the prescription. Still, he was able to look down at his legs. They didn't appear to be seeping blood from the wounds he had sustained from the boat's props. They now looked more like raised pink welts. Bill felt a little better, handing the goggles back to Neal, who promptly put them back on. One of the reasons Bill had decided to swim away from the other two before was the simple fact he didn't want the smell of his blood to be responsible for attracting sharks. Bill figured with his wounds bleeding under water he was done for and there was no reason to share his ill fate with Neal and me.

Neal spoke. "I know what you're thinking, Bill. It won't do us any good. You think about what's swimming below, you'll go nuts. I said it before."

Neal's words made sense. All three of us shook our heads to

Waiting for Morning Time

agree and remained as close as we could to stay together, hoping a big target would scare away any of the smaller sharks. Nothing would help against a Tiger, Bull or Oceanic White Tip.

***

It would be next to impossible to describe the thirst and rawness of throat. The first drops of rainwater hit the back of our mouths and burned like acid, yet we couldn't get enough. We must have each ingested a gallon of seawater since we left the boat.

Only God knows why I thought of a Sprite or was it a Mountain Dew commercial. It popped into my head, where a man who had been stranded in the desert for days appeared in a corner store. He grabbed a bag of chips and ate a handful, exacerbating his desert thirst because he knows a cold soda awaited. I chuckled, "I'm losing it!" Both Bill and Neal looked at me curiously.

Another thought hit me. I pulled out my dentures. I wore false teeth on the top since my early twenties. Now Neal and Bill looked at me like I was crazy, until I held the denture out and found that water could be caught in the shallow bowl. The heavenly rainwater tasted like nectar of the gods ... water had never tasted so good. We drank as much as we could, eventually slackening the awful thirst.

***

The wind calmed and it seemed as if the Gods were putting on a show. Looking up, I could see flashes of blue sky all around. It was as if we were in the middle of massive round theatre, acres big with white and black clouds as the projector screen and lightening dancing across it in all directions, 360 degrees and truly magnificent. We settled back for a time and watched in awe, thankful for the time of rest in Nirvana.

If a massive shark would suddenly surfaced and cut a line for one of us; we would probably have let the beast eat away, no fight. Each of us feeling paralyzed during the short reprieve.

For the first time since we left the Scarab, we could converse without having to yell or worry about being beaten up by the next wave. Neal would be the first to talk as we floated with the easy waves, gently rising up and down. "We need to be spotted before nightfall. This storm will pass, and we'll have three, four hours at best." He turned and looked into my eyes. "How are you?"

I spoke halfheartedly. "I'm in okay spirits, but I'm starting to feel the cold. My legs feel like frozen poles, I know they're there, but... they're disassociated with the rest of my body... numb."

Neal nodded and turned to Bill. "What about you?"

Bill bounced up and down in the chop for a few seconds before answering. "I'm better now... I'm sorry to have put you through a scare. I can't say what came over me. I was delusional."

Neal shook his head. "It's okay to say you were scared. We're all scared, we just show it in different ways, and besides, that's over... move on."

Bill nodded, accepting Neal's words. "Yep ... I'll admit it. I don't like the deep water below me ... it's messing with my head."

Neal grinned. "Not that deep bro ... we're closer to shore than you might think. Could be twenty- or thirty-feet max."

Bill grinned for the first time. "Don't know if that makes me feel any better."

Neal added, "If it's any consolation, the bigger sharks will have been driven to deeper water. They won't like this storm. See all this baitfish." He pointed to the small white and green backed fish swarming around. This stuff will be driven into shore by the weather. It's all here because it knows it won't be eaten."

Bill interjected. "Yeah, and the sharks will follow it inshore once the storm ends."

No one said anything for a few minutes.

Bill's head was beginning to swim from lack of sleep. The

Waiting for Morning Time

sudden calm and reprieve from fighting off the storm caused his vision to blur uncontrollably. It felt like coming indoors from a few hours outside on a cold blustery day. Once relaxed, sleepiness takes over and needles and pins attack the eyes. Sleep would be the only antidote. Bill turned. "Neal ... Nitrox?"

Neal didn't say a word, nor did he hesitate to give each of us a shot of the enriched air. Everyone felt marginally better within seconds, but we knew the waves and storm would soon hit again. We needed to stay motivated, or we would die. It was a miracle to have survived thus far, but there would be another half to follow. Storms like this one traveled in a whirling circle. We were now in the middle.

Neal reached over and poked Bill in the ribs. "Bill, what's the first thing you're gonna do when we get back home?"

He didn't answer right away, but you could tell something was churning in his brain ... the process being slowed by the deepening cold slowly engulfing their bodies.

"Big mother steak... baked potato... beer, lots of it." Bill grinned.

"You're beautiful wife?" Neal smiled at him.

Bill grinned and nodded as if to say ... *yeah, that too.*

"What about you, Lew?"

I chuckled, still thinking about the soda commercial. "Mountain Dew!"

Neal narrowed his eyes, lowering his brow. "Merry?"

"I'm not going to let her out of the bedroom for a day. But right now, to be honest, I couldn't imagine any more strenuous activity. Give me a day or two to rest and she'll be in trouble."

Bill rolled his eyes, too much information coming from a father. Still, he continued the line of question and looked at Neal. "What about you?"

The slender man was quick to respond. "I like your idea... steak, maybe some greasy pizza and wings. Wish you hadn't mentioned food." He turned to Bill. "Gonna hug my kids and that woman's gonna wish I never came home." He laughed.

"How long we been out here now?" Bill asked.

"Gotta be close to twenty-four hours; the storm hit mid to late morning. I figured the boat went down early afternoon. It's close to a day. Man!" Neal showed surprise.

We relaxed and looked up to watch what was left of the light show as the happy, but somber thoughts just spoken created a 'quiet few minutes of pause.'

I became too tired for conversation anyway, the cold creating a disconnect between his brain and tongue. We floated along, enjoying what we knew would be the last minutes of calm before being thrown into the storm once again. Having hellfire to look forward to, filled us with dread. But it seemed academic we would die when the first part of the storm rolled over us—yet we lived. There was hope, however thin it appeared.

I figured I'd used up perhaps the last of my nine lives. Angst filled my heart once again, as I looked at the lightning flash at the inner back wall of the storm now approaching. Once again, the bolts of electricity put on a show worthy of God's approval. I wondered if I'd missed something. Was it a vision? Or simply, something my companions and I were blessed to enjoy. The treasure of light, given to us from Mother Nature, seemed like the last cigarette before the firing squad. I envisioned God high above the clouds surrounded by sunlight and looking down on them. *Okay, you poor souls, I'm going to allow this storm to take you, but I'm going to give you this one last wonder before you pass into my realm.*

I smiled, the sky show truly indescribable. I wondered how many had been blessed to witness God's spectacle. Could it be a private club ... whose members no longer exist?

***

Waiting for Morning Time

The reprieve of floating in the calm of the storm didn't last more than fifteen minutes in clock time. We tried to stay inside the calm area, but the back end of the swirling mass of clouds soon engulfed us. The high waves kicked up, making quiet conversation impossible. The painful wind, howling like a choir of banshees, took over. We found ourselves back tossing and turning in the horrific waves braved only minutes before. Doing our best to stay close, we hurdled down the front of the first rogue wave.

When they hit the water and bounced up Neal yelled at the top of his voice, "Storm's going towards shore. It'll have its own current. Let's try to swim towards it once it passes."

No more needed to be said or could be said as our bodies were tossed down the face of another massive wave. I didn't realize how much damage I'd endured until the first tumble tossed my numb legs askew over my head. I could feel my hip joints straining to keep the ligaments from snapping. Legs flew about, nerves unable to connect with my brain. I'd lost connectivity to my feet many hours ago. It became a helpless endeavor, my body in its own way trying to shut down, pulling what reserves it had towards the brain and heart. Although I suspected my brain didn't receive its equal share. Eyesight and thinking were becoming foggy, shock setting in to protect from the pain and terrors faced. My body was slowly dying.

As the backside of the storm rolled over, I experienced a vision of Merry's face and it didn't look happy. She appeared strong, but worried. I felt close to tears, but sorrow would have been a useless waste of energy, using resources I didn't have to spare.

"I'm sorry," I muttered under my breath.

Still, I couldn't stop thoughts of guilt still seeing my wife's face. What could I be sorry for? We hadn't planned on the catastrophe happening… the emotions were past the point of feeling remorseful about sending her off with Jackie, Anna and the kids. No. I felt sorry I wouldn't get to spend the rest of my days with that marvelous woman. Staring up into the storm clouds, I needed to be honest with myself.

We were not going to be rescued. The last plane had flown right over not seeing us. *How would it get any better?*

Though I experienced extreme despair, I needed to put on a strong front for Bill. While Neal seemed okay, Bill appeared to be going through round two of giving up. Our chances rested upon being spotted *once the storm passed*, or we were in big trouble. I was not an odds maker, but rather, a realist. At this point, I didn't give a thousand to one chance. If we were strong enough, possessed wet suits and flippers the same as Neal ... we *might* ... but, that *might* would be a dicey long shot. I took a deep breath of sea air, filling my lungs before another massive wave shot up to hurdle me into the depths of the water. Once I resurfaced, it took me a minute to compose myself. The only thing I could think to do at this point would be-- to pray. I prayed to God and Jesus and all the angels. I couldn't remember any of their names but pray to them I did. It was not a well thought out prayer. How could it be while spitting saltwater out of my mouth and thinking about my family and Merry. If there is a God, I knew he would understand and that is all that mattered.

***

The storm passed, not quickly, but more of a slow pulling back of the built-up wind and rain. Before we knew it, we were outside the storm the black mass of virulent clouds moving away from towards shore. It felt like a mirage. Within half an hour, to a man we lamented the fact we hadn't drank more rainwater, but then again ... how were we to know?

As the wind died down, so did the waves and so did the tumbling down, but the cold from the Northern front had set in— equally as dangerous as the storm. We were able to bring the rope and bumpers in closer to each other to communicate. It seemed like a couple of hours or so since words were spoken.

Neal looked towards where the sun would be setting behind the grey cold-looking clouds. During late winter, it would be crossing low in the sky, and it would be dark in a few hours. He sighed, knowing no one would be able to find them in the churned up brown and black murky gulf. The weather looked as if it would settle, but not before dark.

Neal looked to me like he could function somewhat normally, if a little stiff. Bill and I could no longer feel our legs and arms making them clumsy without control, the heat leaving our extremities to warm the core of our bodies.

Marbles filled my mouth, yet I initiated conversation. I feared we might all fall to despair and mental numbness if I didn't. I spoke as loudly as I could. "Boys, I think we're gonna have to spend another night out here."

Neal nodded, his teeth chattering. "I didn't want to say so much. I'm pretty okay, but you two must be freezing your tails off. I'm worried for you."

Bill rolled his eyes back into his head. "Are we better floating here, or should we keep pushing towards shore?"

Neal thought for a moment. "There are currents out here, which might make any swimming we accomplish useless." He paused, keeping his head above a sharp rolling wave passing through. "Call me stupid, we need to create some body heat, it's going to get cold real soon—if it's possible to be any colder."

Bill nearly squealed; his voice pitched so high. "What about sharks? These waves are knocking down real fast."

Neal cocked his head to the side. "It's a possibility. Don't think about it."

Neal and I could see the *easy-for-you-to-say* look on Bill's face. We needed to keep the young man calm.

I knew deep in my heart if my son and I were not there, Neal would have left for shore hours ago with the aid of his flippers. "Billy... think about Anna and your kids. They need you to stay strong… not to give up. If the sharks get us, so be it. You can't worry about what you can't control."

Bill put his arm over my shoulder and rested his head for a moment ... a good sign. "We're going to make it." I felt I needed to offer some hope. "I believe that if we can make it through the night, the calmer sea should allow us to be spotted."

Bill turned to Neal, having a horrible thought. "There has to be a normal period of time at which searches for people like us finally get called off. How long do you think they'll keep looking for us?"

Neal took a few moments in his slow, methodical way. "Depends on who's looking. The Coast guard can only take up so many man-hours. They have other situations to deal with. I would think people like us… are never found. Still, I agree with Lew. The water will be much calmer tomorrow if we can just hang in."

Bill said the words none of us wanted to hear. "They might not come out in the morning… they might think we're dead from the storm." His eyes rolled up in his head.

Neal nodded. "Good point. Who'd think we survived that *mother* ... REALLY?"

I smiled, with just enough conviction to fool even myself. "Merry!"

CHAPTER TWENTY

11 a.m. Sunday - Prior to the Storm

JACKIE RECEIVED A CALL from the Coast Guard near noon. Everyone in the kitchen waited patiently for her to finish with their hearts in their throats. Merry gestured towards her with flaying hands trying to mouth questions. It seemed they were living from phone call to phone call.

Jackie shook her head meaning no news. When she got off the phone, Jackie exclaimed, "NADA! They told us to get everyone off the water. I told them the planes were in and Mark had taken harbor in Sarasota. They said they don't want any more disasters."

It seemed like an awkward balance. Everyone knew sooner or later a call would come in stating they were dead or alive. A neutral or informational call didn't spell out disaster. Everyone could breathe a sigh of relief… until the next time the phone rang.

Merry and Niki nodded. Both heard the wind beginning to whip up pretty strong, Anna and the kids, not being used to Florida storms seemed very uneasy. The look on Anna's face showed a mixture of fatigue, panic and fear of the unknown.

Merry hugged Anna. "I know ... we're gonna get through this together."

"I can't imagine Bill out there… anyone out there. I feel so sorry for them."

"I'm with you, honey. The fact you think they are still out there says something to me. We can't give up hope until it becomes... impossible to hope." Merry pulled Billy into the hug, his eyes on the verge of tears. Still, he was being a proper little man, taking in the information, as kids will do, digesting, thinking and... fretting like the rest.

There appeared to be at least twenty people in the house. Pastor Pat concerned friends and members of Lew and Merry's church along with Jackie's relatives bringing food. They had arrived one by one as if by a load of stone, pulling well-wishers and supporters to the Obendorf household, the ensuing tragedy impossible to ignore. People wanted to know, wanted to play a part and help if they could. It was in the DNA of human nature. Within another hour, even more people came to the house. Most everyone congregated in the kitchen, making it feel more like a wake than a vigil.

Pastor Pat became a blessing. Beyond prayers, he helped to keep everyone grounded. Women and men pledge their lives to the Lord, live to do His work in tough situations. Pastor Pat easily fell into that role. He wasn't overly preachy, but more of a solid person and a good friend upon which any and all could draw strength from his conviction and calmness.

The crowd stood as Anna had been in touch with her mother and Bill's sister again, who in turn contacted Bill's mother, Lew's ex. They were all heading down to Florida. Merry felt awkward about Janet coming but felt empathetic. Bill is her son, and she would need to be here.

She appreciated the support... but a thought began to creep into her head. No matter how positive she appeared believing the men were alive, Merry started to run through the scenarios, which might occur should the worst happen. Merry, Anna and Jackie were running

Waiting for Morning Time

on pure adrenalin. If the men were to succumb to the sea, it would be a mess. The news and the reality ... the closeness would be fresh to the new arrivals, and it would be impossible to placate them. Merry and Anna would be incapable of entertaining, let alone comforting them. The three women had been living with the reality of the events for over a day. The news of their deaths would be fresh... ugly to the newcomers. Merry didn't think she would be able to deal with them. She held no animosity towards them, yet she needed to think about the realities of what might come.

***

Niki Butcher took to the adversity and handled it with uncanny strength. The three wives didn't know what they would have done without her. Niki walked into the kitchen wanting to make sure the girls still kept things together. She could see how the new people, who seemed to be arriving by the minute, were taking the three gals off task, demanding their attention and information. Niki drew them into one of the bedrooms by waving her forefinger. Jackie, Anna, and Merry followed her into the room and formed a four-way hug, their heads nearly touching in their attempt to find some privacy.

Jackie spoke up. "Mom, I'm so glad you're here. You've helped us keep things together." She took a deep breath, on the edge of tears. "This is simply crazy... unbelievable."

Niki placed a quieting finger across Jackie's lips. "I know you girls are at your wit's end." She paused, wiping a bead of sweat from her forehead. "I'm trying my best to lift you up. I won't let any of you go down. I believe what we're doing here is going to save our boys. We have to keep each other strong. Only you have the ability to keep pushing, no one else is going to do it for you. The Coast Guard can only keep a search up for so long. They have statistics on this sort of thing. It becomes a matter of priority, probability and manpower."

Anna stood with Billy by her side looking as if she might swoon. Jackie and Merry were not far behind with only a semblance of control present in their eyes.

As Niki continued to talk, the worst of the storm began to hit. The wind intensified. A low humming whistle started up as the air pressure outside began to drop. Loose debris, including furniture, palm branches and anything not tied down began to hit the house. The small lake upon which Jackie and Neal's home resided routinely stayed still like a millpond. Not today. It looked angry, with three-to-four-foot whitecaps spilling over onto the roadway leading to their property.

Merry looked over at Anna. "Why don't you take Billy into another room, catch a few deep breaths? I'll make you some tea."

Anna nodded and retreated as suggested, probably glad to be given the direction. Niki looked to see if she remained within earshot. Merry nodded and spoke. "She just finished bawling... after thinking of Bill out there in the storm. I said to her that by now they would be out of it, probably the better part of a half hour by now. Those words seemed to settle her. We have to keep everyone else calm, but I'll be honest, she puts me to the edge of tears every time she breaks down."

Niki nodded. "You're probably right, Merry." Gathering her thoughts she said, "I just chatted with Clyde ... he spoke with Marshall."

Merry had briefly heard about Marshall a year or so prior while talking with Jackie over a few drinks. Jackie explained that Marshall is a seer of sorts. While Merry didn't believe in the paranormal ... at this point she couldn't care two gosh-darns how they found and rescued their men. She remembered Jackie stating how he painted his toenails purple because it is the color of the future ... therefore, his feet preceding him into the future. Marshall was known as a *forward thinker* within the paranormal community. "What did he have to say?"

Niki took a moment. "He gave a coordinate. Turned out to be one of the dive sites, however, he said in his vision, they were still with the boat. But that doesn't seem to be the case. If they were with the boat, they would have been found."

Merry spoke. "I don't think that they're with the boat."

Anna put a hand on her arm. "What makes you think that?"

Merry seemed nervous to say what she wanted. "Though I haven't slept much, I did have a very vivid dream."

Jackie urged Merry on, if nothing else it would be good for her to talk.

"I saw three male angels forming a ring over the three of them. This is the second such dream. I could see they were in a storm and the rain poured down in buckets. I could see and hear the water hitting the bright white wings of their protectors. One angel looked up at me and smiled. I know they are alive, all three of them as I could see all their heads between the wings. God is with them, but he can only do so much ... God's buying us time. We need to be strong now. It's going to be tough, but if we can pull together and keep out hearts strong, we will find them."

The three women did pull together, foreheads touching. Merry spoke. "I have done all the praying I can for the time being. There is one thing I'm not sure I'll be able to deal with."

Niki prodded Merry to speak up as she massaged Merry's arm.

"If Lew's ex and daughter arrive, and the outcome of the rescue is not what we want? I hope you follow... I won't be able to deal with them in a hospitable way. I love them dearly, but I'm at my wits end as it is right now." Tears formed in her eyes and her bottom lip quivered.

Jackie put her hand behind Merry's head, pulling her close. "Don't you worry, girl. I'm with you one hundred percent. I know it might appear I'm focused on Neal ... well I am. But I love Lew and though I've only met Bill this week, I feel for him and poor Anna and Billy. Don't worry, we'll insulate you."

Niki nodded. "I concur. We're both with you, Merry ... one hundred percent."

Merry sighed, relieved by Jackie and Niki's sentiment.

Everyone in Jackie and Neal's home hunkered down by the storm. It battered the house for the next two to three hours. To some it seemed a normal occurrence.

To others like Anna and Billy, it was truly a frightening experience. The thought of the men having to survive it out on the water was tormenting. Anna didn't know how much more she could take. Bill and Anna met young. He was everything to her. How could God take him away from her now, after taking away her father? She needed to maintain her faith. God wouldn't let Bill go and was doing everything He could to help all three men.

***

Jackie, with her baby in her arms, sat down in her favorite rocking chair by the living room window. She rolled him slowly back in forth trying to get him to fall asleep as the rain slammed against the glass. For the first time since the men had been discovered to be missing, her mind went to a dark place. *What if Neal didn't come back?* She looked down at Robbie as he squirmed to get comfy. *He will never know his father.* She took a deep breath trying her best to choke back a sob. She continued to breathe deeply watching the storm, which Neal would have endured out in the Gulf …unprotected. She hoped that it wasn't an omen of bad tidings.

CHAPTER TWENTY-ONE

JACKIE AND MERRY climbed into the car and closed the car doors behind them. Looking at each other, they took a long deep breath simultaneously. There were too many people in Jackie's house. It seemed a reprieve to be alone in the vehicle for a time. "The silence out here is deafening." Merry shook her head.

Jackie nodded. "I know everyone means well, but it's becoming a bit much."

"We need to remember they're worried just as we are. They need to know what's going on. It's human nature. If my friends were lost at sea, I'd have a hard time sitting by the phone waiting to hear news."

Jackie nodded, rubbing her tired-looking face. She took another deep breath and engaged the ignition. After a few minutes driving in silence, navigating fallen debris from the storm both women seemed to relax.

Merry said, "So, what are we going to say?"

Jackie tapped her long fingers on the steering wheel. "The truth, I don't know what else besides the truth. Heidi said to keep to the facts and not get too personal."

Merry nodded slowly, not knowing what else to say and feeling discomfort as to what they were about to do.

***

They pulled into the boat launch parking lot a short time later. Both their hearts were beating fast, seeing the lonely truck and trailer waiting for the men to return. Its presence underlined the reality of the grave circumstances. There were no other cars in the lot, except for a minivan with NEWS / SARASOTA HERALD embossed on both sides and on the back. A thin man in his forties and another with a camera stood beside the vehicle. When Jackie pulled up beside them, she felt suddenly uncomfortable about doing the interview. She couldn't explain it, but it felt somehow… scary and overwhelming that the world would soon know their— private terror. But she remained steadfast in her belief they needed to whatever they could to help rescue their men.

They got out of the car, timidly and approached the two men. Since the wind died down after the storm moved out, it was not difficult to talk and be heard. Jackie stepped up to the reporter and offered her hand. "Jackie Obendorf ... Butcher."

The man scribbled down the information. "Is that with one F?"

Jackie nodded.

He turned to Merry. "Merry, M E R R Y, Lipsit. I'm Lew Lipsit's wife."

"What are the names of the missing men ... I'm assuming that he's one of them?"

Jackie nodded. "Lewis, L E W I S, Lipsit, William, Lipsit and Neal, N E A L, Obendorf."

The reporter tried his best to stifle a grin; their nervousness seemed almost comical if the situation hadn't been so dire. "So, what's going on? Heidi says your husbands are lost at sea." He pointed to the cameraman. "Do you mind?"

"No." Merry spoke up, looking to Jackie for support.

When Jackie nodded her agreement, the cameraman started to record the interview. Both women took a moment to fuss with their hair being out in the wind.

He stepped in beside the two with the camera facing them head on. "Sam Farthing, Sarasota Herald. I'm here with Jackie Butcher Obendorf and Merry Lipsit, whose husbands have been reported lost at sea."

Jackie took the lead. "Over twenty-four hours at this point."

"When did you first notice they were missing?"

"Yesterday, later in the day." She went on to describe the events as they unfolded, prompted by his questions.

When he finished the interview, the reporter shook both their hands. "Ladies, I wish you the best of luck." His eyes darted to the ground periodically, unable to hold either of their frightened stares.

He shook his head seeing they noticed his unease. "Sorry, ladies ... I get a lot of these types of stories. I hope yours has a happy ending. I'll let you know how and when this gets used. Might end up on tonight's news. I'm going to send it to Heidi at News 40. Thank you."

Everyone shook hands and went their own way.

***

On the way back, they looked at each other thinking the same thing. Jackie spoke first. "That wasn't what I expected. I feel like we were interviewed for a little league game. But I'm glad that we did it, it's given me some hope."

"Hope is a form of prayer. God feeds off our hope." She hesitated thinking about Jackie's further comment. "Little league isn't the right word. I don't think he believes we will find them. He looked very uncomfortable. I don't blame him, I would too."

"I suppose. Well, let's hope that this foray into the unknown helps."

They continued their drive to Jackie's place in silence. When they arrived, the house appeared lit up for Christmas. Walking from the car, they were both dreading the chaos and questions they would be met with inside, their short reprieve over.

***

As expected, the entourage waiting inside the house didn't appear to be able to operate without Jackie and Merry, Anna too upset to direct any of the search activities.

Niki caught the look on Jackie and Merry's faces. She could tell their spirit wavered.

Before Jackie or Merry could do or say anything about the news interview, Niki herded them into a bedroom as she had done earlier and showed anger on her face.

"Stop this now... You do not know that your husbands are dead." She stopped to choose her words. "Don't use up all your energy mourning them tonight. You'll have plenty of time to mourn them later if they are actually gone, but you don't know that yet... so don't do it!"

Merry and Jackie eyed each other before looking back at Niki. Her words hit a nerve, making sense. The kind woman's speech would make the next several hours somewhat easier. Jackie spoke up. "Stay in the present, right?"

Niki gave her daughter a hug, "That's right, sweetheart. It's all you can do."

CHAPTER TWENTY-TWO

THE STORM from start to finish lasted three hours, though it seemed a lifetime to Neal. He watched Lew and Bill slowly deteriorate, realizing he might not be far behind them. All three of them unwittingly ingested a lot of salt water over the last day. The cold drove them to numbness. The last equally insidious threat is sleep deprivation. It slowly took over their bodies and minds. While a shark might cause instant trauma and death; salt could poison and the cold, sure to stop their vital organs; lack of sleep, on the other hand, is sneaky. It never showed signs of taking hold until it took away your ability to concentrate or think about it.

Neal felt the cold, but the wetsuit kept his body temperature moderated. He probably dropped a degree or two, but Lew and Bill were starting to turn pale and blue. Their lips were black from lack of blood flow. What scared Neal the most is the fact that they were no longer complaining about the cold. Both had gone past the tipping point and their bodies were in effect on the brink of death. Lew and Bill were in shock as their bodily systems kept changing to protect the brain from the trauma being experienced over the rest of their bodies.

Thank goodness the surf kept dropping. Neal didn't think they possessed the strength to fight the giant waves they bravely faced during the worst of the storm. Soon their organs would shut down and there was nothing Neal could do about it. He resigned himself to the fact he would have to watch his friends die if they were not rescued soon. He couldn't believe they would make it through another night.

Though somewhat insulated from the cold, Neal was not immune from the salt and lack of sleep. The seawater could tear a man's insides apart, making him thirstier than if he hadn't sipped the water— a deadly paradox. Too much salt could also play tricks with the mind. All three men hadn't been able to keep large amounts of seawater from entering their mouths and nostrils during the storm. Human body cells can prevent some salt from entering through their membranes and the body can normalize sodium chloride concentration to a degree. However, when the salt outside of the cell is vastly greater than within, the cells try to regulate the indifference and transport water out, which invariably creates shrinkage of the cell, or extreme dehydration. The body tries to compensate for the excess sodium and the kidneys will extract more water from the body than is available by creating urine. Extreme dehydration can set in, again, like the cold, shutting down the major organs to include the kidneys, leading to delirium and death.

Though Neal fell prey to the cold and the salt, he struggled most with lack of sleep. He is the type of guy who couldn't make it through a movie without nodding off. They counted their time in the water at approximately thirty-five hours. Taking into consideration being awake for eight hours prior to the boat flipping, they had been awake for forty-three hours. It would be now that their bodies would start to play tricks with the mind, creating hallucinations and forcing the body into snippets of slumber or micro sleeps, which would be impossible for the deprived victim to stop. In extreme cases, the body will shut down, but the three men were not close to that point ... yet.

Neal found himself face down in the water. Suddenly gasping for air like sleep apnea, he awoke. Invariably, he kept drinking more seawater he couldn't afford to ingest. He stopped urinating a few

Waiting for Morning Time

hours ago, which frightened him. The face in the water, waking up suddenly now happened to all three of them. When it occurred, they tried to shake their heads as hard as they could to stay awake. The process became unbelievably painful. Neal figured at this point each of them were having an episode every thirty minutes or so. The monotony of floating made matters worse along with the cold. Of course, nothing could be done about that.

Neal inflated his BC slightly, filling the air bladder to the point where it might pop. He wanted to try and keep his mouth out of the water. The device pressed hard against his chest, causing him some pain. He shook his head, thinking how he had spent all his life on the water, possibly one quarter of his waking hours. He couldn't believe how he got himself here. It had been harmless enough in the beginning, but nothing out of the ordinary for him. Yes, it was the first time he had been with an inexperienced diver in less than favorable conditions. Everything is easy when the water stayed calm. The situation would have been perfectly fine if the weather had been even a little better, but that's the way the ocean worked. No one gets into serious trouble when the weather's balmy... unless you run up on a sand bar at thirty miles per hour, or something stupid like that.

Neal was past laying blame, as it wouldn't solve anything. Still, he continued to review the events over and over again. He had nothing but time as the endless waves rolled past him. The boat and it's taking on water could possibly have been handled better, but then again, Lew is not familiar with the intricate nuances of the Scarab. Neal would have recognized the way it sat oddly in the water, the way it canted in the waves. He couldn't blame the other two men for that first warning missed. He sure wished he hadn't made that last dive, but hindsight is twenty-twenty as they say. They all had their parts to play in the blame game. He tried to resolve not to think about it again, nor mention it to the other two men if they found their way out of this mess. There would be nothing to gain from blame.

Looking at Lew and Bill, he couldn't help but feel awful. There is an unwritten rule, or perhaps it is written somewhere stating how the boat's owner, or the skipper is responsible for its passengers and crew. He knew Lew and Bill wouldn't think that way, but it would be something he would have to live with if he ended up being the only one to survive ... and he gave himself the best odds by a long shot. Their loss would haunt him. Still, he couldn't make it home either. He didn't have it in him to make for shore. A big ole tiger Shark might have to finish him off and put him out of his misery if he wasn't eventually rescued.

The thought did provoke a pang of fear, the water calming would induce the sharks to rise looking for meat. To this point he knew the heavy surf kept the predators at bay. If fate led them to spend another night out in the Gulf, the sharks would be a serious concern for any of the three still breathing.

***

They could hear planes, but they never seemed to come close to where they floated throughout the afternoon, very frustrating. Neal didn't like the way Lew and Bill hadn't spoken in some time. Perhaps they were dealing with their own inner demons, trying to come to grips with what was occurring to them. As he spun around slowly… because no one should ever float facing in only one direction, a continuous slow spin; he swore he could see the shoreline. He waited until he had spun around slowly once again just to make sure he was not seeing things. Yes… the shore, they were probably five to six miles away, but it appeared to be no hallucination.

Neal spoke up. "Bill, Lew!" He waited to get a response. Both only stared at him, raising their brows, too lost in their own thoughts to respond. "Look over there, it's the shore!"

Neal's words brought us out of our stupor. Bill exclaimed. "You're seeing things"

"No. I'm not... look!"

After a time, we could all see it. "Hey, you're right!" I said.

Neal started kicking towards the shoreline. "Come on. We may not make it, but it sure is a lot better than wallowing here. It might get our body heat up... might also bring us closer to boat traffic."

I nodded, Neal's words waking me from one of the mini sleeps. "Those planes we hear, they might see us better if we're splashing around."

Bill couldn't help himself. "What about the sharks?"

Neal grinned. "If they get us, they get us. I'm heading that way."

***

We swam for three hours until the sun began to set. By that time the wind had dropped substantially, and it became somewhat calm. However, that reprieve was short lived as the wind began to switch to the northeast, pushing us back out into the gulf. Regardless, we continued to paddle. Neal figured we could do worse. The constant movement kept our minds busy and creating body heat. He thought Bill and I wouldn't make it through the night sitting still, wallowing in the cold water.

When we stopped for a few minutes to watch the sun set behind the grey overcast sky, Bill spoke up. "Could be the last one I see—even if I can't really see it. They're not going to come out again in the morning. It'll be way over forty hours we've been missing when the sun comes back up." His eyes rolled back up into his skull once again, an act Neal was getting used to, as was I. "I'm not going to be able to make another night. I can't stay awake any longer, it's torture—it really is."

I poked him in the shoulder with his index finger. I looked at Neal as he spoke, then back at Bill. "Do you see Neal or I giving up? No... there's still some fight in these old bones. I know I'm going to keep going until this heart of mine." I patted his chest. "STOPS!"

"Dad, it's okay, I know what you're saying and what you're

trying to do. I'm just being a realist. I don't think we'll make it. I can feel my heart thumping in my chest every beat it makes. It's getting slower and slower. I don't know about you guys, but I've stopped peeing hours ago. I feel like I have to, but nothing comes out. I could stick my head into a bucket of cold water and drink it dry. The salt is killing me. If we get out of this, I'm never putting salt on my food again."

Neal spoke up. "Same here! But Lew's right. The water will be pretty calm by morning. We have to give ourselves that one last chance. I'll agree, it ain't looking so good. They'll have planes up through the night, maybe into the morning."

Bill shook his head. "Come on, Neal, it will have been almost forty-five hours at sunrise. Who would expect anyone to last that long? They'll be crying and writing obituaries by then, and rightfully so."

I smiled, Neal couldn't help but do so himself as he looked at my round parched face, the emotion infectious. "I know the girls won't give up. We're going to be rescued. I don't have a doubt in my mind. Bill, all you have to do is hang in there... and nothing stupid."

"Lew's right, Bill, we keep close eyes on each other. Someone starts to lose it... we shake em out of it. The night's gonna be tough, but we can do it. Let's face it, we just have to float and stay awake. This must be a lot harder on the girls because they don't know if we are dead or alive." He looked Bill in the eye. "We know we are alive, and we need to stay that way."

Bill nodded, none too convincingly.

***

We continued to swim for a time, but became too tired, muscles beginning to cramp and convulse. The daylight and the storm had given us something to focus on. The shoreline became a beacon... a

Waiting for Morning Time

goal. Darkness took away the focus, allowing minds to wander. As night set in and the last vestiges of pink disappeared from the western sky, hallucinations began in earnest. Soon we couldn't see each other's faces or our own hands, it became pitch black— terror set in.

Christopher Bowron

CHAPTER TWENTY-THREE

AS THE EVENING wore on, the first of the news vans set up in front of the house, soon followed by a knock on the front door. The distraction would be a good thing because emotions were running ragged. When Jackie answered, a female reporter with an empathetic face handed her a business card. It was clear she was well informed of the circumstances. "Mrs. Obendorf?"

Jackie looked a bit flustered, pulling at the bottom corner of her t-shirt. "Yes, please come in." The rest of the guests became quiet, shuffling closer so they could hear better, wanting to know what was being said.

"Thank you, Jackie. Linda Carson, ABC News 40. I work with Heidi. I've listened to your interview with the Herald and Heidi wanted me to see if you might do an interview with us. We'd like to get it on the late news."

Jackie looked over at Merry, seeking her assurance.

Both Merry and Niki nodded.

"Okay... we don't want a free-for-all though. What happened to the tape the guy at the Herald took?"

"We'll be using that as well. We're trying to capture the human element. We want to be here when we get news of your husband's

Waiting for Morning Time

rescue." Her cheeks colored slightly.

Jackie frowned. "Or, when we get the news of their deaths?"

Linda grimaced, nodding slightly. "Heidi said she had that talk with you?"

Jackie sighed. "Yes. That's true she did. We ask that you respect our privacy if and when that time comes."

Merry spoke. "That won't happen. They are alive. I can feel it."

Niki jumped in. "I agree, no negative energy will be created until we know the verdict on their survival. I believe energy leaves the room once it's expelled, and people can sense it. Don't let your husbands' sense this. DON'T DO IT."

Everyone in the room went quiet.

Merry spoke up. "She's right." Then she turned to the reporter. "Let's do this."

***

After a short talk with Linda Carson, the cameraman and lighting crew came inside. Jackie could see there were other news crews arriving. A male reporter from Fox 13 tried to barge in with the other crew. Jackie cut that off. "We have an understanding with Heidi Godman, News 40 only. We're sorry." The man left looking none too happy. Soon he could be seen setting up with a film crew outside the house, using the Obendorf residence as a backdrop for his news shoot. There was nothing she could do about that.

Anna wasn't sure she would be able to hold up to do the interview, so she bowed out. Jackie and Merry stood in the kitchen as the shoot began, holding onto a telephone.

The bright lights came on. "Linda Carson, ABC News 40. We're at the house of Jackie Obendorf whose husband, Neal and two friends Lew and his son Bill Lipsit, have gone missing in the Gulf of Mexico."

The camera panned to Jackie and Merry.

"Friends and family have gathered to offer support. The three men have been missing for over thirty-five hours and it's suspected their boat went down mid-day Friday in the choppy Gulf waters. The men were fishing and didn't come home that evening. Any information or sightings of the men and their thirty-foot, white and red Scarab boat can be called into the newsroom. Linda Carson, News 40."

The lights went off and everyone took a deep breath. Linda smiled and said, "Now, that wasn't too bad ... was it?"

Both Merry and Jackie smiled.

"I hope you don't mind, but Heidi's asked me to stay on."

Jackie smiled. "As long as we have an understanding."

Linda nodded.

***

The phone continued to ring nonstop. Evidently, the interview at the marina made its way onto the 7 o'clock news. Calls were coming in from friends, relatives, newspapers, along with radio and television stations.

The three wives were reaching a breaking point. They had endured nearly two days without sleep and their emotions were on edge. Jackie thought about what her mom had said about not grieving for Neal before she knew for sure her husband to be gone. That thought kept her focused on the tasks at hand. Everything else became a blur.

Little Billy was mature throughout the whole series of events. After a while the adults treated him as an equal and he was not left out of any of the delicate conversations, nor were any words candy coated. He stayed very quiet but did his best to calm down his mother. Merry, as time went on, became very concerned about Anna. Billy could see this and did his part helping to keep her together. The boy grew up to be a young man over that weekend.

Jackie called the Coast Guard.

"St. Pete's Coast Guard." She recognized the voice as the dispatch from last night.

"This is Jackie Obendorf."

"Good evening, Mrs. Obendorf. I'm sorry to say there is no news. I know you're not going to want to hear this, but we have to assume your husband's boat went down. With all the manpower, including your friends with Lee County and the Cesena pilot, we've covered the coastline from Boca Grande to Tampa. We would have seen the boat."

"We've been thinking the same. My Dad just arrived and he's not going to go out in the boat again, says it's useless."

"He's probably correct. The only way they're going to be spotted is from above. The Gulf is still a mess. I'm afraid that it's going to be really difficult to identify them in the water, Mrs. Obendorf. I'm sorry. Looking down, all you are able to see are thousands of white flecks... the wave tops. We may have passed right over them and missed."

"How long do you keep searching?"

When he spoke, it sounded more like a well-planned speech, probably given several times a year. It would be tough, like a doctor telling a wife her husband probably will not survive the night after a complicated surgery. "Well... Mrs. Obendorf. The easy answer is ... when there is no chance the missing person is still alive. We have a mission coordinator, who's running the search and rescue. He's in charge of Sarasota and St. Pete's. He organizes all of the planes, boats and choppers. We know the stats and the odds of survival. We'll keep looking until a body is found, but the search will be downgraded to Active Search Suspended ... Pending Further Developments."

"Are we there yet?" Jackie heaved a deep breath, letting it out slowly through her teeth.

"I hate to say too much as it's not my call, Ma'am, but yes. If we feel the area has been scoured sufficiently, we then look at the stats, the temperature of the water. It's called the Cold Exposure Survivability Model. We plug in all sorts of variables. If your men were wearing wet suits, they could survive as long as three to four days. The Gulf today is 69 to 70 degrees. Without proper insulation, no one has survived longer than 40 to 44 hours. At 65 degrees, they wouldn't have lasted a day. The two larger men will stand a better chance. Then there is the salt water… and the marine life… as much as I hate to say it."

"So, our last chance is tonight and the early morning?"

"Yes ma'am."

"We have more planes going up in the morning."

"Make sure that they have their flight plan approved."

Jackie smiled. "We have friends in high places, sir."

"So, I understand. We'll let you know if we find anything. Hang in there, Mrs. Obendorf." He hung up.

The room full of people stood slack jawed as Jackie relayed the information given to her. Anna left the room in another fit of sobbing.

Niki, Jackie, Anna, and Merry were very thankful for the people who came to take vigil with them. They brought food, which was a godsend, as the family nibbled away all day without worrying about where the goodies were coming from.

Clyde, who had only just arrived with Mark and Cheryl spoke up. "So that's it. We need to find them tomorrow morning."

Someone from the back of the room called out, "The police are here."

Clyde couldn't help but exclaim. "My goodness!" He and Niki gathered Jackie and Merry. Together, the four went to the door. Merry held tight onto Jackie's hand.

A Venice Police officer waited at the door. "Jackie Obendorf?"

Jackie stepped forward, her heart pounding. "That's me."

He ushered them away from the front door, away from the media, now a fairly big mass of trucks, cars and reporters all eager to get a scoop, no matter the cost. The cameras were all over the quartet.

The officer spoke quickly. "Jackie, don't be alarmed and I'm sure that me being here has done so. We wanted to let you know two bodies have been found in the Intracoastal Waterway."

All four collectively took in a deep panic-filled breath.

"We wanted to tell you before it ran on the news. Neither one has been identified as your missing husbands. We didn't want you to be shocked or worried when the stations promo *two-bodies-found* for their next newscast. It'll be on all the news programs." He glared back at the media vultures as they hovered.

"Sir, we appreciate your coming here and thank you." Clyde said, before he ushered the three women back into the house.

The officer nodded and headed back to his cruiser.

Before they went back inside, Jackie spoke to the other three. "We are going to have to face the facts tomorrow morning one way or another. I think we should call a press conference tomorrow morning. At that time, we will have a pretty good idea if it's over or not."

Clyde and Niki nodded. Clyde spoke up. "Good idea, Jackie. But, if you think that's gonna get rid of them, it won't. Not until the next big story comes along."

Jackie made eye contact with Merry. "You agree?"

Merry nodded.

She spoke to the dozen people who crowded the front door. "We will give you a chance for your questions tomorrow morning at 9 am. We will tell y'all what we know about our men disappearing and if there is any news regarding the search. Until that time, please respect our privacy." They turned and went back into the house.

The night wore on and it looked as if people were in no mood to leave. Niki and Clyde went to all the visitors and suggested it might be time to go home and they were all welcome again in the morning. Merry spoke up before anyone could leave. "I'd appreciate Pastor Pat saying a prayer for us and our men."

Pat smiled, nodding his acceptance. Once the house cleared, he gathered the family together. "I would ask us all to join hands and create a circle so our prayer will have the strength of many and so it may reach Lew, Neal and Bill."

He waited for everyone to join, nodding his encouragement to those in the room who might not have faith. "We need everyone." Without any reluctance, everyone took part, joining hands in the living room, bowing their heads. He spoke in his smooth upbeat manner. "Lord, give Lew, Neal and Bill the strength they need to survive the fate which nature has offered them. Send your angels to protect them and may Jesus, Mary and Joseph bring them home to finish their lives and continue God's work. Amen."

***

Clyde and Niki waited until everyone left before they said goodnight. Clyde spoke to Jackie and Merry before he went to stew in the camper at the side of the house. "You girls try to get a little sleep. One way or another, tomorrow is going to be an emotional… tough day. You haven't slept in a couple. Even a few hours will help."

"We'll try," said Merry.

***

Merry, Anna, and Jackie laid down on Jackie's large King-sized bed, staring up at the ceiling fan as it spun slowly round and round in the moonlight filled room.

Anna spoke. "Do you think they're still out there… I mean alive?"

Merry didn't hesitate. "Yes. I know that they are. I can feel them… I know that I would sense it if they were gone. Lew and I have been so close for all these years that there is more than a physical bond between us. And I'll say, he's one tough man, been through so much, I know that this won't be the end of it. He didn't

Waiting for Morning Time

kiss me goodbye when they left. This wasn't meant to be the end."

Anna spoke. "What about Bill? I'll be useless without him. I don't have a job."

"Don't you worry honey, all three of them are tough. Lew and Neal are survivors. They won't let Bill fail." Merry didn't know why she said those words the way she did. Somehow, she felt that Bill would be the one having the toughest time. She took Anna's hand in hers before Anna left for her bedroom.

Jackie let out a big breath. "She'll be in big trouble if anything happens to him."

"You've got that right. Let's not focus on the negative. Let's think of all the positive things we can do in the morning to help them."

"You're right."

***

They both fell asleep for a couple of hours. They were woken by the phone. Jackie bolted upright, lifting the receiver, certain it would be the Coast Guard. She froze ... her hand couldn't bring the phone to her ear. She felt numb, her heart racing, thumping so hard in her chest she could hardly breathe.

Merry pushed the receiver into Jackie's ear.

"Hello, this is Jackie?"

"Hi Jackie, this is Bill's mother, Janet. Bill's sister, Debbie, is here with me. I'm so sorry to call you at this hour. We're flying into Ft. Myers tomorrow at noon. We need someone to pick us up."

Half stunned, Jackie could only respond, "Okay, we can arrange that." *4 AM? Couldn't this wait until the morning?*

"Anna has called us, and we need to get down there to support her. Have you heard any news?"

Jackie relayed what she knew to this point, and they ended the call. She looked at Merry. "She has to know we haven't slept."

Merry fell back into the bed. "Maybe she figured we'd be up in vigil?" A more realistic thought popped into her head. "Bill's her son, she's scared to death, poor soul."

"I was ready to have a heart attack there. People should know not to phone during the night. No good news comes from a call in the night."

"Let's try to get another hour. We'll get up and make that list we talked about."

They both fell back to sleep.

Waiting for Morning Time

CHAPTER TWENTY-FOUR

I CRAWLED MY WAY OUT OF THE SURF, the sand squishing through my fingers felt like heaven after forty hours of floating in cold salty water. I looked back and could see Bill and Neal a way behind. I'd been away from Merry longer than I could remember ever being apart, but it was the middle of the night, and I didn't want to wake her and the other girls. My wobbly legs on the soft sand brought me down face first. I spit sand out of my mouth. I tried to rise to my hands and knees… this was going to be a process, my legs disconnected from my brain. I smiled seeing a neon sign across the street from the beach. It beckoned to me-- MOTEL. Somehow I found the strength and climbed to my feet, legs shaking. It seemed to take forever to make it to the edge of the street forcing each leg forward step by step. A thought occurred. *How would I pay for the room?*

    I dug deep into my pocket and found a wet wad of bills: ones, fives and twenties. I pulled them out and tried to count. A room would cost at least a hundred dollars. I shook my head, not sure I had enough. In frustration, I threw down the money. Looking back to the water, I wondered, if Bill and Neal made their way out of the surf yet? I could see them still floating a hundred yards offshore.

    I yelled. "Hey, I need some more money! I'm short twenty bucks."

    Merry would probably be mad at me for not coming straight

home. She is probably mad at me anyway and I felt so tired. I needed to take a nap before I could face her. I needed to get my story straight.

"Lew." Neal must have sprinted out of the ocean to get to me so quickly. Why were his legs not wobbly?

"We're gonna stay the night. I'm too tired to go home. I need to sleep."

"Lew!" This time, Neal shook me by the shoulders.

"Neal, I don't want to be in the water, why did you bring me back in? We need to get to the Motel."

"Lew…!"

I opened my eyes. Then I opened and closed my mouth several times as if talking to Neal. No words came out … I was speechless.

Paper money floated around me, ones and fives mostly. Neal and Bill tried to gather some of it up. "I'm going to the Motel. It's right over there." I pointed into darkness. "It was right there … Right Over There … I need that money, give it back!"

Bill appeared, his hands on either side of my face. "Dad, you're hallucinating."

I looked around at the bills circling me in the water, lit up by tiny bits of bright green algae. I was stunned by the realization … what I had been seeing wasn't real. I looked up at the sky-- blackness. "I'm so cold." My body began to shake. It felt as if I might slip out of reality once more. "I can't stop it, please don't be mad at me."

It was at this point that Bill purged himself from whatever selfish thoughts he might have harbored. Seeing me act this way shook the younger man to the core. I had always been the strong one. I caught snippets of the conversation between Neal and Bill.

"Dad missed taking his heart medication over the past two days. I wonder if it has anything to do with his mental state. He's failing fast."

"Your dad's sixty-six."

"Maybe Dad is doing well."

Bill pulled himself closer to us holding the rope attached to the boat bumpers. The rope had been our savior. Without it, we would have drifted apart well before the storm. It was strange, though we were apart, we could feel the other men on the other end of the line in the pitch dark. It became a comfort. We moved tight, gliding along the rope. We could see nothing above the water, only the rough outline of their bodies below, lit up like ghosts by the bioluminescence.

Neal spoke. "It's gotta be midnight ... long way to go yet. I know we said it a while back, but we have to watch each other a little closer, let's stay tight. Sharks might not be interested in a large mass... we might look like a predator to them."

Bill nodded. "I agree."

I must have blanked out again. I awoke with Bill shaking my shoulders.

"Dad, you look like you're drunk... your head is just rolling on your shoulders."

I couldn't respond.

Neal spoke to Bill. "It's the salt, the cold and we're tired. There's no blame. Maybe you could say a prayer for us Bill. I'm not much into prayin'. I think if we don't get picked up by mid to late morning, we're not gonna make it. I've been holding Lew now for the past four or five hours. I think he's suffering horrifically from exposure. We all are to a degree, but he's not good. I haven't been able to look at him since it became dark, but he's on the way out, I can sense it in his breathing."

"I agree." Bill dropped his head. "I don't think I'm far behind him. When we were swimming towards the shore, I'll admit I was out of it, too. The shore looked real close like I could touch bottom and walk out. I'd let my legs drop, but there was nothing there."

"You don't seem as freaked out anymore?"

Bill didn't quite know how to answer that. "I am, but perhaps it's the fact that nothing has come up and grabbed us yet. I'm getting used to it. Desensitized to what swims in the dark water below me. In the beginning, I envisioned all the things that might be under me... and me not being able to see them ... scared the daylights out of me. I panicked. I'll admit it. I'd appreciate it if you wouldn't talk about it to be honest." He chuckled.

"Yeah, I get that. The deep water's never bugged me. I love it. If it helps, I'm not afraid. If we can keep ourselves strong enough to wait for morning time, we're gonna be spotted. The surf's not half what it was seven or eight hours ago."

"You really think they're still looking?"

"Maybe you don't remember, but there was one of those C-130s from the Coast Guard pass by a mile or so to the south. If they're still looking in the middle of the night, they'll at least try in the morning— we have to hang on until then. We have to hope there isn't some other fresh tragedy to take the Coast Guard away from our cause. By afternoon, I'd have to admit to your line of thinking. We might be old news."

Bill nodded. "I don't remember the plane. I was about to tell you... when we were swimming to shore. For at least a couple of hours, I thought we were in these long canals. I could see the end of them, but we never could get there. The walls on the sides were too high. Like the sides of a lock on the Welland Canal, back home... twenty feet high... so real. When we stopped swimming, I came out of it on my own. Then at one point, I saw the water cooler at work, but I couldn't get to it— more than frustrating! I could cry."

"I've not experienced anything that bad yet. I feel like I'm drifting into sleep though. I can't stop it."

We were quiet for a time, the wind still whistling off the top of the waves. Bill spoke. "The worst is the damn salt. My eyes are so sore. I think it's blinding me. You're lucky that you have your dive mask."

Neal nodded. "Sorry man, it's been a savior, but it's been fogging up and that's made it hard to stay in the present."

"I don't blame you for anything."

Neal wasn't ready for the comment. "Okay... I don't know what to say."

"Say nothing, Neal. When we're done with this, I don't want anyone saying this or that. It happened to all of us and that's it. We were fortunate you were able to take us out. I... feel really bad about the boat."

"Just a boat ... got good insurance. I'll get another one ... maybe?" He smiled.

"I won't screw up my dive gear next time, if you'll take me out again?"

"Yeah, man, we're going out again. You had to see all those Grouper ... unbelievable!"

Bill shook his head. "I wish!"

"I still can't believe you had all that weight on."

Bill chuckled. "I must have thought the BC would be able to counterbalance any amount of weight. I didn't realize it was that excessive."

"You could have gone over the side with one of those army tanks strapped onto you. No BC big enough ... Lucky actually... you could have drowned."

Bill nodded. "You were there to save me. Like you've been saving us these all these past hours."

"Spose I could have. We'd have had to buddy dive. You know about that right? We'd have figured it out."

"What you trying to say, Neal?"

"Nothin really." He went quiet for a time. "I guess what I'm really trying to say is... diving can be wonderful, and it can also be dangerous. If you're not sure about something ... ask. I wish you'd asked me about the belt. Five pounds might've done you."

"I get that."

"Sorry, just trying to pass the time."

"No, you're not. You're driving home some point."

"Bill, forget about it. No blame, no foul."

Bill kept at him. "So, what's you're take then on the sinking of the boat… really?"

"Boat must've taken a few good waves on the stern. Could have been taking on water slowly and then wham, a big wave takes her, over the gunnels. The boat is stern heavy. Can happen."

Bill's eyes seemed to burn but not from the salt. "Even though you're the captain, I still don't blame you. It was a mutual thing. I just wanted you to know."

"I appreciate that. You're talking like this is the end."

Bill pondered the quiet man's words. "Maybe? Maybe not? Of course, I would want to say such things, if I knew it is the end. I mean them all the same… even if by some miracle we're found." He changed directions. "How long will it take to rescue us if someone does see us?"

Neal smiled. "Now, you're talkin. Suppose it depends on who spots us. If it's the Coast Guard sees us? Could only be minutes. They carry rafts in those C-130s. They can drop it out the side door."

Bill said, "Dad needs someone to pick us up right now for him to have a chance."

Neal cut him off. "I think we should leave that up to Lew. You, if anyone, should know he's a pretty tough guy."

***

Neal's mind turned to his own thoughts. He had heard stories over the years about people surviving for long spells, but nothing to compare to this. He had also heard stories of how the Gulf swallowed people up, never to walk the earth again. That's fate. It could happen to them.

Waiting for Morning Time

Neal was surprised how long Bill and Lew had survived. Bill still had a little fight left, but like Bill said, Lew teetered on the edge. He steeled himself to the fact that he would try to get the two men through this to the best of his abilities. If, and only when both of them passed, would he think of himself and try to make a run to shore.

What really played on Neal's thoughts: it wouldn't be long before he might be the only one lucid enough to do anything right down to waving something at a plane flying overhead.

He held no blame to any of them including himself. What happened was a boating accident. It wouldn't deter him from buying another boat if they ever got out of the water. He was raised on the water, and he bore the kind of courage only sailors earn by knowing the waters they're in and having faith in their own abilities. He didn't fear for himself, but Neal did fear for the two people he had brought out on his boat. That boat was not supposed to go down like that… well, maybe it could, but not that fast?

It seemed crazy. He shook the thought out of his head. It wouldn't have happened on one of the sailboats his family owned over the years. Sailboats were different. Unless the hull got cracked somehow, there is no place for the water to get inside. There could be a bad through hole, or leaky gasket around the edges of the hull and deck, or the windows ... but, it would be caught pretty quick. *It was a freak accident, that's it.*

For the first time, he was willing to admit to himself—he was scared, the utter darkness getting to him. It made it hard to stay awake. It seemed like your eyes were closed, but they were not. He reached out to Bill, needing to know that he was not alone. "Hey buddy, you okay?"

Besides the roll of the waves, there was silence for a time. Bill didn't respond, which sent an electric shock through Neal's spine. "Bill!"

"Neal… sorry, I'm dozing. You alright?"

"Kinda. I'll admit, I was getting a little freaked out by the blackness."

"I'm glad that you called out to me. I think I was asleep. I'll be honest. You and Dad have been pretty calm. Well, Dad's out of it now. But, I've been so scared since I jumped off your boat. I'm super scared now, but I'm getting used to it. The darkness though, is adding a new level. I know that I'm close to death. I'm shutting down. So all this other stuff like sharks isn't quite as scary. Does that make sense?"

"Spose so. You've been scared for a while… it's only just hitting me. Man, it's black out here."

Bill chuckled. "If I ever get out of this, I'm going to get a night light in my bedroom so that I never have to be in the dark like this again."

There was quiet for some time. Both men found deep places in their consciousness to hide.

***

Neal's mind drifted to all the crazy stupid things he and his friends had done on the water where they should have had problems. They always survived. Taking his catamaran purposefully out into a storm so he could have a wild ride. He had death rolled the boat, flung fifty feet into the water after burying one of the pontoons only to laugh his head off… get back on and do it again. Neal, of course, felt he was past that sort of thing now, and considered himself an exceptionally safe boater.

He thought about Jackie and Kayla and their baby Robbie. He wanted to give them the biggest hug. Thoughts of hugging reminded him of how much his chest hurt. The BC was applying a lot of pressure right in the middle, just above the solar plexus. It was his lifeline right now though and he was thankful for it. He tried to put some extra air in it to help him hold Lew's face out of the water. He didn't dare deflate it ... just in case.

***

Neal didn't know how he managed to drift this far and not realize it. Somehow he must have fallen asleep and let go of Lew and Bill. *How could he let that happen?* He hoped Bill kept Lew's mouth out of the water. He had drifted into the Intercostal Waterway between the Venice barrier islands and the mainland. When did he lose touch with the other two men? It could have been hours for all he knew.

He became frantic and spun his head around looking for them. They couldn't be far behind. Those who lived near Venice called the Intercostal the Ditch. A lot of it manmade, and often the brown water resembled what one might find in a ditch.

The sun sat high in the sky, and he could feel it beating down on his unprotected head. A woman on the shore beckoned him to swim over to her. "I'll help you out." She extended her hand to him and called to him again, this time from the other shore. He tried to swim to her, though it took some time. He began to get very tired. After all, he had been swimming for over forty hours. *What did she expect?*

The back and forth with that woman on shore went on for some time.

"NEAL!"

He recognized the voice. Someone shook his head. He opened his eyes and saw blackness, Bill right beside him. He could feel that Bill cradled his father in his arms, trying to hold Lew up and give him a shake at the same time.

"Neal, you're hallucinating! You'd let Dad slip under the water. The only way I knew is that I heard him gagging."

All Neal could think to say was. "Man! … it all looked so darn real."

"It's crazy, isn't it? Look, the sun should be coming up soon. Let's get in tight. I need you to hold Dad. My lifejacket is done."

Neal took over. Though what he had just experienced still played out in the back of his head. It scared the bejesus out of him, knowing he had lost control... Neal Obendorf became truly fearful. What would happen if the hallucination swelled up again to grip his soul? He'd lost control.

CHAPTER TWENTY-FIVE

ANNA WAS FIRST UP-- 4 A.M. She hadn't slept for a second in over fifty hours. She poured grounds into the coffee maker, probably for the twentieth time in the past three days. It was something to do and it kept her mind and her hands busy. She bent down on her elbows and watched the dark brown-colored water percolate into the glass pot. She felt so tired. She nearly fell asleep on her elbows. Strange, she could nearly pass out standing up, yet when she lay her head down to sleep, her thoughts tormented her, unable to shut off the workings of her mind. Looking at her face in the mirrored backsplash, her cheeks were puffy, her eyes looked rubbed raw and red. Anna didn't think there could be a tear left in her to shed even if the men didn't get rescued.

From the beginning, Merry and Jackie were all bent on the men being alive. They kept their strong attitude stating the worst couldn't happen to their men because they were *their husbands*. Their belief built on Jackie and Merry's *strong will*.

Anna led a simple life. She looked after Bill and the kids. Anna was practical, a realist… street smart about the sort of things that happened to normal people. Just because Merry and Jackie felt they were above the rim mentally and spiritually, didn't mean their men hadn't already drowned out in the Gulf. No one gets a free pass in life because you feel you deserve one. No one survives that long. She moved away from the coffee maker, startled to see Clyde standing at the edge of the kitchen and den.

He opened his arms and gestured for her to come to him. She accepted the hug and he spoke to her in his matter-of-fact way, which she could appreciate and understand. "Have you come around to accept the worst, Anna?"

She backed away, looking at his white-bearded face. "What do you mean?"

"That they ... could be gone?"

"How did you know?"

"I'm good at reading people. You've experienced your epiphany. You know they could be." His eyes stared at her, filled with empathy. "But I tell you that they are not. They aren't until we have proof as such. I'm a realist, but I am not one to give up. I know that Lew, Neal and Bill are strong people. It's going to take a lot to bring them down. If you can accept the worst, it makes it easier to work towards the best, which we are doing.

Though his words were difficult to take, the way in which they were spoken didn't jolt her into a fit of despair. For the first time, someone spoke frankly and honestly with her. Anna appreciated it and hugged Clyde again.

He walked into the kitchen. "I couldn't sleep either." He looked over at the coffee pot. "Thanks for making this." He helped himself to a cup; double-double and sat down at the counter.

Anna poured herself coffee and sat beside him. "Whaddaya think happened?"

Clyde stared through the dark kitchen window into the night. "At the risk of sounding prophetic, here's my thoughts: For thousands of years, the sea has been taking good men... good sailors. The sea needs to be respected. A small mistake can lead to disaster. The thousands, maybe millions of men since time began who thought themselves impervious to nature, only to lose their lives to it probably felt the same. All of a sudden you are in a predicament and Mother Nature throws you a curve ball."

Anna nodded. "I would never have said that as well as you. But, I'm thinking along the same lines. No one ever wants to have an accident."

"Precisely. What if they took on some water while fishing and didn't notice it? On the way in they were hit by a rogue wave. That boat could've rolled uncontrollably, flipping, possibly swamping and they were not prepared."

"Is this what you think has happened?"

"Something like that. But I do believe that they are alive. Neal and Lew are seasoned boaters and the weather wasn't that terrible when the boat would have experienced trouble—it simply wasn't that bad. They are out there. The boys need to stay sound until we find them, which we will."

"Do you think that they're alive?" She looked up with her teary puppy dog eyes."

"Don't cry, Anna."

"I promise."

"I do have this little spark in me that says—yes. But we need to get to them soon"

"We're on the same page, Mr. Butcher."

***

Their soft conversation in the kitchen and the smell of coffee brewing spurred those now waking up to rise out of bed. Soon Merry, Jackie, Niki, and Billy stood gathered around the island. Clyde looked at them ... one at a time ... and nodded when he saw they could meet his eyes. Finishing with Billy, who smiled back as his eyes lowered shyly.

Clyde put his arm around Billy's shoulders. "These are hard times." He paused, catching a frog in his throat. "We've been through a lot the last day or so, but not more than what those men have experienced, I can guarantee that."

Merry cut in. "God bless."

He acknowledged her sentiment with a nod. "Is everyone ready for what might happen today?"

There were nods, but none with too much conviction

"There's a convoy of news trucks parked out front waiting for a story. I know we've set up a press conference for nine, but they're not going to go away after that. Let's hope the men are found today, but if the worst happens, let's be prepared for it. It could be a really hard day."

"We have planes ready to go up soon. If they aren't found today, it's possible they will not be found alive. I want everyone to be prepared for this possibility, but in the meantime we should all be believing that they are strong enough to survive until we find them."

Merry smiled. "Clyde ... they aren't dead. They are still alive. I know it. I've seen them in my dreams ... protected by angels."

Clyde nodded. "Protected is well enough, if they aren't found by mid to late day, they will die of exposure no matter what's wrapped around them. I've been reading about this and have taken into consideration what the Coast Guard told Jackie last night."

Jackie spoke up. "Okay, let's move on." She was willing to accept her father's words, but only for so long. Jackie needed to get busy so she could deal with whatever eventuality hit them. "Standing around won't do us any good."

Clyde's voice rose above the murmurs as he stared his daughter in the eye. "If you're not willing to accept what could happen, we won't be prepared to face the ravenous media waiting outside." He sighed. "I love Neal like a son. I don't want anything bad to happen to him." He looked at Merry. "If what you believe in your heart and your dreams are true, it will be a miracle. Now, let's hope for a miracle, but be ready should it not happen."

Merry interrupted. "Pray Clyde! Hope is not good enough. We need to put their fate into God's hands."

"I'll take anything at this point, Merry." He paused. "I'm going to head out to the airport and talk to your friend, Rich. I feel like I need to do something."

Niki gave him a hug. She understood. Like Jackie, Clyde would never be one to sit down and do nothing. He needed to be involved somehow.

They all smiled at each other appreciating Clyde's words, however tough they might have seemed, they were the truth and given with good will.

Clyde hugged Jackie and Niki. "I'm meeting the pilots before they go up."

Jackie spoke. "Pilots?"

"Yes. Your friend Rich called me last night. He's been able to find a few more planes. He smiled."

***

Niki tried her best to make something for breakfast from the remnants in the fridge. Most were content with a piece of toast and jam. Billy was happy with peanut butter. Little Robbie woke up crying. Niki shifted her focus and gave him bottle and it quieted him down immediately.

Everyone watched the early news at 5 a.m. their plea-for-help story, getting some good coverage. A picture appeared on the television screen of the boat sitting on the trailer. Hopefully, someone might see the men or the boat and report it. However, it seemed a long shot.

Jackie got a twinge of anxiety when she saw the replay of their marina interview; the empty truck and trailer sitting at the marina, waiting for the men to return. "I've got to get that truck. Someone's going to steal it if I don't."

Niki agreed. "This is southwest Florida."

Jackie nodded, knowing once off the beaten track and away from the coast, the crime rate rose astoundingly high. Someone might spot the truck and trailer on the news and see an opportunity. "The fellas aren't gonna need it now. Why don't you go and pick it up? It'll keep you busy."

Jackie called Cheryl, who had been sitting by the phone waiting for news. She would be pleased to pick up Jackie and take her to the boat ramp. She too, looking for a distraction.

***

While Jackie was gone, Merry took up her station at the phone, manning calls from mostly concerned friends. Merry cut one of the calls short as she saw the US Coast Guard come up on the call display. He heart took an extra beat picking up the phone.

"Hello, this is Merry Lipsit."

"This is Lieutenant Brown from St. Pete's Coast Guard Station, are you Lew Lipsit's wife?"

"Yes. I am. Do you have good news for us?" Merry said louder than normal so she could get everyone's attention.

"I'm afraid not, ma'am. I'm phoning to tell you we will be downgrading the search later this morning. We're sending two C-130's up early and we're going make as many passes as we can before we have to come back and refuel. I hate to be the bearer of bad tidings, but, we're reaching the point where survival does not seem likely."

Merry calmly said, "Though I don't like it, I understand. But, I have to tell you, they're alive.

"I hope this is the case, Mrs. Lipsit. We'll let you know the second we find something." He hung up.

Merry's face dropped, her cheeks turning deep red. "They're

going to call off the search." She slipped down on one of the kitchen chairs looking on the verge of a breakdown. *So, this is how it's going to end.*

Niki spoke up. "From what I could gather, they are still going up this morning?"

"Oh, yes, for one last sweep of the coastline."

"Then we still have hope."

She felt slightly better after Niki's words. "I'm going to call Bill Cameron to make sure he's going up." Merry dialed his number.

He picked up immediately and answered. "How are you ladies making out this morning? Is there any news I should know?"

"We're starting to lose it a bit Bill. Jackie's gone down to the Marina to pick up the truck and trailer."

"That's a good idea, Merry."

"Do you plan on going up today to search?"

"Of course, my pilot can't make it until nine or nine-thirty, then we're taking off."

"The Coast Guard is calling off the search."

Bill let out a heavy breath, knowing they wouldn't be calling it off unless they were pretty sure there is little chance of survival. He had been starting to wonder the same. He had seen the movie too many times and knew the probable ending. These types of searches were rarely successful. Still, he would kick himself if he didn't have one more try. "We're going to find them, Merry, I can feel it." He gave her the words more as a comfort than anything. "I'll be in touch and let you know if we see anything."

"We're so appreciative of all your efforts, Bill."

"Nonsense, you and Lew are like family. I know Lew would do the same for me. I'll send Canda. She's been through a rough night and I'm sure she'd like to help somehow."

"You're wonderful, Bill, and Canda is always welcome."

"Talk soon as we know anything. Bye."

They hung up.

As Merry sipped her coffee, she looked down at her hand as it trembled. She tried to stop the shaking, but couldn't will her hand to respond; the stress of the situation slowly taking over her mind and now her body parts. She suddenly noticed the quiet. Niki and the baby, Anna and Billy were the only ones left there and she could feel their eyes on her. Looking up, Merry smiled weakly. "They're in God's hands now. There is nothing else we can do."

CHAPTER TWENTY-SIX

CLYDE PULLED into The Venice Airstrip. He drove up next to a fuel truck. An older fuel technician looked over at Clyde through the dark morning and rolled down his window, anticipating a question.

"Excuse me. Where might I find Rich Godoy?"

"Y'all part of the search?"

"Yes. I am. My name's Clyde Butcher."

"Right! Y'all called yesterday wanting to pay for the fuel. Like I said, the County's got this covered."

"Yes. I did."

"We're behind you, Clyde. If them boys are out there, I sure as heck hope you find them today."

"Thank you. One of them is my son-in-law."

"See that hanger five-hundred-yards over to the left with the lights on? He's getting the plane ready."

Clyde nodded and pulled up beside the hanger where Rich and two other men were performing the last check on the plane. He could see that there were four other planes also going through the same process.

They turned to smile as Clyde walked towards them.

"Rich?"

"Mr. Butcher. We met a couple years back at Neal's."

"Yes. We did." He shook Rich's hand, recognizing him

immediately.

Rich motioned to the other two men, introducing them to Clyde. The first wore a cast on his right hand and arm, he fist bumped Clyde with the end of it. "This is Shane Steinberg, my spotter."

"Mr. Butcher. We're going to get them today."

Clyde only nodded, not wanting to jinx the sentiment.

He turned to the third man as Rich introduced him. "My brother, Ted, my second pilot and spotter." He gestured to the other planes and their crews. "We're going to have a few more eyes up there today Mr. Butcher.'

Clyde shook his hand and turned back to Rich nodding. "We can use all the help we can get. I've been looking at the tide charts and current predictions. I know you have your own ideas, but I have a feeling they may have swung back towards Venice instead of carrying on up the coast towards Tampa and Anna Maria Island. The wind switched with the Northerner." He stopped, reading the expression on Rich's face. Clyde felt like a new Chef stepping into the kitchen wanting to add too much salt to the pot.

"We may only have so much time. I'd planned on starting up by Anna Maria."

"I know it's a gamble, but I think it's worth it." Said Clyde. "Can we get everyone over here so that we can look at this chart I've brought with me."

Rich called the other men over and everyone was introduced to Clyde. "The Coast Guard will most likely be thinking the same as you, predicting that they may have drifted north. We were also told that they were playing a hunch after someone reported seeing a similar boat and three men fueling up down closer to North Port and Boca Grande. Let's hedge out bets a little and play the middle. I suggest you take a start closer to Venice. You're flying a grid pattern correct?"

Waiting for Morning Time

"We will be once we're all up." Said Rich.

"Can you extend it a little longer and cover a bit more to the south?"

Rich drew in a deep breath. "You're saying that you think they could be back closer to where they started?"

Clyde nodded. "That's my belief."

Rich pursed his mouth, scratching his head. The last thing he needed right before heading up in the air is a change in plans, but he could follow Clyde's logic. If they didn't find them with the first grid search, they would try further north later in the morning. "I'll call it into to the tower once we've plotted it out." He smiled. "It is your son-in-law. We'll take a quick pass to the North while we wait for everyone to get air born, then we'll start our grid where you suggested."

Clyde nodded, pleased with the compromise. "I know it's going against your instincts, Rich." He sucked back some emotion before he could speak again. "If I didn't ask you to do this and we didn't find them? I wouldn't be able to live with myself."

The pilots along with Clyde spent the next hour plotting each plane's flight patterns. Once everyone was satisfied with the plan Rich stood from the table and looked Clyde in the eye. "I'm thankful for your input Mr. Butcher." He shook his hand and could see the emotion welling up in the older man's face. "I still have you're number and you have ours, call us if you have any more hunches." Rich looked at all of the pilots and their crew. Everyone was chomping at the bit to get going.

Clyde spoke. "I think we should say a prayer before you take off."

Everyone nodded.

A large circle was formed, everyone holding hands. Clyde began. "Holy Father, we ask for your guidance and grace to help us find these men. Bless these pilots to steer a true course and that they return safely. Amen."

"To the men," they repeated: "Amen."

Clyde turned slowly to look at each face. Gentlemen. I appreciate your efforts, but I'll say... this is our last chance to find them. If they aren't pulled out of the Gulf this morning, they will be lost. I guarantee it. Go find them!"

Before Clyde could move to leave, Rich asked, "Bill Cameron going up today?"

"That's my understanding, but not until mid-morning. I won't hesitate to call."

"Okay good."

Clyde slowly walked the twenty or so yards to where he'd parked and slid back into his SUV, but didn't start the engine. He stayed a while and watched Rich's plane taxi out of the hanger and eventually take off, heading towards the Gulf, slowly followed by the other planes. Clyde could no longer contain his emotion. He broke down in tears and sobbed uncontrollably. He had been trying to be the strong one, like Jackie and Niki. But, it all became too much, the thought of losing Neal... became overwhelming. He couldn't come to grips with the fact that his daughter's husband, the one who makes her life so complete... father of his grandchildren... could be dead. Clyde and Neal shared a strong relationship. He loved the tall quiet man. He sobbed for several more minutes. After a few deep breaths, he became able to wipe his eyes and blow his nose. The emotion subsided enough to function once again.

His thoughts turned to Lew and Bill. He'd only met Anna shortly yesterday and that morning. He couldn't see how she would be able to handle the loss of Bill... the young kids. Merry... he'd never met a couple so dependent upon each other. He continued once again to cry for a time until he slowly drove away from the airfield.

***

Waiting for Morning Time

Clyde detoured from returning back to Jackie's house. He wasn't sure he would be able to hold things together in front of the rest of his family. Instead, he headed towards the Venice shoreline. He found a place along the break wall and stared out into the Gulf. He looked up at the sky and prayed as the sea crashed against the rocks.

Christopher Bowron

CHAPTER TWENTY-SEVEN

AS THE DAY began to show with a golden orange glow to the east, we greeted it with mute expressions. The front hadn't cleared and the sky remained overcast. While the light became a blessing, we were no longer able to show emotion. We had nothing left, the cold robbing every last ounce of our resolve. Neal looked at us. I rested my head on Neal's shoulder, the BC the only thing keeping Neal up. My life preserver became so water soaked it was doing the reverse, pulling me down into the water with its weight. And yet, it was the only sources of warmth. If Neal let go of me, I would slip under the waves and be gone within seconds. I would die quickly.

Bill hadn't spoken in hours ... none of us had. Bill did, however, have some life left in him. He gave Neal a 'thumbs up' when the first light could be seen rising in the sky. A look of shock came over Bill's face when he looked at me. I tried to smile but couldn't. Neal held my head barely above the water, his arm under my chin and hooked through the life preserver. Neal looked at Bill as he held onto the rope attached to the large white boat bumper. The cold was insidious, and no one knew the true consequences; oblivion taking over the thought processes. Bill and I were beyond feeling the cold. Our internal organs were shutting down. I knew I was in shock, my body protecting my mind from what was happening to me.

***

Neal suddenly thought about what he would do when Lew passed. It would happen soon. Even if spotted by a plane, it could take hours for them to be rescued. The Coast Guard would need to get a chopper out to them, a boat would be useless unless already close by. Neal slipped his hand down to Lew's wrist to check his pulse. It took him a moment or two to locate it, his fingers feeling like cold sausages. He could still detect a beat. "Sure is a tough old guy." He mumbled to himself.

The sun peeked above the eastern skyline through a tiny break in the cloud, Neal never so happy to see it. He shouted over to Bill, trying to gage his state of mind. "Hey, Bro! We made it."

Bill's head lolled to the side with a half-smile forming. He gave another weak thumbs up.

"Your Dad's not doing so well. What should we do if he passes?"

I somehow heard the words and responded with a slurred, "I'm not finished, Merry. I'll hang on long enough to see you again."

Both men smiled.

The surf had calmed considerably to approximately six-foot swells, a heck of a lot better than the twenty they'd experienced earlier.

Bill spoke up. "Haven't heard a plane yet. They ain't coming back out."

Neal smiled.

"I don't see what's so funny, Neal."

Neal pointed north. Bill turned to watch the Coast Guard C-130 passing low over the water, coming from the north. *Too far out*. Neal thought. It continued to the south.

Bill smiled. Too much energy was needed to speak.

"I'm gonna let him go when the time comes, Bill. I'll let you have a few moments with him. Heck… you can have all the time you want. But, we'll just let him sink."

Bill shook his head. "Is that what you're gonna do with me, too?"

"No." Neal smiled. "I'm gonna use your fat arse to fend off the sharks."

"Buzz off, Neal." Both men smiled at each other.

"Let him slip away. Hang on." Bill swam over towards us. He put his hand on the back of my head and kissed me on the lips. "Hey? You there, Dad?"

All I could do was loll my head from side to side. "I'm coming, Merry." I slurred.

"I love you, Dad." He pressed his forehead up against mine. He pulled away shaking his head, holding back a tear. "He doesn't know what's going on anymore."

Neal nodded. "I'll let him go. You okay with that? It's coming soon Bill."

Bill nodded and drifted away holding onto the bumper having said his goodbye. He didn't have anything left in him for more words.

***

I opened the door at Butterfly Palm Drive. I had decided to buy it without Merry knowing. The third-floor condo looked out over the lake at Heritage Palms. It would be a good move. First thing I did was turn up the heat and run a hot bath. I needed to clean myself up before my bride arrived. I asked her to come and have a second look. I wanted to surprise her.

I was thirsty and poured myself a tall scotch and water on ice. The liquor burned the back of my parched throat. I quaffed the whole drink in one long never-ending sip.

Merry would love the place, not getting too mad at me for buying it without first selling the North Ft Myers property. I wasn't worried about it. The canal property would sell in a second.

    I poured another scotch. I had become so darn thirsty and I didn't know why. Going to the lanai at the back of the apartment, I sat down on the tile floor looking at the sun as it rose over the lake. I could sure get used to these mornings. It reminded me of the Niagara on the Lake property. The sunsets over Lake Ontario sinking down under the distant Toronto skyline and Port Weller were sublime. We had made love on the floor of the empty house before we moved in. Turning my head, I looked at the carpeted floor of the new condo. "Why not?" I said out loud.

    I stood ... someone was at the door. Whoever it is didn't knock, but I knew someone was there. As I approached, I could see a light shining around the edges of the door. Bright light like what you might see in an alien movie looking like white sheets of laser beams. When I pulled open the door, the handle felt warm to the touch. I found myself awash with searing light, half blinding me. Still, my eyes could see the silhouette of three figures. While I couldn't see who they were, their hands were beckoning. I wanted to go to them, but first I would have to say goodbye to Merry. I wanted to kiss her one last time. As I walked backward, away from the door, the light dissipated, and the door began to close on its own.

CHAPTER TWENTY-EIGHT

JACKIE WAITED nearly an hour for Cheryl. She could have taken a shower had she known it would take this long. By the time Cheryl arrived, the sun shone over the backside of her house, peeking through clouds. Cheryl pulled into the driveway looking ready for anything; the press conference, the impetus for the makeup and fussed hair.

Jackie slid into the front passenger seat. Cheryl couldn't help herself and blurted out, "Anything?"

Jackie shook her head. She'd been asked the same question a hundred times over the past few days. She could however empathize, Neal being her son. "You won't want to hear this, but the Coast Guard is going to suspend the search after this morning."

Cheryl nearly drove off the road. "You're kidding me, right?"

"No, they get to a certain point where the odds are against survival, something to do with the cold and their projected body temperatures." She probably should not have been so candid. As she looked over at her mother-in-law, Jackie could see her in the throws of holding back tears and profound emotions… her mascara would be ruined.

"Dear God!" She put her hand over her mouth."

"I'm sorry, mom, but it's the truth. You want me to candy coat it after this point let me know."

Through heavy breaths, Cheryl nodded. "No. I appreciate the truth. I made a fool of myself yesterday and I vowed I'd do a better job today."

"It may not be an easy day, but no one blames you— this is horrible."

Cheryl smiled, taking a deep breath. "I'll do better. The shock of it is wearing off some." She smiled again. "I don't have any more tears." As she said the words, a big drop boiled up in the corner of her eye, rolling down her cheek and smudging her makeup. "Shoot."

Jackie smiled. "It was a good plan."

***

It didn't take them very long to arrive at the boat launch, Jackie happy, yet reticent to see the truck and trailer sitting in the middle of the parking lot, marking the beginning of the end to her. Once she retrieved the vehicle, it would be like throwing in the towel. She pointed down to the jetty. "Do you mind going for a walk first?"

"You don't want to go back either?"

Jackie put her arm around her mother-in-law's shoulder and walked so she could see the Gulf still turned up brown and choppy. They both gazed out at the water. It was hard to imagine the men surviving in such terrible conditions. The Gulf of Mexico is fairly calm on a normal day ... turquoise and various shades of blue.

"What do you think? Are they still out there?"

"Neal's a fish. I put odds on him still being with us. The other two men, I'm not so sure about ... as long as he has on his wet suit."

Jackie nodded. "I've been thinking the same thing. Come on, time we got back." She looked out at the brown Gulf. "It's a strange feeling. What have all the other wives felt throughout time... the ones who have lost their spouses to the sea? I don't think there is anything else we might have done. I have a... could this possibly be happening to me feeling? No, it couldn't be… but yet it is. It's surreal. I have to come to the realization that this is happening. Neal most likely is gone."

Cheryl pulled her daughter in law close. She didn't say anything. There was nothing to be said.

CHAPTER TWENTY-NINE

AFTER THE CALLS were made, Merry looked out the front window. She counted four vans and seven cars. It must be an everyday occurrence for the media people, just another gig. She could see them all standing around smoking laughing at the odd bit of humor. For Merry, it caused a lot of stress. She and Jackie made the decision to go public with the men's disappearance. Now, they needed to live with the consequences. The only lead they had received was that of a similar Scarab being fueled in Boca Grand last night.

Jackie dismissed the query instantly. "He wouldn't go to Gasparilla to fuel up, it doesn't make sense. There were cheap gas stations closer to Venice. Why wouldn't they have called?"

Merry sat down with another cup of coffee, away from the others. Pastor Pat arrived bright and early with members of their congregation. A close friend of Merry and Lew offered to pick up Lew's ex-wife and daughter, Debbie, at the Ft. Myers Regional Southwest Airport. Their kindness took a load off of her mind.

Her thoughts drifted back to her best days with Lew. She couldn't remember too many truly bad ones. Getting ripped off by their bookkeeper back in Canada was not a pleasant memory, but Lew had shrugged it off. He never let too much bother him. Merry was different. She sometimes became lumped together as one with her husband. Lew possessed a pleasant outgoing persona. While Merry did too, she still had a practical side, which could see the reality of how a situation be it money or practical family matters would affect them. Merry couldn't slough off everything. Friends of theirs, who followed the sometimes-crazy events of the couple, watching carefully picked up on it. From time to time Merry could get moody.

On that morning Merry was off, much like when the men left for the fishing trip only much worse ... a better than good chance her husband was dead. She had faith in her dreams and prayers, but after a time reality sets in. She could do no more, now she needed to pick up the pieces wherever they might fall. She still felt sorry she had been angry with Lew on Saturday. He didn't meant to slight her. She knew that as a fact. He wanted to make the day special for his son, who he hadn't spent very much time with over the past few years. There existed a disconnect between that side of Lew's life and the one she shared with him. It didn't always mesh. At times, that nuance caused some friction. Wishing Lew could be sitting beside her on the couch, Merry made a promise that if they found her husband, she would be considerate of all facets of his life. She also knew if he was indeed alive, he would be having the same thoughts regarding her. She smiled knowing Lew lived; she could still feel him tugging at her soul; however, the tug was weakening.

Niki walked into the living room. "Merry, there you are. The news lady is at the door, News 40. Linda Carson." She looked excited.

Merry got up and walked into the kitchen with Niki. They met the woman the night before and couldn't feel the same excitement as Niki.

The vibrant female in her fifties with blond short-cropped hair stood talking to Pastor Pat.

She turned and stepped towards Merry, extending her hand. "Good morning!"

"Hello, Linda. Here we go again." Merry tried her best to smile

"Yes, of course. If you don't mind, I'd like to take some footage in the home. It might make for a more organic feeling."

"It's Jackie's home and she's not here… gone to get their truck from the marina. I don't think it would be a problem." She looked over at Niki now shrugging her shoulders.

Niki nodded to Merry. "No, I think Jackie would approve."

Linda smiled, straightening out the hem of her skirt. "Great! We'll try not to be too invasive. We may ask a few questions."

She didn't waste any time. Her cameraman and lighting crew set up in the kitchen within minutes. Linda stood in the middle of the kitchen, where a half dozen people were milling around and jumped right into a take. "Linda Carson News 40 ... I'm standing in the kitchen of Jackie and Neal Obendorf. Neal and two friends have been missing since mid-day Saturday. Their boat is feared to have gone down in the cold Gulf waters off the shore of Venice. If rescued, they will be the longest known survivors to be found alive in open waters. The families have been using the Obendorf home as hub for support of the three lost men. Any news of the men can be reported to the News 40 station, the number is on the bottom of your screen. Linda Carson, News 40."

Clyde arrived just at the end of the first television shoot, stunned at how fast the home managed to fill up with people while he had been gone. He walked over to Merry and Niki as soon as he spotted them through the crowd.

Niki gave him a hug. "You look terrible, Clyde." She could see the redness around his eyes. "Why don't you go have a shower?"

He nodded and disappeared into the master bedroom.

Merry looked at the concern etched upon Niki's face. "He's taking this very hard."

"He is. He took our son, Ted's death badly. I think he fears Neal's possible death more because the wounds have not yet healed. Clyde does not want to feel that hurt again. He and Neal are tight.

He's close to Jackie as well and he knows how much she loves Neal."

Merry gave Niki a hug. "All three of these men are loved. If there is a dark ending to all of this, there will be a lot of people with holes in their hearts."

Waiting for Morning Time

CHAPTER THIRTY

RICH EASED THE CESENA closer to the water as they crossed the long line of sandy beaches stretching both north and south as far as the eye could see. The sun coming up over the horizon to the east, allowed them to see a somewhat calmer Gulf of Mexico. As they passed the half-mile of churned up brown sandy water, normal after a storm, they looked down at the Gulf, Rich shaking his head. The past few days had seen the water a dark blue almost black, impossible to see much, especially when they factored in the white caps. Today, the water looked milky green, not as bad as it had been, but still a difficult backdrop for spotting the men, far from the normal turquoise, like in a photo out of a tourist brochure.

"This is a little better!" Shane yelled out.

Ted and Rich turned, giving him a thumbs-up.

Rich deviated slightly from the route he discussed with Clyde Butcher. Instead of heading immediately south, he turned north towards Anna Maria Island. He wanted to take that stretch of shoreline out of the equation before he went off on a flier.

The flight north yielded little besides the fact they were able to spot a pod of dolphins as the beautiful aquatic mammals chased a school of mackerel a couple of miles offshore. Their black bodies showed up nicely against the green. The visual encouraged them. They knew if they were to get close enough to the men, they might be able to identify them.

Rich radioed into the tower. "Tampa Approach, this is flight number 797. We are going to change course and head south along the coast. We plan on heading due south, four miles west of the coastline where we will commence our submitted flight plan."

"797, this is Tampa Approach. Roger that!"

Rich banked the plane in a wide arc and settled in for the flight south. He brought the Cesena down as low as he dared.

***

Bill Cameron waited at Page Field Airport in Ft. Myers. His pilot, Carman, wouldn't be able to make it until approximately 9 am. Bill became increasingly anxious to get up in the air. He knew if the men were alive, they would be on their last legs. Merry called to tell him the Coast Guard would soon call off the search. He knew it would be a heck of a lot easier for one of the C-130s to help out, if they were already in the air should the men be spotted. He decided to wait in the cockpit of the plane, and tuned in to the VHF radio just in case.

***

Rich kept to the four-mile-out-from-the-coastline course all the way from Anna Maria down slightly past Venice. He checked in with Tampa Approach to let them know of his change in course. "Tampa, this is flight 797."

"Go ahead, 797."

"Changing course ... will be heading due north, five miles out from the coast."

"Roger, we see you. You are clear to proceed."

Rich began getting a little uptight. It was difficult flying, and his neck was becoming stiff. He knew he would continue with the grid until he found Neal and his friends, or when the sun went down. They would have to return to Tampa Approach in a couple of hours to refuel. It was only 7:45 am and lots of daylight ahead. Rich still couldn't understand what had happened. He had been with Neal on several spear fishing dive outings and knew the man to be fastidious when it came to the water. Neal was a real pro. Rich hoped he would get to hear the story. He checked in with the other pilots, the last one just getting airborne.

His brother Ted spoke. "You're a little off target here, Rich. We need to be a half-mile north of here. Correct to thirty degrees."

Rich nodded and banked the plane sharply, adjusting to the new course.

Christopher Bowron

CHAPTER THIRTY-ONE

NEAL APPEARED to be the only one halfway lucid enough to follow the course of the small plane as it passed along what he guessed must be the coast. It soon disappeared into the distance. He took a deep breath and continued to hold Lew's head out of the water, checking his pulse periodically. Bill continued to bob, off in his own world, too tired to care anymore. Bill lost the good sense to keep his head above water, his head lolling around like a rag doll, Neal incapable of helping him. They were at the point of giving up. Funny enough, Neal felt very calm at the notion of dying. He'd come to grips with the fact that both Bill and Lew were on the way out, possibly any moment. He would follow… in time.

Today would be the first time he spotted sharks, though since the beginning he knew they were there. He didn't know if his eyes were playing tricks or not, but he thought he saw a few Black Tip sharks following the bait fish that were plentiful on the surface that morning. Sea birds scoured the wave tops waiting for the scraps from the predators below. The Black Tips wouldn't bother them. It was the Great Hammer Heads, Bulls and Tigers worrying Neal. Where there were small sharks, big ones would follow. He shook his head. It would be their luck to have a plane finally find them, only to become breakfast to one of the large apex predators roaming the Gulf beaches. Bull sharks would tear them to shreds. "Keep your head in the present, nothin' you can do about it," he said aloud to himself.

Lew mumbled something incoherent back to him."

Neal put his head back to rest on his BC vest. He reached into his belt and pulled the Nitrox bottle out and took the last of the air. He didn't know why he thought to do it. He threw the empty canister away.

***

Neal didn't pay any attention to anything but the slow rise and fall of the waves. He resigned himself to the fact that this would be the end. He became strangely calm, the thought of dying no longer frightening.

The plane appeared as if out of nowhere, banking over their heads. He must have been in such a daze not to hear it. He grabbed for one of the children's lifejackets tied to the rope. He hoped he could free it on time to wave it before the plane disappeared.

CHAPTER THIRTY-TWO

"FLIGHT 797, this is Tampa Approach."

"Go ahead, Tampa."

"You have moved off your proposed course."

Rich spoke into the handheld microphone. "Roger that Tampa, we're adjusting."

"I told you so," said Rich's brother, Ted.

"Hey, I'm getting punchy and I'm doing my best." Rich banked the plane sharply towards the coast allowing the left side of the plane a clear view of the water below. They were directly off the coast of Venice and the airstrip.

Shane yelled out, "Holy S@#$! Stop the plane!"

Both Ted and Rich laughed. Ted yelled back, "Whaddaya mean?"

"I think I see something black against the green. A man in a dive suit ... no wait... three of them, one's waving a life jacket."

"Are you POSITIVE?" Rich yelled back.

"It's them, unless it's another lost group! No. I'm sure."

Rich took another pass over them. That time, all three in the plane could see them. Rich spoke up. "Ted, write down our GPS coordinates."

Waiting for Morning Time

"Got it!"

All three became a little panicked, their words jumbled, falling over each other until Rich finally exclaimed, "Calm down, everyone!"

Rich called it in. "Tampa Approach, WE FOUND THEM!"

Silence .... "Are you certain, 797?"

"Affirmative, Approach. We're going to continue circling."

"797, I'll contact the Coast Guard. Can you give us your coordinates?"

Rich relayed the location to Tampa Approach.

After a couple of minutes, Tampa came back to them. "797. The Coast Guard is on their way. They have asked that you vacate the area. Hang on.... 797, we see another plane approaching from the east. Can you make a visual?"

Shane yelled. "MAN! They're coming right over the top of us, one of the planes from the Sundowners."

Another voice came on the air. "Flight 610, hailing from Venice...we found 'em."

Rich lost his cool. "610, get the heck out of here. We found them four minutes ago. Clear out of the airspace."

Tampa conferred. "610, leave the airspace immediately. 797, take a course east northeast 75 degrees. You've done your job and congratulations! A C-130 has an ETA of two minutes. Let them do their job."

Rich responded. "10-4, Approach. We're heading home."

***

Neal startled as the plane seemed to come out of nowhere. He continued waving the children's lifejacket. The other two were in no shape to move. He worried that the plane hadn't spotted them in the horrible chop.

He smiled to himself as he saw the white Cesena bank again to fly over top. He knew that he would be saved, but would they be able to get the rescue in place soon enough to help Lew and Bill?

***

Rich took his cell phone out of his pocket and dialed Jackie's house.

A female answered. "Hello?"

"Who am I speaking to?"

"Merry Lipsit. Who's calling?"

"Merry, it's Rich Godoy. Is Jackie there?"

"Hello, Rich, no she's gone to get Neal's truck from the marina."

"We found them!"

CHAPTER THIRTY-THREE

THE NEWS CREWS began to set up in the sunroom just off the kitchen. The crowded house became—pure chaos. More supporters arrived: church members, friends and relatives. Merry answered her cell.

"Hello?"

"Merry, it's Cheryl. I know Jackie said she'd give you call when we were on our way back to the house, but she's left her phone in my car."

"No problems with the truck?"

"No. Everything seems fine. We should make it back in plenty of time for the press conference."

"Thanks, Cheryl. We'll wait for you in case you get delayed." She hung up.

Niki and Clyde looked at her questioningly. "It's okay, the truck's fine and they're on the way back."

Both of the Butchers nodded.

Linda Carson walked up to the three of them. "How would you like to do this? I'll tell you how these things normally go, if you don't mind?"

Clyde motioned for her to continue speaking with a flourish of his hand.

"Okay. We should give each station a chance to do their lead-ins.

Then, if you don't mind, I'll go last, giving a brief synopsis of the events and begin with a question. At that time, you will be allowed to answer them as you best see fit. I'll moderate the floor. Once we get going, you'll be fine."

Merry, Niki and Clyde nodded in agreement. Over the hubbub of the house, Merry heard the house phone ring. They had kept that line clear except for calls to the Coast Guard and Pilots.

She moved quickly to pick up the cordless phone.

"Hello?"

"Who am I speaking to?"

"Merry Lipsit, who's calling?"

"Merry, it's Rich Godoy. Is Jackie there?"

"Hello, Rich, no she's gone to get Neal's truck from the marina." Merry felt her heart thud in the center of her chest as her breath quickened.

"We found them!"

The people milling about the house had fallen into a rhythm over the past few days, where everyone would become quiet with each incoming call. The only background noise to be heard were crews banging the legs of camera stands and lighting equipment. Everyone else tried to glean a sense of the conversation by watching the expression on Merry's face along with her body language. One of the cameramen sensed an opportunity and began taping the sequence.

"Are you positive?"

"There are three PIWs, one waving a life jacket."

"PIW?"

"People in the Water."

"Are they all alive?"

A murmur ran through the room.

"Where did you find them? Are they all alive?"

"Six miles out from Venice, and we can only confirm one person to be alive ... the lifejacket waver. The Coast Guard has been contacted and should be here any moment. I'll have to sign off, Merry. They want me to vacate the airspace."

"I can't tell you how thankful I am … we are. Please, thank your crew."

"My brother, Ted, and my friend, Shane."

Merry murmured something low under her breath. "My three angels…"

"What's that, Merry?

"...Thank you again, Rich!"

"The Coast Guard will let you know their status. We're not out of the woods yet. Bye for now." He hung up

Merry looked up, suddenly aware of all the faces staring at her, the lights and the cameras panning on her. Merry yelled, "THEY'VE BEEN FOUND!" She raised her arms up in the air. The room erupted into pandemonium; everyone including the news crews jumping up and down ... hugging each other.

Once the room quieted, Linda Carson made a questioning nod towards Merry, beckoning her towards the camera.

"Let me call Jackie first." Merry insisted.

"Of course," the blond-haired reporter butted in.

Merry dialed Jackie's number.

"Hello?"

"Jackie?"

"No, it's Cheryl, remember, Jackie left her phone in my car."

"Right … they found them!"

"What?! You're kidding me?"

"No. I just got the call. We're not sure what condition they're in."

"I can't believe it. I'm going to hang up and try to get Jackie's attention. We're about ten minutes away!" Cheryl hung up.

Linda Carson stepped in beside Merry as the camera began to record and the cameraman silently counting down from four with his fingers. "Linda Carson, ABC News 40. I'm here at the residence of

Neal and Jackie Obendorf, where we've just been told three men: Neal Obendorf, Lew Lipsit, and his son, Bill Lipsit have been spotted floating in the Gulf. The men have been missing for over forty-five hours. We're told the Coast Guard has begun rescue procedures. I'm with Merry Lipsit, Lew's wife. Merry, how can you explain what you are feeling right now?"

It took Merry a few seconds to calm her heart before she could talk, a gamut of emotions flowing through her. "Elation... Shock... Relief. I can't say anything more."

Linda motioned to cut the camera. "Thank you, Merry."

Clyde, Niki, and Anna shuffled Merry off to a corner of the room, where they all hugged each other and shed tears of joy. As they looked around, most of the other faces had tears running down their cheeks, the outpouring of emotion uncontrolled.

Clyde spoke to the three women. "This isn't over, girls. They've been in the water a long time and their lives are still in peril. Where were they picked up, Merry?"

"Almost straight off Venice ... six miles out."

He nodded and smiled. "Just as I figured, and they'll bring them in at Venice Airport. I won't be able to sit still, I'm driving up there."

Niki knew not to question Clyde's motives. She gave him a long hug and a kiss.

***

Jackie could see the headlights of Cheryl's car flashing on and off and hear her horn blaring. She felt sorry for her mother-in-law throughout the ordeal. Jackie knew Cheryl didn't meant to lose control of her emotions. Jackie couldn't imagine how she might feel if one of her children were in a similar situation. Cheryl loved Neal. They were very close. Jackie looked back at the car, the lights still flashing on and off. What could? The hair on Jackie's arms stood on

Waiting for Morning Time

end as she remembered her cell was in Cheryl's car. Had their bodies been found?

Pulling over to the side of the road, Jackie jumped out of the truck and ran back to the driver's side window of her mother-in-law's car. "What is it, mom?"

Cheryl stuck the phone out of the window. The poor woman could hardly catch her breath to tell Jackie, "They've been found!"

Jackie grabbed onto the side of the car to keep from dropping to her knees. "Are they alive!?"

"I'm told that one of the men was waving."

Jackie took her phone and ran back to the truck. She knew that the one man who was able to wave would be Neal. Her heart soared momentarily until another thought hit her. *What if the other two were dead?* It would be a miracle if Lew lived, with his age and heart. She suddenly felt badly for Merry... for Anna—she had her doubts for Bill.

***

Bill Cameron sat in the cockpit of the Lee County twin-engine Cesena, monitoring the police channels as well as the Coast Guard. As he flipped the channel to monitor the Coast Guard, he came in halfway through a conversation.

"Dispatch, we're firing the smoke cannon ten feet to the left of the PIWs." Silence.

"We should be able to get them outta the water within twenty minutes. Smoke canister has been deployed successfully. We're gonna swing around and drop a life raft."

"Roger ... ambulance assistance will be ready at Venice airstrip after pickup."

Bill slammed his hands onto his knees and yelled, "YES!" He quickly climbed out of the plane and slipped into the driver's seat of his Lee County Sheriff's unmarked cruiser. He could be in Venice within three quarters of an hour. He called Canda, as he knew she was at Jackie Obendorf's house.

"Canda, It's Bill. They've been found!"

Canda answered in her southern drawl. "Yes. But we don't know what condition they're in?"

Bill responded. "They're being taken to Venice airstrip. I'm on the way there now."

CHAPTER THIRTY-FOUR

I WAS CLOSE TO DEATH and didn't watch nor even know what went on. I can only recount what I've been told. Bill and Neal held my head up out of the water. It became a two-man job. Neal and Bill watched as the massive C-130 came in low from the Northwest, with maybe a couple hundred yards of altitude. As the Coast Guard plane drew in almost over us, it looked like they were firing a canon down at us. The loud concussion bounced off the water. A canister the size of two cans of tennis balls on top of each other, hit the water, the sound of the can discharging its payload startled even me from my comatose state. Grey blue smoke issued forth from the missile, marking our location in the surf.

At that moment, Neal and Bill knew they were saved, the smoke one of the best things either of them could remember seeing in a very long time. Neal couldn't help but feel a pang of worry as the plane banked off to the east in a wide arc. He looked closely at Bill's wrinkled face and could see twinges of fear in his eyes as well.

Bill spoke up. "I'd hate to make it all this way to get eaten by something now."

"Don't think about it, Bill. Think of your family, your kids. You're gonna see them again!"

Tears began to well up in Bill's eyes. He tried to smile. "I'll try. I feel so vulnerable." He looked down into the water. "The sound of that smoke bomb's gotta' attract something."

"Don't think about it, man. Look!" Neal pointed to the north. "Here she comes again."

They watched as the C-130 made its next pass, it seemed an eternity for it to reach them. They watched as a large red box sort of thing was dropped out of the side of the plane. It looked as if it might hit them on their heads, but the payload had been expertly deployed. As the red box hit the water, sensors triggered the condensed air canisters to inflate the large round life raft.

Neal grabbed onto the circular rope ladder, floating out to the side and around the raft. He tossed his flippers in and slipped his foot onto the ladder, the corner of the raft dipping down into the water. His legs felt dead, the blood having been diverted towards his core. He heaved himself up and laid down on his back, basking in the heat from the sun. He didn't know where he would be able to find the strength to help the other two up the ladder. It would be difficult, basically three hundred plus pounds of dead weight.

Bill yelled at me. "Dad... you're gonna have to help out here."

My head lolled from side to side. "Help what... I'm sorry, Merry."

"Dad, Merry's in the life raft."

"Okay." I put an arm onto the edge, but that would be the extent of my efforts.

Bill put both feet into the rungs of the rope ladder and tried to push me up. Neal worked from above to pull on my life preserver, but the raft was not very stable, and he found it difficult to gain leverage. Both men at that point, using ninety-nine percent of their reserves of energy felt like it might take more than they possessed to get me up and in.

They struggled for another five minutes of pure frustration, where I would slip back into the water just when they thought I might be up.

Neal finally said. "This is my last try, Bill. I got no more. We're going to have to both hold onto him in the water if we can't get him in. It might take some time before they can get a chopper out here."

"One more time, Neal, we gotta get him outta the water. He doesn't have that much time left!"

Between Neal pulling and Bill pushing, they finally rolled my body up and into the raft. Neal fell back exhausted.

It took Bill a couple of minutes to get himself up into the raft with Neal's help. He lay across both of both of our legs. Not being able to move for several minutes. He looked over at Neal and smiled. They used up that last percent of energy to perform a high-five. "I'm not going diving with you next week, Neal." Both men cracked up laughing, but the levity would be short-lived as their eyes reverted back to me. They said that I didn't look well. My color appeared ashen grey, my lips blue and my tongue hung out of the side of my mouth. Neal and Bill later told me I looked like a dead man. My legs were white-grey with no sign of any blood flow. The warmth provided by the sun felt lovely, but neither of them thought for a moment it would be enough to resuscitate me.

***

It took nearly half an hour for the Coast Guard Air Sea Rescue Chopper to arrive. The sound of the massive blades could be heard coming toward us before it could be seen. The sun on our bare skin did wonders to bring us around. Bill couldn't stop shaking for the first fifteen minutes. I really didn't do much of anything except speak gibberish. Fifteen minutes later as the chopper neared, I opened my eyes and registered what was occurring around me.

None of us saw the diver as he jumped from the helicopter. I resting my head on the inflated side panel and startled as the man appeared in his scuba gear from apparently nowhere. "Good morning, gentlemen. How are we all doing here?" He shouted. The downward wash of the spinning blades flattened the sea out somewhat, but the noise of the engines made it difficult to hear the man's words.

"Not so good today, thank you." I said.

"Don't y'all worry, we're going to have you up and into the chopper *tut suit*." He looked into our faces most likely to see who was in the worst shape. He pointed to me. "Sir, I want you to slip over here and back into the water. I know you're cold, but it would be easier to get you into the basket. He did the same thing for Bill. In reality, he wanted to shock us a bit to keep our adrenalin running, or we might shut down.

I nodded, needing the help of Neal and Bill to get back into the water. The cold felt like acid as I slipped back into the ocean. The frogman was ready and guided me into the basket.

"Hold on, sir."

I nodded and was quickly winched into the large chopper, hovering above us. The diver went along for the ride to help me out once we reached the large red craft. The empty basket was lowered again after a couple of minutes. In turn, Bill and Neal were raised up into the Coast Guard Chopper. The frogman caught a ride up with Neal at the end.

For a large helicopter, there wasn't much room in the Holding Bay. Neal, Bill and I, along with the two-crew members, crammed into the small space. I didn't help matters much as I couldn't sit up, monopolizing much of the space.

The man who operated the electric winch spoke up. "You fellas are lucky. Most of our pickups after that amount of time are half eaten or long dead."

Bill frowned at the man's comment as he tried to lie down. The diver waved his finger at him. "Sit up! No laying down. It'll be the death of you. In fact, let's get up, Mister?"

Bill spoke up. "Bill Lipsit and that's my father, Lew Lipsit, and he's our friend, Neal Obendorf."

Waiting for Morning Time

The diver nodded. "We knew the names, but not the faces belonging to them." He smiled. "Let's get Lew sitting up." He shook me, trying to keep me awake. With the help of the other Guardsman, he pulled me upright against a bulkhead. "Cannot let you guys off the hook that easy."

"What the heck do you mean?" Bill said with some irritation.

"There's been too much adrenalin running through your veins for the past day or so. When folks like you are rescued after a long trauma, we need to keep you active. Your brain all of a sudden says ... okay I'm safe and stops the flow of adrenalin, which right now is still needed to keep your hearts pumping... whammo and you die. For the next hour or so, we need to keep you awake and moving, until we can get the proper fluids and nourishment into your bodies."

"Speaking of nourishment ... do you have any water?" asked Bill.

The diver nodded, opened up a backpack and offered him a bottle of water. "You know there was food and water in the raft we dropped?"

Neal nodded. "We were too exhausted to look. As you can see, we're not with it at the moment."

The diver spoke. "To be expected. You guys must have gone through a heck of a time. Sharks left you alone?"

Neal nodded. We thought we saw a few, but they didn't bother us."

"You're lucky, probably the storm. They can be devils, especially the Bulls."

Bill downed the entire bottle of water in a couple of seconds, probably the best water he had ever tasted. In fact, he could have downed five more bottles.

Neal and I looked to the man expectantly. He shook his head. "That was supposed to be for the three of you. The doctors are going to give me heck. We're not supposed to give you more than a few sips."

Neal spoke up. "There's no more?"

"Let me see." He rummaged around in the pack for a moment, finally pulling out a can of Coke. "This might go down rough."

I put out my hand. "I need to have something, let me have it."

The diver handed it to me after pulling the tab open.

I took a long swallow, quickly gagging it back up, spitting it all over my chest and belly. "Are you trying to kill me? That's burning like crazy." I began to cough.

Neal shook his head when it was offered to him. "I can wait," he croaked and eyeing Bill, sideways.

***

The ride back to land didn't take much more than twenty minutes. As I came back to what might be called consciousness, I thought about our ordeal. I didn't have the strength to join in the small talk between Bill, Neal, and the two Guardsmen.

From the moment we hit the water, I had known we were going to be spotted. I didn't think it would have taken so long. It was only after the chopper had gained some altitude that I looked out the side window that I realized what the three of us had been up against.

The Gulf was calmer now. Looking down, I realized how impossible it would have been to spot three little heads bobbing in the surf. So many people scoff at the safety measures enforced by the Coast Guard. Though Neal's boat would have complied, I could think of a few other measures that should be taken into consideration for safety sake. Notably, some sort of floating emergency pack containing a signaling device, at least a dozen flares, and inflatable life rings. Someone could make money off that idea, I smiled.

I swatted away the Guardsman as he tried to poke me. Though I knew why, it became irritating. My thoughts drifted back to Merry, as they had over the entire ordeal. I feared it might have been the end of our love story and promised to myself I would never say goodbye to

Waiting for Morning Time

her or go to sleep without giving her a kiss. Sounded corny, but it is difficult to do if you are angry with someone. The moral of the story being, I didn't ever want to be apart again with any angst in my mind. A tear came to my eye at the thought of never seeing Merry again ... worse, dying without saying goodbye.

The pilot spoke over the intercom. "Two minutes to touch down at Venice. It looks like we have a party going on down there."

***

The chopper settled down smoothly. After a few seconds the side door opened up. Bill being closest would be the first man helped out. The diver assisted him down the metal steps extended from the craft. His legs felt wobbly, entities unto their own. Still, they forced him to walk a hundred steps to a golf cart waiting for him. They could have had it parked beside the chopper, yet they made him walk. Electric shocks ran up and down his legs and were intensely painful. His feet felt like they were on fire. Yet he remembered what the Coast Guard men said in the chopper. "If we treat you nice and take away your pain, your adrenalin will stop, and you will die." And so he gritted his teeth and did his best. When Bill stumbled, the Diver kept him from falling. In the distance, he could see a throng of reporters and photographers held back by the Venice Police. There were two men he didn't know, allowed to approach the helicopter along with men from the Coast Guard and the Police. One looked to be about forty in a dark suit and the other large man in overalls had a thick white beard and rubber boots. They watched as the paramedics carted him away to an ambulance.

I was next off. I needed more assistance. Like Bill, I would be forced to walk a distance. I couldn't hide the pain caused by the return of blood to my limbs. Embraced by Bill Cameron and then Clyde Butcher, I didn't have the strength for words and I feared what emotions might appear if I did try to talk. My friend Bill along with a Guardsman helped me to another golf cart, where I spread out my legs as my knees were so swollen, my legs unable to bend.

Neal was the last to exit the chopper and remarkably, he could walk on his own. Still, he looked like a wounded bird with his arms extended away from his body, his scuba mask still hanging around his neck.

Clyde's heart nearly broke when he saw his son-in-law. He ambled over to him and embraced him. "We were so worried."

Neal half smiled. "I know you were. I'm so darn happy to see you, too, Clyde."

"Nobody gave up, Neal. It's a miracle you were found."

Neal felt overcome with emotion and couldn't speak. He put his hands to his eyes, unable to hold back his tears. He did manage to croak. "Jackie, the kids?"

"I understand their going to take you to Venice Bon Secours Hospital. I've let them know where you'll be. Let's get you onto that golf cart.

CHAPTER THIRTY-FIVE

JACKIE ARRIVED at her house ten minutes later, closely avoiding an accident in her panic. Irritated to see her entire laneway taken up by news crews and cars, Jackie walked several hundred yards to get to her own house; the last hundred, hounded by the press. Microphones and cameras stuck in her face.

Niki watched for her and quickly rushed Jackie away from the mob.

Entering the kitchen, she was swept up by Merry and Anna, in a three-way-group-hug by the wives of the rescued men. Jackie couldn't get over how the other two ladies looked revived and healthy now that they were given true hope.

Merry said, "We should call the Coast Guard. I didn't want to do so until you got back." Merry could see the relief now in Jackie's eyes. It must have shown on all of their faces. Life can play cruel games. One minute you can be washed with sorrow, the next, bathed with hope and joy. "We still don't know if they are all okay. Let's pray to God they're all safe." In the back of her mind, Merry felt sure Lew lived, but she'd heard it was not easy to shake off the effects of being exposed to the cold for a long period of time. Nonetheless, the call was made with a lump in her throat.

As Jackie prepared to make the call, the media were now in the house crowding out some of the well-wishers to get better shots of her phone call.

The phone rang.

Jackie looked surprised. "It's the Coast Guard, St. Pete's dispatch."

"Yes, this is Jackie Obendorf. We were about to call you. You've found them?"

"Yes. Mrs. Obendorf, three PIWs were located seven miles offshore between Venice and Sarasota. They have been identified as Neal Obendorf, Lew Lipsit and Bill Lipsit."

"Are they all Okay?"

"Ma'am they are all alive, but I say that with a caution. Sometimes the next day or so can be… difficult. Their bodies and minds have been through a lot. They are being taken to Venice Bon Secours. I would suggest that you give them some time to be examined before heading to the hospital. They are exhausted and we're still worried about Lew Lipsit."

"Thank you! The Coast Guard has been wonderful, and all three families have appreciated everything you have done."

"You're welcome, Mrs. Obendorf, and I wish you the best over the next few days. God bless." He hung up

Jackie put down the phone and yelled, "They're all alive!"

The room erupted again; maybe not to the same level as fifteen minutes before, but close to it.

***

Shortly after, the children were brought home and Pat Thurmer and Niki asked if everyone might give the families space and time to rest. There were grumblings from the press, but soon the house was empty except for Niki, Jackie, Reverend Thurmer, Merry, Anna, Billy, Ashley, Kayla and baby Robbie.

The phone rang. Jackie picked it up. "This is Jackie."

"It's Dad. They're alive!"

"Yes, we've heard, but it's a little touch and go for Lew?"

"Yes, I'm afraid so. I would pull yourselves together and get down here as soon as possible."

"Merry and I were thinking the same thing, but the Coast Guard told us to hold off."

"Damn what they said. These poor men are in a bad way, even if they are cognizant, their bodies are in danger of shutting down as we speak. I wouldn't wait."

CHAPTER THIRTY-SIX

BILL AND I shared a room, while Neal rested in a single suite. We were all encased in a bubble wrap with warm air blown under it. We were told it was the best way to slowly bring our body temperatures back to normal.

I was the first to be poked and prodded by the medical staff. There was concern over my heart and the fact I had been off my medicine for three days. As the doctors wrapped up their exams with Bill and I, the chief of staff came in to speak to us. He seemed like a nice man in his mid-sixties.

"You are all very fortunate to have survived. I'll start with your body temperatures. The normal temp is 98.6 degrees. You are both suffering from hypothermia, where your body temp drops below 95 degrees. At the time you arrived at the hospital, your core temperatures were approximately 93 degrees. We can assume you've warmed a bit since your pickup. I would hesitate to guess you may have gone as low as 91-92 degrees. You're not supposed to be alive. Much longer and we wouldn't have been having this conversation. Your wounds caused by the salt water will heal quickly. There is no risk of infection. The salt water is in fact a disinfectant."

I spoke up. "What about all that blood work they did and my heart?"

The doctor laughed. "It's not supposed to work this way, but... your blood work now is better than it was two months ago. We accessed your last chart from your family doctor. Once we get you warmed up and hydrated, we'll be sending you home."

Bill asked. "How's Neal?"

"We've not assessed him yet, but your friend has another issue. He was lucky to have been wearing the wet suit. His core temperature only dropped a couple of degrees. But, the combination of the tight suit and the ingestion of salt water has caused his Pancreas to swell up."

"How serious is that?" asked Bill.

"It can be life threatening. I'm glad we caught it. Hopefully, the meds we've given him will calm things down."

As he turned to leave the room, the doctor stopped and looked back. "I want to congratulate the two of you. It's truly a miracle you survived the stress put on your bodies. You're lucky to be alive. Take care, gentlemen."

After he left, Bill turned to me. "You okay?"

I smiled. "Never been better, Billy. I could use a scotch and water though."

"That's not funny, Dad."

"I'm serious. I've just been given another chance to live after sitting at death's door." I thought back to what may have been a hallucination: the door and the men beckoning me to follow them through it. I hoped it would be some time before I ever saw that doorway again. "It truly doesn't get any better than that. Most people in our situation don't get a second chance."

"Suppose you're right. It brings things into perspective."

"Darn straight it does. Maybe it'll bring what we were talking about back on the boat ... religion into perspective."

Bill nodded. "In the middle of the night ... our last night out there,

I prayed a lot and I promised God if He found it in His will to let me live, I would find a bigger role for Him in my life."

"That's all that He can ask."

"I also think I've been chasing things in my life that didn't really matter; booze, strip joints and fun friends who are really only drinking buddies ... not true friends. What I should I have been doing is looking out for my family; being a big part of my kids growing up instead of being a bystander. That's going to change big time."

"It's worth it to me to hear those words, Bill. Now… aren't you glad I took you out fishing?" I smiled.

"Sometimes we need a life changing experience to see the need to make changes in our lives. I would have liked our life changing experience to have been a little less torturous though. These past three days were a form of hell, both mentally and physically. It's impossible to put into words what I personally experienced: the highs, the lows, the terror of the deep water and sharks. I'll never forget my struggle to pull things back together … and to find the will to go on during that last night." A tear formed in his eye. "It really got bad when we thought we were going to lose you. Neal and I had to talk about what we would do with your body. We didn't want to lose you ... I didn't want to lose you, Dad."

I smiled. "I'm sure as heck glad you didn't lose me."

Bill chuckled. "Enough! Hey? Who was the big guy with the fluffy white beard and wearing overalls?"

I laughed. "That's Neal's father-in-law, Clyde, Jackie's Dad."

"I kept thinking, who the heck is this guy?"

"He walks around in the Everglades taking nature pictures."

"That explains it."

***

Neal tried to close his eyes and sleep. The task made difficult by the

Waiting for Morning Time

fact that his father-in-law had fallen asleep in the chair next to the bed. Clyde's snoring reverberated off the walls. Neal didn't have the heart to wake him. From what he had been telling Neal, the man suffered from the same amount of sleepless hours as him. Now that he had found Neal, he probably didn't want to take his eyes off him while waiting for Jackie to arrive. Sleep could wait. But what Neal couldn't wait for was his family ... Jackie, Kayla, and the baby, along with his Mom, his brother Mark and Holly. There were moments out there in the Gulf when Neal truly didn't think he would see any of them again.

In the beginning, he had felt he could have been able to swim for shore with the scuba gear and flippers. He held onto that thought until the start of the second night. It was at that point he realized he would have to gut things out with Lew and Bill, truly tied to their same fate. There is no way he would have the strength and fortitude to make that long swim. In the end, he questioned if he would have been able to make it in the beginning. However, it was all a moot point now. He looked forward to seeing his family and, never been one to take those beautiful people for granted.

Soon enough, he finally fell asleep regardless of the snoring.

CHAPTER THIRTY-SEVEN

MERRY SAT on the end of Jackie's bed looking in the mirror as she put on a change of clothes. She sighed, seeing her reflection. The woman looking back at Merry had aged over the past few days. Merry needed a few minutes to catch her breath. Her nerves were still on edge, even with the knowledge the men were saved.

She was glad that Jackie was in agreement that they needed to get to Bon Secours ASAP. Her heart went out to Lew. She remembered meeting him at the fortune telling machine, the dumbfounded look on Lew's face when he saw how their colors and order matched up. He looked guilty, like he didn't want her to think he might have set it up. She read his face at that moment and could tell him to be an honest man and for the next fifteen years he never let her down. Always there at her side, Lew became a part of her. The thought of him dying and leaving her side, created a void within her, one Merry is not sure she could live with… the emptiness during the rest of her days.

She nearly lost the big lovable man. How would she survive without Lew? He completed her. Merry's next heavy sigh led to a sob, her raw emotion venting without control ... without restraint. Her worry and fear rained out of her.

Jackie and Anna must have heard her wail. Both rushed into the bedroom. Seeing Merry struggle with her emotions, they quickly moved to hug and support her. Merry's pent up heartache spilling down her cheeks became infectious. Soon all three of the women were sobbing uncontrollably.

The first to pull away was Jackie, wiping her eyes with her shirtsleeve. She spoke between choking on her breaths. "Well, that outpouring must've been needed. We must look like three crying fools." She chuckled.

Jackie's subtle laugh broke the crying spell for both Anna and Merry. Within seconds they were all laughing.

"I'm sorry," Merry apologized. "I've been holding back for the past few days. The hurt and pain wouldn't stay in any longer. I'd been deflecting my fears and emotions by replacing them with practical notions."

Anna nodded. "I understand, Merry. Look at me, I've been a blubbering crybaby for three days. I lost my filter a few weeks back."

"Yes, honey, with good reason. You've been through so much these past months."

Jackie was on the verge of tears again. "Anna, you've done amazingly."

A smile crossed Anna's face showing off her pretty features. "It's all okay, girls. I didn't want to lose my biggest love. I… I didn't want to be a bother, I couldn't help it." She seemed to relax, no longer afraid of the unknown.

Jackie brightened. "Okay girls, we have a big day ahead of us. Let's stop all the blubbering and let's get to our fellas. And, it would seem our story hit the big time. I just watched Linda Carson on the morning news. The media is touting what's happened as being a *miracle*. We've received calls from three producers. The men are wanted for appearances on the Today show with Katie Couric and Brian Gumble. Can you believe it? The boys are wanted by Sally Jessie and The New York Times. We've received a call from Canada, the Toronto Star."

Merry's eyes popped. "It is mind-boggling … really it is." She smiled. "Let's go see those men. I want to give Lew the biggest hug, and I don't plan on letting go."

CHAPTER THIRTY-EIGHT

WHEN THE PRESS figured out the three families were setting out to meet with the survivors, Bon Secours Hospital was mobbed by reporters and cameramen. Linda Carson, with the inside scoop was first on the scene. Standing in front of the entrance, she watched the cameraman as he counted down with his fingers from four to zero. She was the lead in by news anchors Heidi Godman and Monica Yadis back at the News 40 studio.

Heidi: "An amazing story of survival. Three men missing for days off the Gulf Coast are found. Good evening... I'm Heidi Godman."

Monica: "And I'm Monica Yadis. Three men took off on a dive trip and didn't come home. But tonight, folks are celebrating in Venice in what some are calling – a miracle. The three have been found alive. News Forties Linda Carson joins us live at the hospital where the three men are at. Linda, how's it going?"

Linda: "It is amazing, Monica. Three friends, Mr. Neal Obendorf of Venice, His friend, Mr. Lew Lipsit sixty-six of Ft. Myers and his son Bill from Canada were found this morning and rescued by the Coast Guard. It was about ten am when the Coast Guard spotted them. They were hanging onto floatation devices way out in the Gulf. They were rescued and brought here to Venice Hospital. Neal is expected to go home tonight. Lew and Bill will be spending the night in the Hospital." A broad smile formed on Linda's face.

"The families of the men have been waiting and praying ever since the three divers set out on a dive trip aboard the thirty-three-foot Scarab Saturday morning."

A picture of the boat is shown on the television screen.

"They didn't return when they were supposed to. That Saturday night, they were joined by friends and family in the search. They had searched everywhere from Ft. Myers to north of Tampa.

This morning the call came. The three men had been spotted eight miles off Venice. Their boat sank Saturday afternoon. Ever since, they've been waiting for help to arrive. Everyone agrees that their rescue is nothing short of a miracle."

*Excerpt from the actual newscast March 5th, 2001, ABC News 40.

***

The wait at the hospital had been agonizing for the women. The girls were followed by the Press the moment they left the house. Photographers acting like Paparazzi, sticking cameras in their faces. When they reached the Hospital, they were hounded as they waited to see their men.

After waiting what seemed hours, Jackie, Anna and Merry were let in to see the men. It was brief. Bill and Lew were asleep. Merry and Anna hovered over their men, touching their hands and cheeks gently as not to wake them. Jackie smiled looking in. She'd been more concerned for Lew and Bill once they had been rescued, somehow knowing that Neal was okay. She smiled left the two women to their husbands. She'd been a little nervous talking to Merry, fearing the worst as the morning wore on.

Jackie was directed to Neal's private room. She pushed the door open with trepidation. Peeking in, she saw Neal sitting up straight in the bed. Her father was no longer in the room. He'd gone home to have a proper sleep in a bed. He smiled when he saw her. She rushed in and hugged him for all she was worth, not letting go until he patted her on the back.

"Jackie, my chest hurts."

She sat bolt upright. "I'm so sorry."

"It's from the BC. I had to overinflate it to keep myself and Lew's head out of the water the last day."

Jackie put her hand on his. She could see that he was wired on adrenalin. "Tell me what happened... I'm dying to know!"

Neal recounted the story as best he could remember it. Jackie listened intently, nestled up beside him in the bed, a look of wonder etched on upon her face.

As he was finishing up, a nurse came into check his vital signs, frowning slightly. "Mrs. Obendorf. I'd like Neal to see the Doctor and I think it's time he had some rest."

Jackie looked at her—concerned.

"His blood work came back indicating that his enzymes were irregular. We want to keep an eye on it. The Doctor thinks that his Pancreas could be enflamed."

Jackie kissed him on the cheek and said goodbye. "See you a little later. I'll bring the kids to pick you up."

He smiled. "I'd like that."

***

Late Monday afternoon

The three families including the kids, who had created homemade cards for their fathers and grandfathers, gathered in the hospital waiting room along with the reporters and cameramen eager to film the long-awaited reunion with the three survivors.

The men were pushed in wheelchairs, their legs still too swollen and sore to walk.

Neal was met by Jackie and Kayla, little Robbie, asleep in

Jackie's arms. Their family embraced, Neal taking the baby in his arms. Jackie and Neal were too emotional to speak. No words were said, except for a big shout from Kayla. "Daddy!"

A similar reunion was experienced by Anna and Bill and their two children Billy and Ashley. Everyone acted more than happy to have their father and husband back. Anna was not too shy to give her husband a big kiss on his lips.

I looked at Merry tearing up, her chin starting to quiver. I reached up and took her hand in both of mine holding on tightly. Merry reached down and kissed me. "I should have done that before you left."

I smiled. "Maybe I didn't deserve it."

"Never say that, Lewie." She paused. "I never gave up hope."

"I know you didn't, and that's why I'm sitting here now."

She fell into my arms, unable to control her joy, regardless of the cameras and people who watched.

THE END

EPILOGUE

Shortly after being released from the hospital, and on the way home from an interview with The Today Show, Neal became extremely ill and was re-admitted to Venice Hospital with a severe case of Pancreatitis. His condition was touch-and-go and unknown as to whether he would survive. Doctors felt the cause was due to the fact he had over inflated his BC, Buoyancy Control Vest, and wore it too long. The extreme pressure placed on his Pancreas caused it to swell. Neal did overcome Pancreatitis and is in good health today.

NEAL AND JACKIE reside in Venice at the same home where people gathered during the 2001 search. They work with Clyde and Niki Butcher, selling his magnificent photography and picture books at their galleries in Venice and Big Cypress Gallery halfway along highway 41 in the middle of the Everglades. They recommend taking a swamp tour at the Everglades gallery.

BILL AND ANNA believe that the rescue was a miracle from God. Bill, after being rescued gave up drinking and smoking, now focusing on his family. Bill and Anna have been together over 40 years and enjoy spending time with their children and grandchildren. The book is a tribute to his Dad's life and the fact that he lived it to the fullest.

MERRY AND LEW sell real estate in Ft. Myers. Lew recently endured another life-threatening event with a blood clot in his leg. After seven surgeries, he eventually lost his leg and now uses a high-tech prosthesis. Lew states the new leg helps his golf game. I would agree. I wrote this story five years prior to the present day. With great sadness I have to state, Lew passed away in April 2022. After a heart attack the summer before, Lew would succumb to Covid 19, his body not strong enough to fight off the virus. As I finished the formatting of this novel, I was saddened by a call from Bill Lipsit. Merry had taken a turn for the worse after the death of Lew. Merry passed away from natural causes in the Fall 2022

ACKNOWLEDGEMENTS

The process of bringing this story to print has been long in the making. I'd like to thank everyone who let me interview them. It was a process which took a few years. Thank you Merry and Lew. Though it was everyone's story, it was your friendship that allowed me to hear the story. May God bless you and I hope that you are together up above enjoying your next crazy journey. I could not have finished this work without the help of Bill Lipsit, whose spirit, faith and prodding pushed me over the finish line. I'd like to thank my readers, John Wright, Audrey Wright, Bev Hodgson and most of my family. I'd like to thank Amy Shannon for her edits.

Christopher Bowron

Author's Note of Gratitude

I am thankful to have had the pleasure of meeting and interviewing most of the individuals who played important parts in their true adventure. I enjoyed getting to know them through conversations, both in person and over the phone.

I wrote this story from a basis of faith. It is not that I am overtly faithful- I believe in God and went to church on a weekly basis as a kid and still do from time to time. Many of those involved in the calamity at sea are strong in faith. It is their belief that without their faith in God, the miracle which occurred in 2001 would not have happened.

I slanted the story more through the eyes and ears of Merry and Lew Lipsit and their perspective. Not because they were more important than the others. I've known the couple for over forty years. During that time, I cannot remember the two ever being apart. They have always presented themselves as *one person*. They enjoy a special connection. It might have been the strength of their *special connectivity* that brought about the miracle that is their rescue. My kids grew up listening to their retelling of the events and never tired of the tale ... nor did I. It is a miraculous story worth *telling* and *reading* and *believing*.

This is the way it was told to me.

Printed in the USA
CPSIA information can be obtained
at www.ICGtesting.com
BVHW050309040823
668183BV00004B/12

9 781999 441326